**PEARSON
BACCALAUREATE**

History

20th Century World

The Cold War

KEELY ROGERS • JO THOMAS

PEARSON

Pearson Education Limited is a company incorporated in England and Wales, having its registered office at Edinburgh Gate, Harlow, Essex, CM20 2JE. Registered company number: 872828

www.pearsonbaccalaureate.com

Text © Pearson Education Limited 2008

First published 2008

13 12 11 10
10 9 8 7 6 5

ISBN 978 0 435994 37 2

Designed by Tony Richardson
Typeset by Tech-Set Ltd
Original illustrations © Pearson Education Limited 2008
Illustrated by Tony Richardson
Picture research by Bea Ray
Printed in China (SWTC/05)

Acknowledgements
The authors and publisher would like to thank the following publishers for permission to use extracts as written sources:
Extract from *The United States and the origins of the Cold War 1941-1947* by John Lewis Gaddis on p.39, copyright © 1972, Columbia University Press. Reprinted with permission of the publisher.
Extract from *The Cold War: An International History* by David Painter on p.87, copyright © 1999, Taylor and Francis. Reprinted with permission of the publisher.
Extract from *Thirteen Days: A Memoir of the Cuban Missile Crisis* by Robert F. Kennedy on p.102, copyright © 1968 by McCall Corporation. Used by permission of W. W. Norton & Company, Inc.
Extract from *Khrushchev Remembers: The Glasnost Tapes* by Sergei Khrushchev on p.102, copyright © 1977, Andrew Nurnberg Associates.
Extract from *The Cold War* by John Lewis Gaddis on p.169, copyright © 2005 by John Lewis Gaddis, permission of The Wylie Agency.
Extract from *Mastering Modern World History* by Norman Lowe on p.183, copyright © 2005, reproduced with permission of Palgrave Macmillan.
Extract from 'Why did the Cold War arise and why did it end?' by Raymond L Garthoff in *The end of the Cold War: its meaning and implications*, Michael J Hogan (ed) on p.213, copyright © 1992, Cambridge University Press. Reprinted with permission of the publisher.

The publisher would like to thank the United Nations Organization for permission to reproduce the organizational chart on page 165. This material was downloaded on 28 November 2007.

The assessment statements and various examination questions have been reproduced from IBO documents and past examination papers. Our thanks go to the International Baccalaureate Organization for permission to reproduce its intellectual copyright.

This material has been developed independently by the publisher and the content is in no way connected with nor endorsed by the International Baccalaureate Organization.

For photo acknowledgments, please see p.261.

Websites
There are links to relevant websites in this book. In order to ensure that the links are up-to-date, that the links work, and that the sites are not inadvertently linked to sites that could be considered offensive, we have made the links available on our website at www.heinemann.co.uk/hotlinks. When you access the site, the express code is 4280P.

Contents

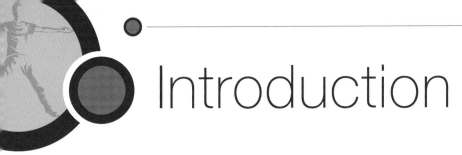

Introduction

How will this book help you in your IB examination?

This book is designed to be your guide to success in your International Baccalaureate examination in History. It covers the Cold War topic and aims to equip you with the knowledge and skills that you will need to answer essay questions on Paper Two, and document-based questions on Paper One.

The book identifies the key themes and topics of the Cold War and includes within each chapter:

- analysis of the key events
- a summary of, or reference to, up-to-date historiography
- discussion on how to answer essay and document questions
- essay planning techniques for each topic and the key themes required
- timelines to help you put events into context
- review and research activities to help you develop your understanding of the key issues and concepts,
- key themes discussed and analysed.

How this book works

Information boxes

As well as the main text, there are a number of coloured boxes in every chapter, each with their own distinctive icon. These boxes provide different information and stimulus:

Theory of Knowledge
There are ToK boxes throughout the book. These boxes will enable you to consider ToK issues as they arise and in context. Often they will just contain a question to stimulate your thoughts and discussion.

ToK Time
How do political leaders attempt to maintain their 'credibility'? Which is more important for this – using reason, morality or emotion when addressing the public?

Interesting facts
These boxes contain information which will deepen and widen your knowledge, but which do not fit within the main body of the text.

The Little Red Book
The 'Little Red Book' was a small red book of Mao's thoughts and sayings that became an essential accessory during the Cultural Revolution.

Essay questions
These boxes are placed near the beginning of most chapters. They contain essay-type questions for you to consider while reading the chapter.

In this chapter, consider the following essay questions:
- What were the key causes of Sino-American hostility from 1949–1970?
- Why was there a Sino-American détente in the 1970s?

Examiner's hints

These boxes can be found alongside questions and exercises. They provide insight into how to answer a question in order to achieve the highest marks in an examination. They also identify common pitfalls when answering such questions and suggest approaches that examiners like to see.

● **Examiner's hint:**
For Document question 1, make sure you include quotes from Document A to back up your answer.

Selected biographies

Important individuals have mini-biographies in the Selected Biography section on pages 243–245. If a person has an entry the name will be highlighted in the text and the Selected Biography icon will appear in the text margin.

Key terms

Important terms or concepts are highlighted in the main body of the text and explained in the glossary.

Weblinks

Relevant websites are recommended in the Further Reading section at the end of the book.

IB History assessment objectives

This book covers the six IB assessment objectives that are relevant to the core externally examined papers. So, although this book is essentially designed as a textbook to accompany the Paper Two Cold War topic, it addresses *all* of the assessment objectives required for both Paper One and Paper Two. In other words, as you work through this book, you will be learning and practising the skills that are necessary for each of the core papers. In addition, as listed below, assessment objectives that are also relevant to Paper Three and the Internal Assessment (IA) are covered.

Specifically these assessment objectives are:
- to demonstrate historical understanding through the acquisition, selection and effective use of knowledge (Paper One, Paper Two and IA)
- to demonstrate an understanding of historical context, cause and effect, continuity and change (Paper One, Paper Two, Paper Three and IA)
- to evaluate different approaches to, and interpretations of, historical events and topics (Paper One, Paper Two, Paper Three and IA)
- to comprehend, analyse and evaluate historical sources as evidence (Paper One)
- to present historical explanations using arguments that are clear, coherent, relevant and well-substantiated (Paper Two and Paper Three)
- to compare and contrast issues or events across time and space (Paper Two and Paper Three).

There is one more assessment objective for both Standard and Higher students:
- to undertake individual research and present results using a formal plan of organization and presentation (IA).

This final objective is focused on the Internal Assessment, and although this book suggests research activities, it is not done within the formal 'plan of organization' and 'presentation' that the IB requires.

Higher level students also have to cover Objective 8:

- to demonstrate in-depth historical understanding of a period of regional history through the critical evaluation and synthesis of appropriate knowledge and concepts (Paper Three).

This objective is not specifically covered, although there is some material that is relevant to each regional in-depth paper.

Mark schemes

For Paper One there are individual paper-specific mark schemes for each examination. This is also true for Paper Two and Paper Three. However, for Paper Two and Paper Three there are also generic 'markbands' that should be used by teachers and students when planning and when writing essays. These are essential 'rubrics', which offer students a better understanding of what is wanted from the essays in their examinations.

The Cold War: key themes

As you read and work through this book, you will be covering the major themes of the Cold War topic. At the end of the book these themes will be reviewed by considering how to answer possible 'thematic' essay questions.

Origins of the Cold War

The ideological differences, mutual suspicion and fear, as well as the key events that led wartime allies to become post-war enemies are covered in Chapter Two and Chapter Three.

The nature of the Cold War

The core ideological opposition between the superpowers is discussed specifically in Chapters Two and Three. However, it is also a feature that is developed in every chapter, as ideological differences are relevant to each area and each event during the Cold War.

The superpowers and their spheres of influence is another dominant theme in this book. Beginning with the development of superpower spheres of influence in Europe in Chapters Two and Three, it then follows the consolidation and spread of these areas of influence around the globe.

There is discussion and analysis of alliances such as NATO and the Warsaw Pact throughout the book. Diplomacy is addressed not only through the dealings of the superpowers with each other and their allies, but also in their attempts to influence the United Nations and the non-aligned states.

Development and impact of the Cold War

The global spread of the Cold War is analysed in Chapter Five, and its impact on the globe is considered in case studies in Europe, Asia, the Middle East, Africa and Latin America. The important Cold War policies of containment, Brinkmanship, peaceful co-existence and détente are addressed in Chapters Two, Three, Four, Five, Six, Seven and Thirteen.

The role of the United Nations and the Non-Aligned Movement is the subject of Chapters Fourteen and Fifteen, while the role and significance of individual Cold War leaders is questioned in Chapter Eighteen.

The Arms Race is the theme for Chapter Ten, which considers both proliferation and the attempts to find nuclear strategies during the Cold War. In addition, Chapter Thirteen, on détente, analyses the attempts at arms limitations.

The end of the Cold War

The longer-term undermining of Soviet control is the subject of Chapter Sixteen, while the end of the Cold War is then analysed in detail in Chapter Seventeen. Chapter Seventeen also considers the events and impact of one pivotal year, 1989, at the end of the Cold War.

Theory of Knowledge

History is a Group 3 subject in the IB Diploma. It is an 'area of knowledge' that considers individuals and societies. In the subject of IB History, many different ways of obtaining knowledge are used.

When working through this book you should reflect on the 'ways of knowing' utilized, not only by professional historians, but also by yourself as a student of history. The methods used by historians are important to highlight, as it will be necessary to compare and contrast these with the other 'areas of knowledge', such as the Group 4 Sciences (Physics, Chemistry and Biology).

1 WHAT WAS THE COLD WAR?

This book is concerned with the period 1945–1989, the years recognized as the 'Cold War' era. Cold War is the term used to describe periods of hostility and high tension between states that stops just short of war. In the period 1945–1989, this was the situation that existed between the two great post-war **superpowers**, the United States and the USSR. The USA and the USSR had emerged as the two competing superpowers following the defeat of Nazi Germany in 1945. Rather than being traditional enemies, expected at some time to enter into conflict, the rapid escalation of nuclear armament by both of these countries made the results of any possible direct conflict unthinkable. It was of paramount importance to find new strategies to avoid escalation to the level of nuclear warfare. This situation led to 45 years of **ideological** conflict, a conventional and nuclear arms race and wars fought by proxy on the battlefields of Asia, Africa and Latin America. It also involved economic rivalry and the development of huge espionage networks, as each side tried to infiltrate the other to discover military and strategic secrets.

It was American journalist Walter Lippman, writing for the *New Herald* in 1947, who popularized the term 'Cold War' to describe the relationship developing between the USA and the USSR, while the U.S. president of the time, **Harry S Truman**, preferred the phrase, 'the war of nerves'.

Communism versus Capitalism

To understand the fundamental differences that existed between the USA and the USSR in 1945, and why these two countries were perceived by many as inevitable enemies, it is important to understand the key differences between their economic and political philosophies, that is, the opposing ideologies of Capitalism and Communism.

The **Bolshevik Revolution** in Russia in 1917 saw Lenin and the Bolshevik Party establish the world's first Communist state based on the ideas of the 19th-century economic philosopher, **Karl Marx**. For the leaders of the United States and other countries in the West, these ideas seemed to threaten the very basis of their societies.

TWO RIVAL IDEOLOGIES	
The West	**The USSR**
Economic differences: Individuals should be able to compete with each other with a minimum of state interference and make as much money as they wish. This is known as Capitalism. Individuals are thus encouraged to work hard by the promise of individual reward.	**Economic differences:** Capitalism creates divisions between rich and poor. Thus all businesses and farms should be owned by the state on behalf of the people. This is Communism. Goods will be distributed to individuals by the state. Everyone will thus get what is needed and everyone will be working for the collective good.
Political differences: Individuals choose the government through voting. There is a range of political parties to choose from. Individuals have certain rights, such as freedom of speech and freedom of the press. This is known as liberal democracy.	**Political differences:** There is no need for a range of political parties, as the Communist Party truly represents the views of all the workers and rules on behalf of the people. Individual freedoms valued by the West are not necessary. This is a one-party state.

Increasing hostility

The mutual suspicion between the West and the Soviet Union manifested itself in various ways between the Bolshevik Revolution (1917) and the start of World War Two (1939):

- the intervention of the West in the Russian Civil War (1918–1922) supporting the conservative forces – the Whites – in their attempt to overthrow the new Bolshevik government

- the fact that the USSR did not receive diplomatic recognition nor join the **League of Nations** until the 1930s

- the **appeasement** of Hitler and the Nazis in the 1930s by the West; this was partly motivated by a fear of Soviet Communism, which at the time was stronger than the fear of German fascism

- the **Non-Aggression Pact** (**Nazi–Soviet Pact**) between the Soviet Union and Nazi Germany signed in 1939, which allowed Hitler to concentrate on attacking the West.

Idealism versus self-interest

The USA and the USSR each believed that its particular political philosophy was the 'right' one, that their respective system was the most fair and the best for creating a just society. How they translated these opposing ideologies in practice is outlined below. You can see that each side believed that it offered the only true path to 'peace, freedom, justice and plenty' for all. However, behind the idealism, the USA and the USSR were also motivated by their own self-interests.

USA	USSR
What ideals underpinned the view of each country?	
• Idealism of Presidents Woodrow Wilson and **Franklin D. Roosevelt** • Struggle for a better world based on collective security, political self-determination and economic integration • Peace, freedom, justice and plenty	• Marxist idealism and Stalinism • Struggle for a better world based on international socialism • Peace, freedom, justice and plenty
How was this to be achieved by each country?	
• Achieved by democracy / Capitalism and international co-operation	• Achieved by spreading Soviet-style Communism
What elements of self-interest lay behind each country's ideals?	
• The need to establish markets and open doors to **free trade** • The desire to avoid another economic crisis of the magnitude of 1929 • President Truman and most of the post-war U.S. administration's belief that 'what's good for America is good for the world'	• The need to secure borders • The need to recover from the effects of World War Two • The need to regain strength as the 'nursery of Communism' • Stalin's belief that what's good for the USSR is good for workers of the world

So, what really motivated the foreign policies of the USA and the USSR – idealism, or simply old-fashioned **imperialism**? It could be a matter of 'perception'. As you will see from the events after 1945, it is sometimes very difficult to separate actions based on ideology from those based on self-interest.

What was the significance of Stalinism?

At this juncture it is important to establish what the Soviet leader Josef Stalin's own particular 'brand' of Communism meant. It was a Soviet Union driven by 'Stalinism' that faced the Capitalist powerhouse of the United States in 1945, and some historians believe that this was a key factor in the development of the Cold War. (For further discussion on the historiography of the Cold War, see Chapter Four.)

Stalin had taken over the leadership of the Soviet Union after the death of Lenin, becoming sole leader by the late 1920s. His policies included the ruthless **collectivization** of all farms, which led to the deaths of millions of agricultural workers. He also started a series of 'Five Year Plans' in industry, which dramatically increased industrial production and put the USSR into a position where it could greatly contribute to the defeat of Nazi Germany in 1945. In the 1930s, Stalin launched the Great Terror, which resulted in **purges** of all political opponents, as well as millions of ordinary people who were executed or sent to the gulags (slave labour camps).

By 1945, Stalinism meant:

- the dominance of Stalin over the party, and the party over state institutions
- a powerful state security machine
- the ruthless maintenance of power by the elimination of opposing leaders, groups or entire sections of the population
- the development of a regime associated with paranoia and violence.

Josef Stalin, leader of the Soviet Union, 1928–1953.

Stalin's role in World War Two

Stalin had hoped an attack from Hitler could be delayed indefinitely by signing the Nazi-Soviet Pact in 1939. However, in June 1941, the Germans felt they could no longer hold off action on the eastern front and, despite the fact that Britain had not yet been defeated, launched Operation Barbarossa against the Soviet Union.

The Red Army was ill-prepared to resist the Nazis, having had most of its experienced and talented officers killed in Stalin's purges. Stalin had also ignored repeated warnings from the West. The Ukraine was quickly overrun and the German army besieged Leningrad and reached the outskirts of Moscow. However, the Soviets were able to prevent the Germans taking Moscow and after the Soviet victory at Stalingrad, the Nazis were slowly pushed back towards Berlin.

Stalin's key role in the final victory over Nazi Germany in Europe not only made him more secure and more powerful in the Soviet Union, but it also put him in a strong position to emerge as one of the leading powers of the post-war world.

The cost of World War Two

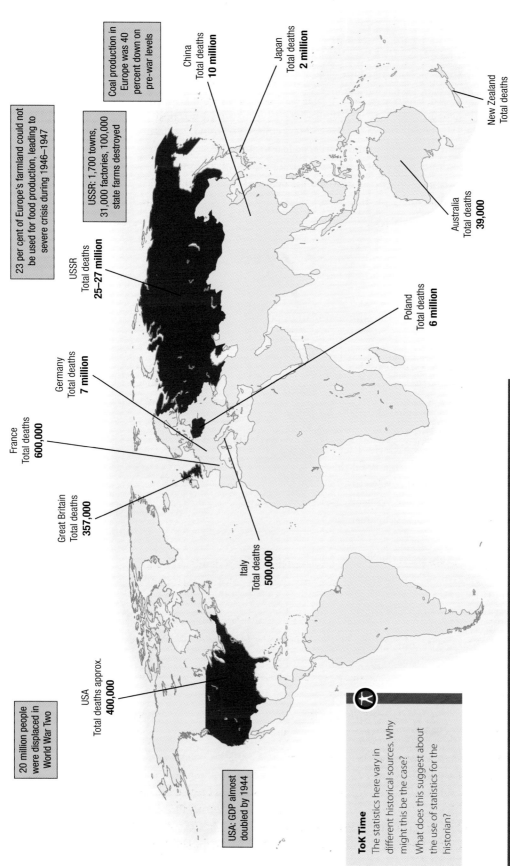

20 million people were displaced in World War Two

23 per cent of Europe's farmland could not be used for food production, leading to severe crisis during 1946–1947

Coal production in Europe was 40 percent down on pre-war levels

USSR: 1,700 towns, 31,000 factories, 100,000 state farms destroyed

USA: GDP almost doubled by 1944

USA
Total deaths approx.
400,000

Great Britain
Total deaths
357,000

France
Total deaths
600,000

Germany
Total deaths
7 million

USSR
Total deaths
25–27 million

China
Total deaths
10 million

Japan
Total deaths
2 million

New Zealand
Total deaths
12,000

Australia
Total deaths
39,000

Poland
Total deaths
6 million

Italy
Total deaths
500,000

ToK Time

The statistics here vary in different historical sources. Why might this be the case?

What does this suggest about the use of statistics for the historian?

STUDENT STUDY SECTION

Map question

What do these statistics indicate about the different positions of a) the Soviet Union and

b) Europe as a whole compared to that of the USA in 1945?

Why did the USA and the USSR emerge as superpowers after 1945?

American statesman and politician Dean Acheson wrote of the situation in the aftermath of World War Two, 'The whole world structure and order that we had inherited from the 19th century was gone.' In 1945, the 'Old Powers', that is Britain and France, had been shown to be no longer able to maintain peace on their own, while the USA and USSR emerged from World War Two as significantly more powerful than they had been before the war. Why was this?

Military reasons

- To defeat Germany, the USA had become the number one air-force power in the world.
- To defeat Germany, the USSR had become the number one land-force power in the word.
- France and Britain's inability to defeat Germany had changed the balance of power. They had become 'second rank' powers.
- The USSR now lacked any strong military neighbours. This made it the regional power.

Economic reasons

- The USA's economy was strengthened by the war. It was now able to out-produce all the other powers put together.
- The USA was committed to more 'open trade'. Its politicians and businesspeople wanted to ensure liberal trade, and market competition flourished. The United States was willing to play an active role in avoiding the re-emergence of the disastrous pre-war pattern of trade-blocs and tariffs.
- The USA had the economic strength to prevent a return to instability in Europe.
- The small Eastern European countries that had been created after World War One were not economically viable on their own, so they needed the support of a stronger neighbour, and the USSR could replace Germany in this role.

Political reasons

- For the West, the outcome of World War Two showed that the ideals of democracy and international collaboration had triumphed over fascism. Thus the political system of the USA was the right path for the future.
- For the Soviet Union, it was Communism that had triumphed over fascism. Indeed, Communism had gained widespread respect in Europe because of its part in resisting the Germans.
- The USSR's huge losses, and the role of the Red Army in defeating the Nazis, gave Stalin a claim to great influence in forming the post-war world.
- The USSR had the political (as well as military) strength to prevent a return to instability in Eastern Europe. Communism could fill the political vacuum there.

Given the new positions of the USA and the USSR in 1945, and their relative strength compared to the weakened European countries, it is not surprising that they were to become the key players in setting up the post-war settlement in Europe that created the new political map. It was during this process, however, that the Alliance set up during the war collapsed, and by 1949 – only four years after the end of the war – the state of Cold War had come into existence. This international situation was to last forty years until the collapse of the Soviet Union in 1989.

Cold War timeline

Key stages in the Cold War are outlined in this timeline, which is useful for quick reference when constructing essay plans and document-based responses.

USA

USSR

USA	Timeline	USSR
1945	**Origins of Cold War:** Division of Europe	**1945**
Truman		Stalin
1950	**Shift to Asia & beyond** NSC-68 & Korean War	**1950**
	The Thaw New Leaders & New Ideas Sino-Soviet split	
1955		**1955**
Eisenhower	**Crisis & Nuclear Confrontation:**	Khrushchev
1960	• U-2 • Berlin • Cuba	**1960**
Kennedy		
Johnson **1965**		**1965**
	Détente: new relationships Sino-U.S. rapprochement	
Nixon **1970**		**1970** Brezhnev
Ford **1975**		**1975**
Carter		
1980	**Second Cold War**	**1980**
		Andropov
Reagan **1985**		Chernenko **1985**
	Glasnost & Perestroika **Collapse of USSR**	Gorbachev
1990		**1990**
Bush	**End of Cold War**	Yeltsin

Research questions

1 From what you have read so far, identify the main ways by which the superpowers waged the Cold War from 1945.

2 How does a society become Communist? Research Karl Marx's theory of revolution and explain the stages through which society must pass.

3 In 1945 was the USSR a Communist state?

4 What was the idealism of Roosevelt and Wilson in international relations? (refer to the table on page 2)

5 What examples exist of U.S. economic imperialism in the century before 1945?

6 Do you think that ideology or self-interest was a more important factor in motivating the USA and the USSR after 1945?

Key political definitions

It is important to understand not only the basic differences in ideology between the USA and the USSR, but also the following political concepts and ideas:

Liberalism Liberals put their main emphasis on the freedom of the individual. Economically they believe in minimal interference by the state, and in foreign policy they promote the ideas of free trade and co-operation. They strongly believe in:
- civil liberties (freedom of conscience, freedom of speech)
- universal suffrage
- parliamentary constitutional government
- an independent judiciary
- diplomacy rather than force in relations between states.

Fascism This ideology is rooted in ideas that are the very opposite of liberalism. Fascists believe in:
- limiting individual freedoms in the interest of the state
- extreme nationalism
- use of violence to achieve ends
- keeping power in the hands of an elite group or leader
- an aggressive foreign policy.

Socialism This ideology developed in the early 19th century in the context of the industrial revolution. (Note that Marxist ideology uses the term socialism to apply to the transitional stage of the revolution before the state withers away.) Socialists believe in:
- a more egalitarian social system
- governments providing for the more needy members of society
- international co-operation and solidarity.

Conservatism This generally implies a belief in maintaining the existing or traditional order. Specifically, conservatives believe in:
- respect for traditional institutions
- limiting government intervention in people's lives
- gradual and/or limited changes in the established order.

Maoism This is a form of Communism adapted by **Mao Zedong** to suit China's situation. Mao believed:
- revolution could be achieved by the peasants, not necessarily by the urban proletariat, as Marx had envisaged
- class conflict was not as important in revolution as using the human will to make and remake revolution, hence his use of the 'mass movement'
- revolution should be 'on-going', or continuous.

ToK Time

Consider your answer to Question 6, and reflect on how a historian works. Historians select the evidence they identify as the most important and/ or relevant and interpret the value and limitation of different sources. Is historical truth thus really just opinion or can there be objective historical truth? Are there definitive answers to questions such as Question 6?

Right-wing and left-wing

The origin of the terms 'left' and 'right' dates back to the French Revolution. In the Estates General of 1789, nobles who supported the King sat on his right, while radicals who wanted a change in the political system sat on his left. As a result, 'right' was used to describe people who wanted no change, and 'left' was used to describe those who wanted radical change. Right-wing now tends to describe groups who favour free-market Capitalism, emphasis on law and order, limited state interference and traditional values in society. Left-wing now tends to describe those groups who favour more equality in society and thus more government intervention in the economy in order to try to secure this situation.

Questions

1   Which of these ideologies (also include Communism and Stalinism) can be categorized as left-wing and which of them can be categorized as right-wing?

2   Where would you place each of the ideologies on this line?
Left-wing -- Right-wing

3   Do the political parties of your own country fit into any of the definitions given above or do they contain elements of more than one ideology? Where would you place them on the line?

4   What similarities exist between extreme left and extreme right political parties?

5   Is a straight line the best way to represent the positions of the different political ideologies? Could you find another way of doing this?

2 STEPS TO THE POLITICAL, ECONOMIC AND MILITARY DIVISION OF EUROPE: PART I

By the end of 1949 Europe had been divided into two separate 'spheres of influence'. In September 1949, following the Berlin Blockade, the Federal Republic of Germany (FDR), also known as West Germany, was established. A month later the German Democratic Republic (GDR), also known as East Germany, was established. Thus the two Germanys became the heart of the physical dividing line between the two superpower blocs. The eight key steps listed below show the events that led to this division:

1949
NATO established, April
West Germany established, September
East Germany established, October

Berlin Blockade, June 1948	8
Czech Coup, February 1948	7
Red Army Occupation of Eastern Europe, 1945–1947	6
Marshall Plan, June 1947	5
Truman Doctrine, March 1947 and Cominform, October 1947	4
Churchill's Iron Curtain Speech at Fulton, Missouri, March 1946	3
Kennan's Long Telegram, February 1946	2
Wartime Conferences: Tehran 1943, Yalta 1945, Potsdam 1945	1

These steps are covered in this and the next chapter.

As you read these two chapters consider the following essay questions:
- Was the breakdown of the wartime **Grand Alliance** inevitable?
- Can any one personality or country be blamed more than others?
- What issues in post-war Europe caused the most tension?

Timeline to European Division

1939 German invasion of Poland: Britain and France declare war on Germany
Beginning of Winter War between USSR and Finland
1940 Hitler's **Blitzkrieg** through Europe: takeover of Norway, Denmark, the Netherlands, Belgium and France
Battle of Britain
1941 Germany begins 'Operation Barbarossa' and invasion of USSR
Britain and USA sign Atlantic Charter
Pearl Harbor attack by Japan brings USA into the war

1942 German assault on Stalingrad
German defeat at El Alamein in North Africa
1943 German defeat at Stalingrad
Allied invasion of Italy
Tehran Conference
1944 D-Day landings by British and American forces begin in Normandy
Rome falls to allied forces
1945 Warsaw falls to Soviet troops
Yalta Conference
Russian forces enter Berlin
President Roosevelt dies and is replaced by Truman
United Nations meets for the first time in San Francisco
Germany surrenders
Potsdam Conference
Nuclear bombs dropped on Hiroshima and Nagasaki
Japan surrenders
1946 Kennan Telegram
Iran crisis
Churchill's Iron Curtain speech at Fulton, Missouri
1947 Announcement of Truman Doctrine of aid to Greece and Turkey
Marshall Plan for economic recovery of Europe proposed
Creation of Cominform
1948 Czechoslovakian Coup
Marshall Plan passed by Congress
Berlin airlift
1949 COMECON established
NATO established
Berlin Blockade ends
USSR explodes its first atomic bomb
Federal Republic of Germany established
German Democratic Republic established

The breakdown of the Grand Alliance

When the Nazis attacked Russia in June 1941, both British Prime Minister **Winston S. Churchill** and Roosevelt sent aid to the Soviets. This marked the beginning of the Grand Alliance. However, this did not mark a change in how Stalin's Soviet Union was seen, particularly by the British. Churchill retained his dislike of the Soviet leader, remarking to his secretary, 'If Hitler invaded Hell, I would make at least favourable reference to the Devil in the House of Commons'. Thus, relations between the West and the USSR were still clouded by mutual suspicion, as they had been in the 1920s and 1930s.

Despite the fact that the two Western powers sent a considerable amount of aid to the USSR, Stalin demanded *more* action – nothing less than the opening of a 'second front' in Europe to take some of the pressure off the USSR in the east. The **Allies** agreed to this 'in principle', but said that they would not be able to open this 'second front' until the time was deemed right. Stalin was suspicious that they were deliberately delaying this offensive in the hope of seeing the Soviet Union permanently weakened by the continuing German onslaught.

At the first of the three wartime conferences, Tehran in 1943, relations between the **Big Three** seemed to improve a little, as the Western leaders proposed a definite date for the Normandy invasion: May 1944. In return, Stalin promised to declare war on Japan once Germany was defeated.

Step One: The wartime conferences

During the war, the decisions of the Grand Alliance determined the territorial and political structure of post-war Europe. There were three historic conferences between the Allies before the end of World War Two. The key issues under discussion at the conferences fall into the following categories:

- the state of the war
- the status of Germany, Poland, Eastern Europe and Japan
- the United Nations.

The Tehran Conference, 1943

The first conference was held in Tehran, Iran in November 1943. Those present were Josef Stalin representing the USSR, President Franklin Roosevelt representing the USA and Prime Minister Winston Churchill representing the United Kingdom. This was the first meeting of what became known as the Big Three. Their discussions focused on these key areas:

The state of the war: By 1943, the Allies had begun to win the war, following critical turning-point victories in 1942. The Soviets were now pushing the Germans into retreat on the Eastern front, while the Americans and the British had driven the Germans from North Africa and had invaded Mussolini's Italy. However, the UK and the USA had not yet launched the kind of second front that Stalin had been demanding. Therefore, Stalin continued to press his allies to take on more of the burden of confronting the German war machine from the USSR by invading north-western Europe. There was discussion of the war against Japan in the Pacific, which had entered its brutal 'island hopping' phase.

Germany: The key question for the Allies was what to do with Germany after it had been defeated. The Soviets had very different views about the future of Germany from those of the USA and Britain. Many of these differences stemmed from the varied wartime experiences of the Allies, the 'lessons' that seemed to have been learned from the failure of the Treaty of Versailles, and their widely differing ideologies. Thus there was no agreement on the future of a defeated Germany. However, they did confirm that 'unconditional surrender' of Germany was their objective. Roosevelt also supported 'Operation Overlord' (the Allied invasion of northern France that began with D-Day on 6 June 1944) as a priority.

Poland: Stalin's main concern was 'security'. This coloured not only his demands over the future of Germany, but also over the shape of Poland's post-war borders. Stalin wanted to secure his western border by gaining territory from Poland, and by ensuring that Poland had a pro-Soviet government. He argued that Poland had been the traditional launching pad for invasions of Russia. It was thus agreed that the USSR was to keep territory seized in 1939, and Poland in turn would be given territory on its western border from Germany. By agreeing to this, the Allies created a situation that no truly independent Poland could agree to, and also ensured future hostility between Germany and Poland. Thus, a **puppet regime** in Poland looked like a real possibility, and that regime presumably would have to look to the USSR for security. Tensions between the Poles and Soviets were increased in 1943 with the discovery of a mass grave of 10,000 Polish soldiers in the Katyn Forest. These soldiers had been captured by the Soviets in 1939. The Soviets blamed the Germans for the massacre, but many Poles suspected (rightly) that the Soviets were responsible.

Eastern Europe: The Soviets demanded the right to keep the territory that they had seized between 1939 and 1940. This meant remaining in control of the Baltic States, parts of Finland and Romania in Eastern Europe. With much reluctance, the Americans and the British agreed to the Soviet annexation of these territories. However, this was against the 1941 'Atlantic Charter' agreement between the United States and the United Kingdom.

The Atlantic Charter of August 1941

The Atlantic Charter was an agreement between the USA (before it had entered the war) and the UK, which broadly set down their mutual 'vision' of the shape of the post-war world. The charter focused on the future of occupied territories, which would return to selfrule. Both countries also agreed on free global trade, and the charter's high moral ideas provided the first steps towards the formation of the United Nations.

Japan: The United States and the United Kingdom pressed the USSR to enter the war with Japan. They wanted Stalin to open a Soviet 'second front' in Asia. However, Stalin could not be convinced to do this until the war with Germany was won.

The United Nations: The Americans, in particular, were very keen to establish a replacement for the League of Nations. The British and the Soviets gave their general approval to the idea of a new international organization being established. This would, again, be designed to settle international disputes through collective security. The USA hoped that lessons would have been learned from the 'mistakes' that were made in the structure and make up of the League of Nations and that the proposed United Nations Organization could more successfully fulfil this brief.

Conclusions: There were two main positive outcomes from the Tehran Conference:

- agreement on a new international organization
- agreement on the need for a weak post-war Germany.

Roosevelt and Stalin seemed to work reasonably well together. Indeed, on his return to the USA, Roosevelt publicly stated in a radio broadcast: 'I got along fine with Marshal Stalin … I believe that we are going to get along very well with him and the Russian people…' However, as the war continued, the next meeting of the Big Three revealed a growing gap between Stalin's post-war aims and those of the Western powers, though these differences seemed more acute between Stalin and Churchill. Churchill did not trust Stalin, and Roosevelt hoped to play the role of 'mediator' between the British and the Russians. Roosevelt seemed to believe that the more serious problem for post-war stability was British imperialism, rather than Soviet strength. Roosevelt is supposed to have told Stanislaw Mikolajczyk, the leader in London of the Poles in exile, '…of one thing I am certain, Stalin is not an imperialist.' Roosevelt did not appear overly concerned about the future of Poland, nor was he worried about the Allies taking the German capital, Berlin, before the Soviets.

The Yalta Conference, 1945

By the time of the February 1945 Yalta Conference on the Black Sea in the southern Ukraine, Stalin's diplomatic position was greatly strengthened by the physical fact that the Red Army occupied most of Eastern Europe. Once again, the Big Three powers were represented by Stalin, Roosevelt and Churchill. The topics under discussion were the same as at Tehran:

The state of the war: Germany was now on the verge of being defeated. With the Normandy landings in 1944, a second front had finally been opened. The Soviets had driven the Germans from Eastern Europe, and were now ready to invade Germany itself. The British and Americans had forced the Germans from France, and were now poised to cross the Rhine and invade Germany from the west. Japan was still fighting on, but had been under heavy aerial bombardment from the Americans. The USA was now in control of the air and sea in the Pacific, and the Japanese were preparing for the final desperate defence of their homeland.

Germany: The Allies decided that Germany would be disarmed, demilitarized, de-Nazified, and divided. It was agreed that post-war Germany would be divided into four zones of occupation between the USA, the USSR, the UK and France. This division was to be 'temporary', and Germany was to be run as one country. An Allied Control Commission (ACC) would be set up to govern Germany. Stalin demanded a large percentage of reparations from Germany after the devastation that the war in the East had wreaked on the Russians. It was agreed that Germany would pay $20 billion, and 50 per cent would go to the USSR.

Poland: Poland presented the greatest problem – where would the lines of its borders be drawn, and what would be the political make-up of her post-war government? At Yalta the new frontiers of Poland were decided. The border between Poland and the USSR was to be drawn at the 'Curzon Line' (see map below). This put the frontier back to where it had been before the **Russo-Polish War of 1921**. The Poles were to be compensated by gaining territory from Germany. This would be east of the 'Oder-Neisse Line'. Thus, Stalin had got what he had wanted territorially. In return, he agreed to the establishment of a more democratic government in Poland, following 'free elections'. This developed into the key area of disagreement between the British and the Soviets. The British supported the group known as the 'London Poles', who were the pre-war government that had fled to England in 1939, while the Russians wanted the Communist-dominated Lublin Committee in Poland to form the new post-war government.

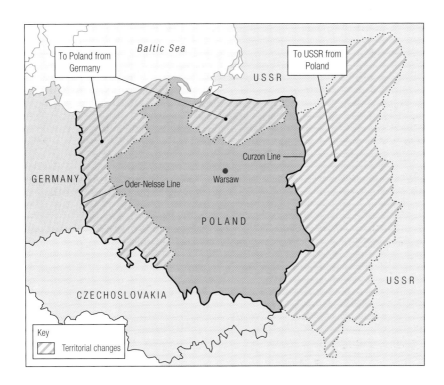

This map shows the new borders of Poland.

Eastern Europe: There seemed to be agreement at Yalta over the future nature of the governments of Eastern Europe. Stalin agreed that the countries of Eastern Europe would be able to decide who governed them in 'free elections'. This was perceived as a major victory for the USA and Britain. Indeed, for the British and Americans this was seen as the most significant of the wartime deals made with the Soviet Union.

Japan: Stalin now promised to enter the war with Japan, as soon as the war in Europe was won. However, the Soviets demanded territory in return from Japan as a 'reward'. This would include South Sakhalin and the Kurile Islands. The Americans and the British accepted these terms.

United Nations: Stalin agreed that the Soviet Union would join the United Nations Organization. The Allies agreed that there would be five permanent members of the Security Council, each with the power of the **veto**. Stalin went on to demand that all 16 Soviet Republics have separate seats in the UN General Assembly. The British and Americans agreed in the end to only three seats for individual republics: Russia, the Ukraine and Belarus.

Conclusions: There were three main positive outcomes of the Yalta Conference:

- agreement on the United Nations
- Soviet agreement to join the war in the Pacific against Japan
- the Big Three signing a 'Declaration for Liberated Europe' pledging their support for democratic governments based on free elections in all European countries, including Eastern Europe.

Who were the London Poles and the Lublin Poles?

The London Poles: Many thousands of Poles managed to escape from Poland during the two assaults on their country by German and Soviet forces in 1939–1940. These included members of the Polish government and armed forces. Approximately 100,000 refugee Polish troops regrouped in France and contributed to the Allied war effort. Although the Polish government in exile initially was also in France, it moved to London after the fall of France in 1940.

The London Poles were led by General Wladyslaw Sikorski until he died in a plane crash in July 1943. He had also been Commander-in-Chief of the Polish armed forces. He was succeeded as Prime Minister-in-exile by Stanislaw Mikolajczyk, who had been leader of the 'Peasant Party'. Mikolajczyk was fairly left-wing, and open to the idea of reaching an agreement with the Soviets. However, the new Commander-in-Chief of the army, General Kazimierz Sosnkowski, together with other leading Poles, was opposed to any deals with the Soviets.

Churchill had a very tough time persuading the Poles to accept a shift in their border to the west of the Curzon Line (see map on page 13). The Poles insisted that if they were to sacrifice the land they had gained in war (1920–1921), then they must have cast-iron guarantees that Poland's government would be 'free' after the war.

But, as Soviet forces moved west in 1944, it seemed increasingly unlikely that Poland's future government would indeed be free of Soviet interference.

The London Poles played an important part in the doomed Warsaw Rising of August 1944. When the Red Army reached Warsaw on its advance to Germany, the Polish underground forces, commanded by the London Poles, rose up against the Germans. Instead of moving in to assist the attack on the Germans, Stalin ordered the Red Army to stop its advance. The Red Army waited outside Warsaw until the Nazis had brutally put down the rebellion, killing almost 200,000 resistance fighters. The Soviets then moved in and 'liberated' Warsaw and Poland, putting in their own provisional government – the Lublin Poles.

The Lublin Poles: Not all Poles were anti-Soviet, and some had felt just as patriotic supporting the Communists. In July 1944, a Committee of National Liberation was set up in Soviet-occupied Lublin, a large city in eastern Poland. This group then came to be known as the Lublin Committee, and they stated that they were a coalition of democratic and patriotic forces, who wished to work with the Soviet Union. This group agreed to the Curzon Line boundary and committed itself to a far-reaching programme of social and economic reform. The USSR recognized this group as the only lawful authority in Poland. Indeed, the Red Army was instructed to co-operate only with representatives of the Lublin Committee.

Towards the end of the war, these Lublin Poles became more influential inside Poland than the London group. Although the Lublin Poles were supposed to liaise closely with the London Poles in the post-war Government of National Unity, they dominated post-war politics in Poland. Leading members of the Lublin Committee were Wladyslaw Gomulka and Boleslaw Bierut.

STUDENT STUDY SECTION

Document analysis

Behind the scenes at Yalta

The letter below was written by President Franklin Roosevelt to Stalin on 6 February 1945 while both were at Yalta. It is about the situation regarding Poland:

> February 6, 1945
>
> My dear Marshall Stalin:
>
> I have been giving a great deal of thought to our meeting this afternoon, and I want to tell you in all frankness what is on my mind.

In so far as the Polish Government is concerned, I am greatly disturbed that the three great powers do not have a meeting of minds about the political setup in Poland. It seems to me that it puts all of us in a bad light throughout the world to have you recognizing one government while we and the British are recognizing another in London. I am sure this state of affairs should not continue and that if it does it can only lead our people to think there is a breach between us, which is not the case. I am determined that there shall be no breach between ourselves and the Soviet Union. Surely there is a way to reconcile our differences.

I was very much impressed with some of the things you said today, particularly your determination that your rear must be safeguarded as your army moves into Berlin. You cannot, and we must not, tolerate any temporary government which will give your armed forces any trouble of this sort. I want you to know that I am fully mindful of this.

You must believe me when I tell you that our people at home look with a critical eye on what they consider a disagreement between us at this vital stage of the war. They, in effect, say that if we cannot get a meeting of minds now when our armies are converging on the common enemy, how can we get an understanding on even more vital things in the future.

I have had to make it clear to you that we cannot recognize the Lublin Government as now composed, and the world would regard it as a lamentable outcome of our work here if we parted with an open and obvious divergence between us on this issue.

You said today that you would be prepared to support any suggestions for the solution of this problem which offered a fair chance of success, and you also mentioned the possibility of bringing some members of the Lublin government here.

Realizing that we all have the same anxiety in getting the matter settled, I would like to develop your proposal a little and suggest that we invite here to Yalta at once Mr Beirut [Bierut] and Mr Osubka [Osóbka] Morawski from the Lublin government and also two or three from the following list of Poles, who according to our information would be desirable as representatives of the other elements of the Polish people in development of a new temporary government which all three of us could recognize and support: Bishop Sapieha of Cracow, Vincente [Wincenty] Witos, Mr. Zurlowski [Zulawski], Professor Buyak [Bujak], and Professor Kutzeva [Kutzeba]. If, as a result of the presence of these Polish leaders from abroad such as Mr Mikolajczyk, M. Grabski, and Mr Romer, the United States Government, and I feel sure the British government as well, would be prepared to examine with you conditions in which they would dissociate themselves from the London government and transfer their recognition to the new provisional government.

I hope that I do not have to assure you that the United States will never lend its support in any way to any provisional government in Poland that would be inimical to your interest.

It goes without saying that any interim government formed as a result of our conference with the Poles here would be pledged to the holding of free elections in Poland at the earliest possible date. I know this is completely consistent with your desire to see a new free and democratic Poland emerge from the welter of this war.

Most sincerely yours

Franklin Roosevelt

Document Questions

1 What is the general 'tone' of this letter to Stalin from Roosevelt?

2 Roosevelt shows sympathy for which of Stalin's key concerns?

3 What suggestions are made for resolving the disagreement over the Polish government?

4 What does this suggest about the relationship between Roosevelt and Stalin?

● **Examiner's hint:** Questions 1 and 4 are asking you to 'read between the lines', i.e., to show the examiner that you understand what Roosevelt's attitude was towards Stalin. Look carefully at the language he uses and quote any useful words or phrases that support your answer.

The Yalta Conference, 1945: ▶
Churchill, Roosevelt and Stalin.

What were the crucial developments that took place between the Yalta and Potsdam Conferences?

There were some crucial events that radically changed the atmosphere of, and the influences on, the next meeting of the Allies in 1945.

- President Roosevelt died in April 1945 and was replaced by Truman, who was to adopt a more hardline, or 'get tough', policy towards the Soviets.
- Germany finally surrendered unconditionally on 7 May 1945.
- Winston Churchill's Conservative Party lost the 1945 UK general election and Churchill was succeeded as Prime Minister by the Labour Party leader, Clement Atlee.
- As the war in Europe ended, the Soviet Red Army occupied territory as far west as deep inside Germany.
- On the very day after the Potsdam Conference began, 17 July 1945, the United States successfully tested its first atomic bomb.

The Potsdam Conference, 1945

The Potsdam Conference took place in July 1945 in Potsdam, Germany. Those participating were Josef Stalin representing the USSR, President Harry S Truman representing the USA and Prime Minister Clement Atlee representing the UK.

The state of the war: In May 1945, Germany surrendered 'unconditionally'. Although war in the Pacific raged on, the Americans were now poised to invade the mainland. By the time the Potsdam Conference began, the USA was planning to use their new atomic weapon against Japan – if the tests on it proved successful.

Germany: The Allies had agreed at Yalta to disarm, demilitarize, de-Nazify and divide Germany, but at Potsdam they could not agree how this should be done. Finally it was decided that they would carry out the de-Nazification and demilitarization of Germany in their own ways in their own respective zones of occupation. The German economy was to be run as a 'whole', but it was to be limited to domestic industry and agriculture (at 74 per cent of 1936 levels). The Soviets were to receive 25 per cent of their reparation bill from the Western zones. The more agricultural Eastern zone was to give food in exchange.

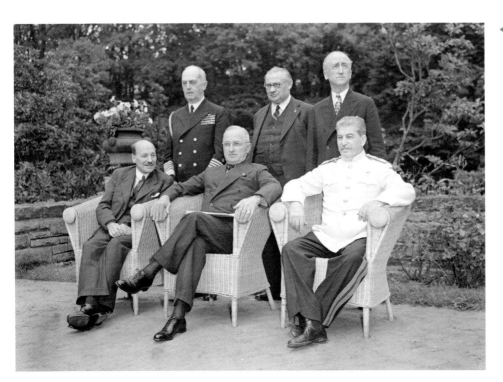

Poland: The new U.S. president, Harry S Truman, was not happy with the agreements over Poland, so he challenged the decision over the new western frontier between Poland and Germany (the Oder-Neisse line). Truman also insisted that the Polish government be 're-organized'. In other words the Americans wanted an entirely new government. They did not feel that there had been a 'free and democratic' vote, and Stalin's offer to include more 'London' Poles within the predominantly 'Lublin'-led government did not appease the USA.

Eastern Europe: The new U.S. leadership was also unhappy about the so-called 'Percentages Agreement' that had been made **bilaterally** between Stalin and Churchill in October 1944 (see page 18). Spheres of influence had been discussed in terms of 'percentages' when deciding the future fate of countries in East and South-eastern Europe. Truman challenged the influence that this agreement had given Stalin over Romania and Bulgaria. However, Soviet military control of Eastern Europe was a fact – the Red Army was literally standing on the territories. Thus, it was very difficult for the West to force Stalin to make any changes. Truman did not want to see Eastern Europe become a Soviet 'sphere of influence', but without threatening to push the Red Army back with ground forces there was little practically that the United States could do. The Red Army from the East, which had come to liberate the area from the Nazis, was beginning to look like an army of 'occupation' to the Americans.

Japan: Truman was told during this conference that the atomic bomb tests had been successful. On 6 August 1945 the first atomic bomb used in war was dropped on Hiroshima. Three days later another atomic bomb was dropped on Nagasaki. Soon after the Japanese finally agreed to 'unconditional surrender'. However, although the Americans liaised with their British allies, Truman did not tell Stalin the 'full story' about this new 'super weapon'. And, for the first time, at this conference the Americans did not encourage the Soviets to join in the war against Japan.

United Nations: The United Nations became a reality. It was officially created at the Treaty of San Francisco in 1945. The USSR was the only Communist power of the 'Big 5' (the USA, the USSR, France, Britain and Nationalist China), who were the permanent members of the UN Security Council. Stalin used the power of veto this gave the USSR to block any initiatives that he perceived to be against Soviet interests.

Conclusions: There were two positive outcomes from the Potsdam Conference:

- agreement for the immediate, practical control of the defeated Germany
- the establishment of the United Nations.

The Percentages Agreement of October 1944

On 9 October 1944, at a meeting in Moscow, Stalin and Churchill devised what is known as the 'Percentages Agreement', which relates to influence and control the Western Powers and the USSR would want to have in various areas after the defeat of Germany. Churchill apparently was concerned that it would appear rather cynical that the two leaders scribbled the fate of millions on a piece of paper. He suggested to Stalin that he burn the paper it was written on. 'No, you keep it,' said Stalin.

Romania
- Russia 90%
- Others 10%

Greece
- United Kingdom 90% (in accord with USA)
- Russia 10%

Yugoslavia
- 50% – 50%

Hungary
- 50% – 50%

Bulgaria
- Russia 75%
- Others 25%

STUDENT STUDY SECTION

Review questions

1 Look over the issues that were discussed at the three conferences. Which issues were satisfactorily resolved?

2 Which decisions were likely to cause tension in the future?

3 From what you have read so far in both Chapters 1 and 2, what do you consider to be the 'seeds' of East–West conflict that were sown from 1917 onwards?

Key developments 1946–1947

Before moving on to Step Two it is important to look at some key developments that were to have an impact on U.S.–Soviet relations.

Salami tactics

One way the Soviet Union gained increasing political control over Eastern Europe was by the method known as 'salami tactics'. This term is said to have come from a remark made by the Hungarian Communist leader, Rakosi, commenting on how the USSR secured Communist control in Eastern Europe, 'like slicing off salami, piece by piece':

- Stage One: The Soviets supervised the organization of governments in the Eastern European states, initially establishing a broad alliance of 'anti-fascists'.
- Stage Two: Each of the parties was 'sliced off', one after the other.
- Stage Three: The Communist 'core' was left, and then ultimately the local Communists were replaced (if need be) with Moscow-trained people.

By the end of 1946, the so-called 'Baggage Train' leaders had returned to Eastern Europe. These were the men who had spent much of the war in Moscow, and were considered by the Soviets to be 'trustworthy', for example, Bierut (who returned to Poland), Kolarov (who returned to Bulgaria), Pauker (who returned to Romania) and Rakosi (who returned to Hungary).These leaders would thus ensure that the post-war governments of their respective countries would be dominated by Moscow-backed, 'Stalinist' Communists.

Case study: Poland The 'free elections' promised by Stalin at Yalta to occur in a matter of 'weeks', were not held until 19 January 1947. Before the elections there had been a campaign of murder, censorship and intimidation. It is estimated that over 50,000 people were deported to Siberia before the elections.

During the elections in January, Mikolajczyk's Polish Peasant Party had 246 candidates disqualified; 149 were arrested and 18 murdered. One million voters were taken off the electoral register for some reason or another. As Desmond Donnelly contends in his book *Struggle for the World*, 'In these appalling circumstances of intimidation, it was not surprising that Bierut's Communists secured complete control in Poland'.

The Soviet perspective on these elections was quite different from that of the West, where they were seen as a breach of the Yalta agreements. The Soviets, however, saw them as a victory over 'Western expansionism:

The political goals set by Mikolajczyk in cahoots with Churchill required that Warsaw be liberated (by British and American) forces before the Soviet army reached the city. That way a pro-Western government supported by Mikolajczyk would already be in control of the city by the time the Soviets arrived. But it didn't work out that way. Our troops under Rokossovsky got there first.

Nikita Khrushchev in Khrushchev Remembers, Volume One *(Little, Brown and Co., 1970)*

This pattern of securing Soviet-Communist-style governments was emerging in the other Eastern European countries that the Red Army had occupied at the end of World War Two – Bulgaria, Romania and Hungary. In Czechoslovakia and Finland there remained only a semblance of democracy.

Soviet pressure on Iran

Another place in which the USSR tried to increase its political control in the aftermath of the war was Iran. At the Tehran Conference, it had been agreed that both the British and the Soviets would withdraw their troops from Iran after the war. The UK took its troops out, but Stalin left 30,000 of his in the north, claiming that they were needed there to help put down internal rebellion.

However, these Soviet troops encouraged a Communist uprising, and the Iranian government complained to the USSR's former allies. The British and Americans demanded that Stalin remove his troops immediately. They also saw this as another breach in the wartime agreements. On 1 January 1946, Stalin refused. He believed that after the war he had as much right to the Black Sea Straits and to Iranian oil as did his former allies. Four days later, Truman wrote to his Secretary of State, James Byrnes. In this letter Truman revealed that he thought the USSR was planning an invasion of Turkey and the Black Sea Straits. He also wrote, '… unless Russia is faced with an iron fist and strong language, war is in the making'. In March the United Nations had its first crisis to deal with – Iran. Iran had made a formal protest to the UN concerning the continued presence of Soviet forces. Under this new pressure, Moscow finally pulled its troops out.

Instability in Greece and Turkey

After World War Two there were anti-imperialist, nationalist and, to a certain extent, 'pro-Communist' rebellions in Greece and Turkey. The British, and to a lesser degree the USA, believed that these rebellions were being directed and supported by the Soviets. Churchill, in particular, was annoyed at Stalin's apparent disregard for their 'Percentages Agreement'.

Communist parties in Italy and France

Communist parties in both these 'Western democracies' grew stronger in post-war Europe, their membership increasing due to the economic deprivations and hardships at the end of the war in Europe. The Americans and the British were suspicious that these newly popular Communist parties were receiving 'encouragement' from Moscow. Indeed there was concern that Italy and France could be 'weak links' in anti-Communist Western Europe.

Cartoon analysis

1   Who is the dancer in the cartoon?

2   What do the daggers represent?

3   What is the message of the cartoon?

• **Examiner's hint:** In Question 3 you need to make sure that you structure your answer clearly. Start your answer with 'The overall message is …' and then give details from the cartoon to support your answer.

This French cartoon from 1950 is entitled 'Caucasian Dance'.

Step Two: Kennan's long telegram, February 1946

George F. Kennan, U.S. diplomat in Moscow.

In February 1946, a key U.S. diplomat in Moscow, **George F. Kennan**, sent a telegram to the U.S. State Department on the nature of Soviet conduct and foreign policy. His views on the motives behind Soviet foreign policy were to have a lasting influence on the State Department. The key idea in this telegram was that the Soviet system was buoyed by the 'threat' of a 'hostile world outside its borders', that the USSR was 'fanatically and implacably' hostile to the West: 'Impervious to the logic of reason Moscow [is] highly sensitive to the logic of force. For this reason it can easily withdraw – and usually does – when strong resistance is encountered at any point'.

To summarize, the key points of Kennan's telegram were:

• The USSR's view of the world was a traditional one of insecurity.

• The Soviets wanted to advance Muscovite Stalinist ideology (not simply 'Marxism').

• The Soviet regime was cruel and repressive and justified this by perceiving nothing but evil in the outside world. That view of a hostile outside environment would sustain the internal Stalinist system.

• The USSR was fanatically hostile to the West – but they were not 'suicidal'.

Kennan's 'logic of force' argument helped to harden attitudes in the USA and was to play a key role in the development of the U.S. policy of containment (see Chapter Six).

Step Three: Churchill's Iron Curtain Speech, March 1946

On 5 March 1946, former British Prime Minister Winston Churchill gave a speech at Westminister College in Fulton, Missouri, with President Harry S Truman sitting just behind him on the speakers' platform. This speech is now seen as one of the defining moments in the origins of the Cold War.

Churchill's speech warned of a new danger for Europe:

A shadow has fallen upon the scenes so lately lighted by the allied victory. Nobody knows what Soviet Russia and its Communist international organization intends to do in the immediate future, or what are the limits, if any, to their expansive proselytizing tendencies. I have a strong admiration and regard for the valiant Russian people and for my war-time comrade, Marshal Stalin. There is sympathy and goodwill … toward the peoples of all the Russias … We understand the Russian need to be secure on her western frontiers from all renewal of German aggression. We welcome her to her rightful place among the leading nations of the world … It is my duty, however, to place before you certain facts about the present position in Europe.

From Stettin in the Baltic to Trieste in the Adriatic, an iron curtain has descended across the Continent. Behind the line lie all the capitals of the ancient states of central and eastern Europe – Warsaw, Berlin, Prague, Vienna, Budapest, Belgrade, Bucharest and Sofia. All these famous cities and the populations around them lie in the Soviet sphere and all are subject in one form or another, not only to Soviet influence but to a very high and increasing measure of control from Moscow … The Russian-dominated Polish government has been encouraged to make enormous and wrongful inroads upon Germany, and mass expulsions of millions of Germans on a scale grievous and undreamed of are now taking place. The Communist Parties, which were very small in all these eastern states of Europe, have been raised to pre-eminence and power far beyond their numbers and are seeking everywhere to obtain totalitarian control. Police governments are prevailing in nearly every case … Whatever conclusions may be drawn from these facts … this is certainly not the liberated Europe we fought to build up. Nor is it one which contains the essentials of a permanent peace …

On the other hand I repulse the idea that a new war is inevitable; still more that it is imminent … I do not believe that Soviet Russia desires war. What they desire is the fruits of war and the indefinite expansion of their power and doctrines … Our difficulties and dangers will not be removed by closing our eyes to them. They will not be removed by mere waiting to see what happens; nor will they be relieved by a policy of appeasement … From what I have seen of our Russian friends and allies during the war, I am convinced that there is nothing they admire so much as strength and there is nothing for which they have less respect than for military weakness … If the western democracies stand together in strict adherence to the principles of the United Nations Charter, their influence for furthering these principles will be immense … If, however, they become divided or falter in their duty … then indeed catastrophe may overwhelm us all.

Winston S. Churchill, Address at Westminster College, Fulton, Missouri, 5 March 1946

STUDENT STUDY SECTION

Document and review questions

1   Why did Churchill use the phrase 'iron curtain' to describe events in Europe?

2   In what way does Churchill allude to the idea of 'salami tactics' taking place in Eastern Europe?

3   Imagine that you are Stalin reading this speech. What might your reaction be?

What was the basis for the Iron Curtain speech?

In his Iron Curtain speech, Winston Churchill was referring to the fact that by 1946, Soviet-dominated Communist governments were set up in Poland, Hungary, Romania and Bulgaria. This was in spite of the hopes expressed at Yalta that there would be free and democratic elections in Eastern Europe after the war. Communist regimes not linked directly to Moscow had been established in Albania and Yugoslavia as well. Within two to three years this Soviet influence would be extended to East Germany and Czechoslovakia. His remarks were also prompted by the presence of the Red Army in those countries 'liberated' from Germany by the Russians – and by the cloak of secrecy which descended over Eastern Europe within a few months of the end of the war.

Soviet reaction to Churchill's speech

The response from the Soviet leadership was quick and one of outrage. Within a week Stalin had compared Churchill to Hitler. He saw the speech as both 'racist' and as 'a call to war with the Soviet Union'. Within three weeks the Soviets had taken several steps:

- They withdrew from the International Monetary Fund (IMF).
- They stepped up the tone and intensity of anti-Western propaganda.
- They initiated a new five-year plan of self-strengthening.

Therefore, the 'Iron Curtain' speech led to a further hardening of opinions on both sides. Churchill had defined publicly the new front line in what was now being seen as a new war.

STUDENT STUDY SECTION

Document analysis

Document A

In this Soviet cartoon Churchill waves flags reading 'An Iron Curtain is over Europe' and 'Anglo-Saxons Must Rule the World'.

Document B

Stalin's March 1946 response to the 'Iron Curtain' speech:

'Hitler began his work of unleashing war by proclaiming a "race theory", declaring that only German-speaking people constituted a superior nation. Mr Churchill sets out to unleash a war with a race theory, asserting that only English-speaking nations are superior nations, who are called upon to decide the destinies of the entire world … There can be no doubt that Mr Churchill's position is a call for war on the USSR.

'It is absurd to speak of exclusive control by the USSR in Vienna and Berlin, where there are allied control councils made up of the representatives of four states and where the USSR has only one-quarter of the votes. The Soviet Union's loss of life [in the war] has been several times greater than that of Britain and the USA put together. Possibly in some quarters an inclination is felt to forget about these colossal sacrifices of the Soviet people, which secured the liberation of Europe from the Hitlerite yoke. But the Soviet Union cannot forget about them. And so what can there be surprising about the fact that the Soviet Union, anxious for its future safety, is trying to see to it that governments loyal in their attitude to the Soviet Union should exist in these countries?'

Questions

1 Explain the message of the Soviet cartoon on page 22.

2 In what ways does the cartoon support the ideas expressed in Stalin's speech?

Review activities

Review these key Cold War issues up to 1946. Add brief notes to the bullet point sub-headings. In your notes, consider how each point added to tension between East and West.
* The opening of a second front
* The Warsaw uprising
* Tensions at Yalta
* Clear divisions at Potsdam
* Hiroshima
* Red Army in Eastern Europe
* Salami tactics
* Germany
* Iran
* Kennan's 'Long Telegram'
* Churchill's Fulton speech
* Instability in Greece and Turkey
* Communist party success in Italy and France

ToK Time
How can changes in 'language' affect our understanding of the past? In what ways can our culture impact on our interpretation of historical events?

● **Examiner's hint:** In Question 2 you are looking for ways in which the sources say the *same* thing. Focus on this and not on differences. Be specific in your comparisons: pick out phrases in the speech which you can quote in support of the cartoon.

3

STEPS TO THE POLITICAL, ECONOMIC AND MILITARY DIVISION OF EUROPE: PART II

Confrontation and containment

In Steps One to Three in Chapter Two, we examined the breakdown of the Grand Alliance of World War Two. In this chapter, Steps Four to Eight, the confrontation between the USA and the USSR intensifies as political, economic and military divisions develop.

Step Four: The Truman Doctrine

Truman made a key speech to the U.S. Congress on 12 March 1947. In this speech he put forward the belief that the United States had the obligation to 'support free peoples who are resisting attempted subjugation by armed minorities or by outside pressures'. This became known as the 'Truman Doctrine'.

It was a radical change in U.S. foreign policy, a policy which had been traditionally **isolationist**. Truman's new 'doctrine' was in response to the unstable situations in Turkey and, in particular, Greece. At the end of the war the British had restored the Greek monarchy, but Communist guerrillas continued to resist in the countryside. The British government could no longer offer assistance to the Greek government, as its own economy had been devastated by the war, leaving the British government £3000 million of debt. In February 1947, the British told the USA that they could no longer maintain troops in Greece. The United States did not want to risk a potential Communist takeover of a strategically important European country, so Truman issued his 'doctrine' and, in the name of preserving democracy over Communism, U.S. aid and military advisers were sent to Greece.

The Soviets saw this as evidence of the determination of the United States to expand its sphere of influence, and they did not recognize any legitimacy in this new American involvement in Europe. Truman's decision was affected not only by Churchill's perception of the expansionist threat, as outlined in his 'Iron Curtain' speech, but also by George Kennan's Long Telegram. As already mentioned, this 'doctrine' marked a departure from the United States' traditional policy of isolation, and it was the beginning of the American policy of 'containment' of Communism. The philosophy of containment would, in the years to come, draw the USA into the affairs of nations well beyond Europe.

On the longer-term significance of the Truman Doctrine, political historian Walter LaFeber wrote:

The Truman Doctrine was a milestone in American history ... the doctrine became an ideological shield behind which the United States marched to rebuild the Western political and economic system and counter the radical left. From 1947 on, therefore, any threats to that Western system could be easily explained as Communist inspired, not as problems which arose from difficulties within the system itself. That was the most lasting and tragic result of the Truman Doctrine.

*Walter LaFeber in **America, Russia and the Cold War**, 5th ed (Knopf, 1985) pp.57–8*

The Truman Doctrine is announced:

At the present moment in world history nearly every nation must choose between alternative ways of life. The choice is too often not a free one.

One way of life is based upon the will of the majority, and is distinguished by free institutions, representative government, free elections, and guarantees of individual liberty, freedom of speech and religion and freedom from political oppression.

The second way of life is based upon the will of a minority forcibly imposed upon the majority. It relies upon terror and oppression, a controlled press and radio, fixed election and the suppression of personal freedom.

I believe that it must be the policy of the United States to support peoples who are resisting attempted subjugation by armed minorities or by outside pressures.

I believe that we must assist free peoples to work out their own destiny in their own way.

President Truman, in address to the U.S. Congress, 12 March 1947

Questions

1 What justification does Truman give for his Doctrine?

2 Identify the key words that Truman uses to describe the West and key words he uses to describe countries under Soviet control. Why do you think he uses this type of language?

3 How important is this document for explaining the development of the Cold War?

Step Five: The Marshall Plan

In January 1947, the U.S. Secretary of State, James Byrnes, resigned and was replaced by General **George Marshall**. Marshall believed that the economies of Western Europe needed immediate help from the USA. In a broadcast to the nation he declared, 'The patient is sinking while the doctors deliberate'. The 'Marshall Plan' seemed to follow quite naturally on from the Truman Doctrine – it was the economic extension of the ideas outlined by the President. Marshall introduced his plan in a speech at Harvard University on 5 June 1947:

It is logical that the United States should do whatever it is able to do to assist in the return of normal economic health in the world, without which there can be no political stability and no assured peace. Our policy is not directed against any country or doctrine, but against hunger, poverty, desperation and chaos. Its purpose should be the revival of a working economy in the world so as to permit the emergence of political and social conditions in which free institutions can exist … Any government which is willing to assist in the task of recovery will find full co-operation … on the part of the United States Government.

Before the United States Government can proceed much further in its efforts to alleviate the situation and help start the European world on its way to recovery, there must be some agreement among the countries of Europe as to the requirements of the situation and the part those countries themselves will take in order to give proper effect to whatever action might be undertaken by this Government. It would be neither fitting nor efficacious for this Government to undertake to draw up unilaterally a program designed to place Europe on its feet economically. This is the business of the Europeans. The initiative, I think, must come from Europe.

George C. Marshall, Address at Harvard University, 5 June 1947, in Department of State Bulletin XXVII, 15 June 1947, pp.1159-6

Dollar imperialism?

The Marshall Plan was designed to give immediate economic help to Europe. The problem of whether or not to 'allow' the Soviets to join the plan, or indeed to avoid specifically excluding them, was solved by setting down strict criteria to qualify for American economic aid. This involved allowing the United States to investigate the financial records of applicant countries. The USSR would never tolerate this condition.

Thus, the United States invited the USSR to join the Marshall Plan and claimed that this 'aid' was not directed for or against any country or doctrine. The stated aims of Marshall Plan aid were to:

- revive European working economies so that political and social stability could ensue
- safeguard the future of the U.S. economy.

However, to avoid the interpretation that the United States was in any way coercing European governments to accept the aid plan, it was made clear that 'the initiative must come from Europe'.

The bill allocating the four-year aid programme of $17 billion did not pass the U.S. Congress until March 1948. The eventual success of the bill was due mainly to the effect of the Czechoslovakian Coup of February 1948 (see Step Seven).

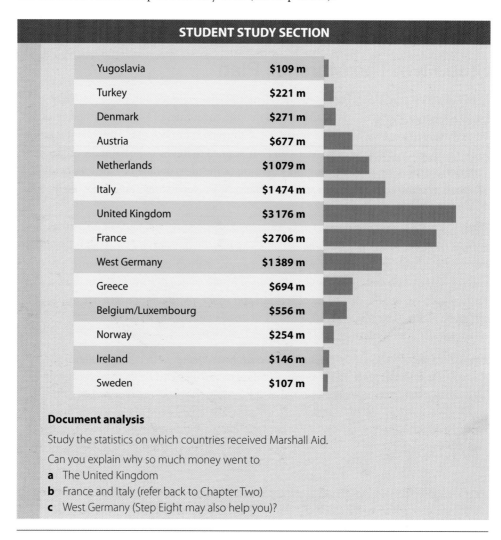

STUDENT STUDY SECTION

Country	Amount
Yugoslavia	**$109 m**
Turkey	**$221 m**
Denmark	**$271 m**
Austria	**$677 m**
Netherlands	**$1 079 m**
Italy	**$1 474 m**
United Kingdom	**$3 176 m**
France	**$2 706 m**
West Germany	**$1 389 m**
Greece	**$694 m**
Belgium/Luxembourg	**$556 m**
Norway	**$254 m**
Ireland	**$146 m**
Sweden	**$107 m**

Document analysis

Study the statistics on which countries received Marshall Aid.

Can you explain why so much money went to
a   The United Kingdom
b   France and Italy (refer back to Chapter Two)
c   West Germany (Step Eight may also help you)?

Soviet reaction to the Marshall Plan

The Soviets rejected the Marshall Plan – as the USA probably intended them to – because the Americans had asked to see recipients' financial records. The Soviets saw this as a prime example of American 'dollar imperialism'. In other words, the Soviets felt the USA was establishing a European empire, and that its method was economic domination and dependence, which would ultimately give it political control.

Soviet Foreign Minister Vyshinsky gave the following speech at the United Nations in September 1947:

The so-called Truman doctrine is a particularly glaring example of the way in which the principles of the United Nations are violated, of the way in which the United Nations is ignored. The United States has moved towards giving up the idea of international co-operation and joint action by the great powers. It has tried to force its will on the other independent countries, whilst at the same time obviously using the money distributed as relief to needy countries as an instrument of political pressure.

This is clearly proved by the measures taken by the United States government with regard to Greece and Turkey, which ignore and bypass the United Nations. This policy conflicts sharply with the principle expressed by the General Assembly in its resolution of 11th December 1946, which declares that relief supplies to other countries should, at no time, be used as a political weapon.

The Marshall Plan is merely a variant of the Truman Doctrine. It is becoming more and more evident to everyone that the implementation of the Marshall Plan will mean placing European countries under the economic and political control of the United States and direct interference by the latter in those countries.

Moreover this plan is an attempt to split Europe into two camps and, with the help of the United Kingdom and France, to complete the formation of a bloc of several European countries hostile to the interests of the democratic countries.

'A view of the Marshall Plan', a cartoon on the cover of the Soviet humour magazine, *Krokodil*.

STUDENT STUDY SECTION

Discussion and review questions

1   To what extent was the Soviet objection to the Marshall Plan 'ignoring' or 'bypassing' the United Nations valid?

2   Vyshinsky suggests that the Marshall Plan will lead to the formation of 'two camps' in Europe. Why?

3   Now look at the cartoon above from *Krokodil*. Which part of Vyshinsky's speech supports the cartoon's message?

Previously the United States had attempted to unite the West with economic tactics; now they were on a path towards military unity. Historian Walter LaFeber pointed out the significance of the Marshall Plan:

The plan's approach … soon evolved into military alliances. Truman proved to be correct in saying that the Truman Doctrine and the Marshall Plan 'are two halves of the same walnut'. Americans willingly acquiesced as the military aspects of the doctrine developed into quite the larger part.

The Soviet response

In response to the Marshall Plan, the Soviets came up with the Molotov Plan, which was a series of bilateral trade agreements aimed to tie the economies of Eastern Europe to the USSR. The outcome was the creation of COMECON in January 1949. COMECON was the Council for Mutual Economic Assistance. This was a centralized agency that linked Eastern bloc countries to Moscow. It was designed to 'stimulate' and control their economic development, and support the collectivization of agriculture and the development of heavy industry.

STUDENT STUDY SECTION

Cartoon analysis

1 How are:
   a the USA and
   b the USSR portrayed in the *Punch* cartoon?

2 What is the message of the cartoon regarding Stalin's policy in Eastern Europe?

Punch cartoon, June 1947. Passengers are being given a choice of two buses, one driven by Stalin and the other by Truman.

THE RIVAL BUSES

Cominform and the 'Two Camps' doctrine

Before moving on to Step Six, it is important to consider two developments on the Soviet side of the Iron Curtain:

Cominform: This was the Communist Information Bureau set up in September 1947. It was created as an instrument to increase Stalin's control over the Communist parties of other countries. It was initially comprised of Communists from the USSR, Yugoslavia, France, Italy, Poland, Bulgaria, Hungary and Romania. The West was concerned that this organization would actively spread Communism (and destabilize the democratic governments) in the West's own 'sphere of influence' – Western Europe.

Stalin's 'Two Camps' Doctrine: Soviet leader Josef Stalin developed his idea of a Europe divided into two opposing camps in the 1920s and 1930s. Following World War Two, this idea, in the divisive context of post-war international relations, became a firm foundation for Soviet foreign policy. Indeed, in February 1946 (before Churchill's Iron Curtain Speech) Stalin had delivered a speech emphasizing the creation of 'two camps' opposing each other. At the inaugural meeting of Cominform in Warsaw, Soviet delegate Andrei Zhadanov delivered an important speech on Soviet foreign policy. He stated that the Americans had organized an 'anti-Soviet' bloc of countries that were economically dependent upon them – not only those in Western Europe, but also in South America and China. The 'second camp' was the USSR and the 'new democracies' in Eastern Europe. He also included countries he deemed 'associated' or 'sympathetic' to their cause – Indonesia, Vietnam, India, Egypt and Syria. This Soviet doctrine was very similar to the 'new world order' outlined by Truman.

Step Six: Red Army occupation of Eastern Europe, 1945–1947

The Soviet Union came to control various Eastern European states by creating what became known as a 'satellite empire'. These countries kept their separate legal identities – separate from each other and the USSR – but they were tied into following Moscow's line by the following factors:

- Soviet military power (later formalized in the Warsaw Pact in 1955)
- 'Salami tactics' (see Step One) which transferred the machinery of government into the hands of obedient, pro-Soviet Communists
- State police and security/spy networks
- COMECON (see Step Five).

As discussed under Step One, Soviet control was in place in most East European countries by 1947. There just remained Czechoslovakia. Salami tactics were taking a little longer there, and Stalin decided that a coup to finally oust non-Communist members of the government would be necessary (see Step Seven).

Thus, by the end of 1948, the satellite states were economically and militarily under the control of the USSR. The USA and its Western allies saw this 'occupation' of Eastern Europe as a direct breach of the agreements made at Yalta and Potsdam and, perhaps more importantly, as clear evidence of Soviet expansionist policies in practice.

The 'Mr X article'

Before moving on to Step Seven, this is a good point to look at the now infamous 'Mr X article' written by George F. Kennan for *Time Magazine* in 1947. In it he says:

> It is clear that the main element of any United States policy towards the Soviet Union must be that of a long term, patient but firm and vigilant containment of Russian expansive tendencies … It is clear that the United States cannot expect in the foreseeable future to enjoy political intimacy with the Soviet regime. It must continue to regard the Soviet Union as a rival, not a partner, in the political arena.

An extract from the 'Mr. X article', Time Magazine, *July 1947*

Kennan was still a strong influence on President Truman, and his reputation as the United States' key expert on Soviet policy also gave him influence over American public opinion. In view of the Soviet takeover of Eastern Europe, a policy to contain the spread of Communism seemed all the more essential.

STUDENT STUDY SECTION

Discussion point

From what you have read so far, whom do you consider to be most responsible for the growth of hostility between East and West up to 1947, the USA or the Soviet Union?

Step Seven: The Czechoslovakian Coup, February 1948

The Soviets continued into 1948 to attempt to consolidate their control over Eastern Europe. Czechoslovakia, however, was seen as moving towards the West. What was most worrying to Stalin was that Czechoslovakia had expressed interest in receiving aid from the Marshall Plan. In addition, there was a certain amount of sentimental feeling in the West for the Czechs after their 'abandonment' (or, as some would say, betrayal) in the **Munich Agreements** of 1938.

In February 1948, Stalin organized pressure on the Czechoslovak coalition government. Twelve non-Communist members were forced to resign. The Czech Communist Party leader demanded the formation of a Communist-led government. Under heavy pressure from Moscow, coupled with loosely veiled threats of armed intervention, Czech President Eduard Benes agreed. He felt that his country, once again, was isolated.

Two weeks later, the staunchly independent Czech Foreign Minister, Jan Masaryk, was found dead, in suspicious circumstances. President Truman responded quickly, calling the events in Czechoslovakia a 'coup'. He also said that through the cynical application of force the Soviets had 'sent shock waves throughout the civilized world'.

At this point, the financing for the Marshall Plan had not been passed by Congress. This was mainly due to hesitation over the huge amount of money it would commit the United States to invest. Truman now used the events in Czechoslovakia to push the bill through. Thus, the 'Czech Coup' was directly responsible for the implementation of the Marshall Plan in Europe. Bloody purges of non-loyal Communists continued during 1948, not only in Czechoslovakia, but throughout the Eastern bloc. Nevertheless, there remained a key area of 'weakness' in the heart of Stalin's sphere of influence and control – Berlin.

Step Eight: The Berlin Crisis of 1948
Post-war Germany

The fact that Germany had been invaded on several fronts by Soviet and Western forces meant that, unlike Japan, it was much more difficult to leave it undivided during

occupation at the end of World War Two. Accordingly, at Yalta and Potsdam, it was agreed that Germany should be divided temporarily into four zones of occupation, administered by the **Allied Control Council (ACC)**, with Berlin's governance being the responsibility of the Allied *Kommandantura* made up of four military governors. This was all seen as a temporary arrangement while Germany's future was being worked out at a peace conference yet to be arranged. It is important to note, however, that at all times it was the intention to treat Germany as one economic unit, and it was expected that Germany would eventually emerge as a united independent state again. However, by 1949, Germany had become permanently divided into two separate states.

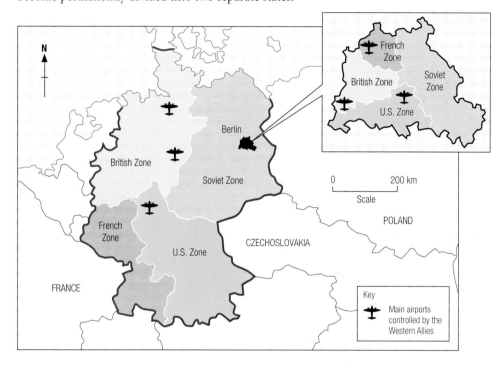

This map shows the division of Germany between the four powers, and also the division of Berlin into sectors.

Why did the post-war powers fail to unify Germany?

This was due to several factors.

- **Germany's key strategic position and the differing aims of the main powers**. Germany's geographic position in the centre of Europe, and its potential economic strength, made it an area of vital concern to all countries, and an area over which they could not agree. The USSR did not wish to see a resurgent united Germany that would pose a threat to its security. At the same time, it wished to get as much out of Germany as possible in terms of reparations. The Soviets were looking for **reparations** of some US$20 billion. France likewise feared a united Germany rising again on its eastern flank and was not keen to hasten Germany's recovery after the war. The USA had come to see that the best hope for European peace would lie in the rapid economic recovery of Germany, and that the best way of containing the spread of Communism would be to bolster the war-torn economies of Western Europe with massive injections of U.S. aid. The UK found it best to endorse the U.S. view. As it was almost bankrupt, it would greatly benefit from American aid.

- **The increasing lack of trust between East and West as the Cold War developed**. The differences in aims and attitudes that the four Allied Powers had in 1945 would have been enough on their own to delay any permanent peace settlement for Germany. However, as the Cold War developed, mutual suspicions between the USSR and the Western powers began to harden. Both the West and the Soviet Union became concerned that a powerful Germany could be a threat if it ever joined forces with the other side. Thus its speed of recovery after 1945 was a central issue in the early days of the Cold War. By 1946 it became very apparent that Germany was, and would probably remain, divided in both economic and political terms between the Soviet Zone on the one hand and the Western Zones on the other.

- **The specific disputes between the post-war powers within Germany itself**. Specifically, the division intensified for a number of reasons. One major factor was economic conflict. Reparations were the key problem. The arrangements set up at Potsdam whereby the USSR was to take 25 per cent of German industrial equipment from the Western Zones in return for supplying those zones with food and raw materials did not work. Food was a huge problem in war-torn Germany, especially with the flood of refugees from Eastern Europe swelling the population. The USSR was not delivering enough food to the Western Zones and was also being increasingly secretive about what it was taking from the Soviet Zone. Thus the United States and the United Kingdom stopped supplies to the Soviet Zone. German coal was another important area of disagreement. The Soviets wanted coal from the Western Zones, but the Americans wanted to use German coal from these areas to assist in the economic reconstruction of Western Europe. Accordingly, 25 million tonnes of Western Zones coal was exported to Europe, rather than to the USSR. Then, early in 1947, the British and American zones were merged into one unit called Bizonia.

There was also political conflict. New evidence suggests that Stalin was planning as early as 4 June 1945 to incorporate a reunified Germany within Moscow's sphere of influence. This was to be done by using the Red Army to control the Soviet Zone while the Communist Party of Germany (KPD) would attempt to get popular support in the other zones. As a first step to achieving this, in April 1946 the Soviets forced through a merger of political parties in their zone to form just one party – the Socialist Unity Party (SED). However, this party was not successful in winning over the West Germans. Several political parties had been established after the war and West Germans were unlikely to vote for a Soviet-controlled party, which, even if it might lead to a unified Germany, would bring minimal economic assistance (compared to the promise of Marshall Aid after 1948) and no chance of democracy. As they saw the impossibility of the situation, the SED leaders began planning their own separate regime in the East.

Similarly, by 1948, the Western powers were beginning to think seriously about consolidating their occupation zones and establishing within them a provisional German government. The **London Conference of Ministers** in 1947, which should have considered the German peace treaty, ended in the Western powers and the Soviets throwing recriminations at each other, indicating that any agreement on Germany's future was remote. Therefore, at the London Conference in 1948, France, Britain and the United States met to draw up a constitution for a new West German state, which would come into existence the following year. As part of the plan of setting up a new West German government, it was also agreed to introduce a new currency into the Western sectors. The old German currency had lost its value and in many areas Germans were operating a barter economy. Stalin rightly saw that the introduction of the new currency signalled the establishment of a new Germany in the West. His action in setting up the blockade of Berlin was to thwart this plan. Stalin also probably hoped that his action would force the West out of Berlin.

- **The Berlin Blockade, 1948**. As agreed at Potsdam, Berlin had been divided between the four occupying powers. The problem for the Western powers was that Berlin lay 100 miles within the Soviet occupation zone, which had been sealed off from the rest of

Germany since 1946. The Western forces in Berlin and the West Germans in Berlin thus had to rely on receiving their food and energy supplies from the West, delivered along road, rail and air 'corridors'. (See map below.)

In March 1948, Stalin started putting a stranglehold on Western interests in West Berlin, mainly through transport restrictions. Then, in response to the introduction of the new currency into the Western sectors of Berlin, Stalin began the total blockade of Berlin on 23–24 June 1948. The roads, railways and waterways linking West Berlin to the Western sector of Germany were all closed. The supply of electricity from East to West was also cut. The USSR also left the Berlin *Kommandantura*, having already left the ACC in March.

This was the first crisis of the Cold War and direct military confrontation was always a possibility. However, the West did not try to defeat the blockade by force, but rather supplied Berlin from the air. During the blockade, American and British planes flew more than 200,000 flights to Berlin in 320 days, and delivered vital supplies of food and coal to 2.2 million West Berliners. Always there was the threat of a Soviet military response. By early 1949, it was clear that Stalin's gamble was failing and he finally ended the blockade in May of that year.

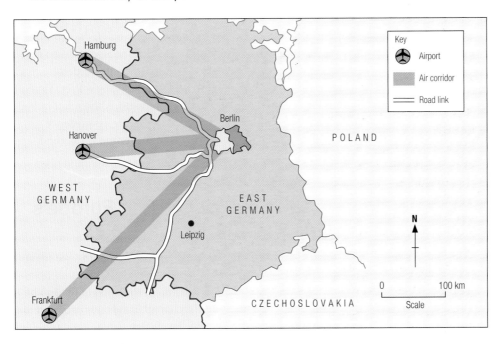

This map shows the position of Berlin and routes in from West Germany.

What were the results of the Berlin Blockade?

This was the first time since 1945 that war had become a possibility and it had a significant impact on the development of the Cold War. It was now clear that any agreement between the two sides would be difficult, if not impossible. Therefore, the failure of the Berlin Blockade had three important consequences. It led to:

- the division of Germany
- the continuation of four-power control in Berlin
- the formation of the North Atlantic Treaty Organization (NATO).

The division of Germany: The failure of the blockade meant that the division of Germany was bound to go ahead. The West moved quickly to set up the Federal Republic of Germany (FRG). It came into existence in September 1949 and a month later Konrad Adenauer became the first Chancellor of the FRG (West Germany).

In response, the Soviets set up the German Democratic Republic (GDR) in the Soviet occupation zone. The inevitability of these arrangements stemmed from the fact that neither side could contemplate the idea of a united Germany which could possibly become an ally to the other side. Certainly, for the West, a divided Germany protected by the USA was preferable to a neutral united Germany. Europe was now clearly divided both economically and politically.

The continuation of four-power control in Berlin: The division of Germany meant that Berlin also remained a divided city. It remained under four-power occupation within the new GDR. As will be explained in Chapter Eight, this continued to be a major source of friction between the West and the Soviet Union.

The formation of the North Atlantic Treaty Organization: The Soviet threat to Berlin, following the Czech coup, reinforced the suspicions that the West already had about Stalin and, combined with the resource demands of the Berlin airlift, emphasized the need for a U.S. defence commitment to Europe. This resulted in the formation in April 1949 of NATO between the USA, Canada, the **Brussels Pact** powers, Norway, Denmark, Iceland, Italy and Portugal. At the same time the U.S. Congress approved a military assistance programme to help build up Europe's armed forces. Thus, from this time, there was a major U.S. military presence in Europe, which was clearly a departure from previous U.S. foreign policy.

In May 1954, West Germany was admitted to NATO. This confirmed the Soviet Union's worst fears concerning the dangers of a return of an armed Germany on its borders. Within a week, the Soviet Union had announced the formation of the Warsaw Pact. This brought all the states of Eastern Europe into a single military command. Although it lacked organization, and was initially more of a political than a military alliance, its existence nevertheless meant that Europe was now divided militarily, as well as economically and politically.

ToK Time:
Consider the events leading up to the Berlin Blockade. How does hindsight affect our understanding of the causes of the blockade? How would perspectives differ in the Soviet Union, the USA and Germany at the time of this crisis, compared to views from other countries around the world?

What conclusions can be drawn about Europe's situation at the end of 1949?

- Europe was now clearly divided along political, economic and military lines. (See again the diagram on page 9.)
- Germany was not to be reunited as had been the original aim of the Allies at the end of World War Two. There were now two clear states, although neither side was prepared to recognize the existence of the other (until *Ostpolitik* in the 1970s).
- The USA had abandoned its peacetime policy of avoiding commitments and was now involved economically – through the Marshall Plan – and militarily – through NATO – in Europe.
- No peace treaty had actually been signed with Germany, which meant that the borders of Central Europe were not formalized. This was particularly worrying for Poland as it now included territory taken from Germany in 1945. (This was not finally resolved until 1975.)
- Western countries had developed a greater sense of unity due to the Soviet threat.

What did this situation mean for international relations beyond Europe?

- From this time on, many conflicts, wherever they were in the world, would be seen as part of the struggle between Communism and Capitalism.

- The USA's policy of containment, which had been developed to fight Communism in Europe, was to lead the USA into resisting Communism anywhere in the world where it perceived that Communism was a threat. This would involve the USA fighting in both the Korean War and the Vietnam War.
- The United Nations was never to play the role envisioned in the original discussions between Roosevelt and Churchill at the time of its foundation. With the USA and the USSR now opposing each other and able to use their respective vetoes, the UN could not act effectively to resolve international conflicts.

STUDENT STUDY SECTION

What is a history essay?

Essays are a central part of your IB course. They are the means by which you demonstrate your historical knowledge and understanding.

The diagram below outlines the key points that you must remember each time you write an essay. Use it as a guide each time you have an essay assignment.

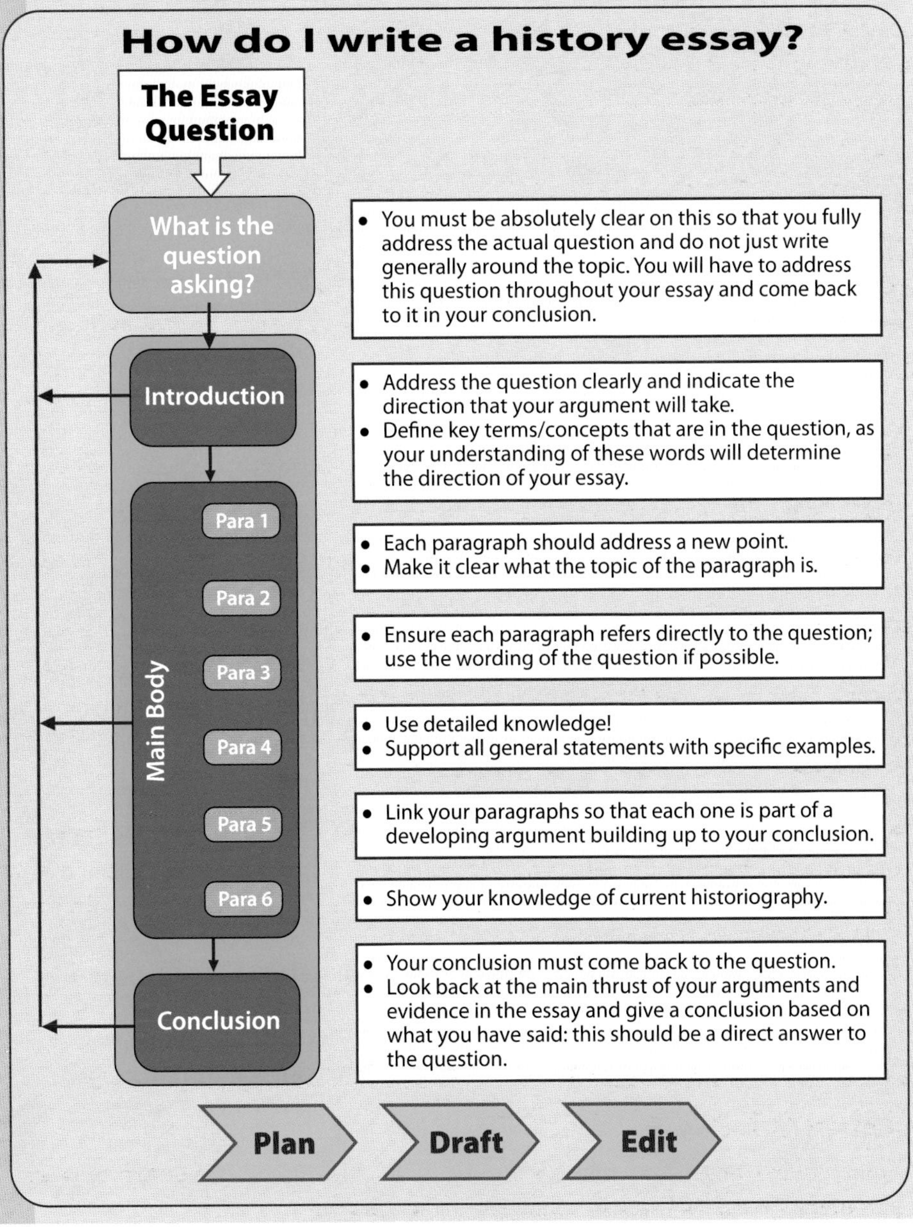

How do I write a history essay?

The Essay Question

What is the question asking?
- You must be absolutely clear on this so that you fully address the actual question and do not just write generally around the topic. You will have to address this question throughout your essay and come back to it in your conclusion.

Introduction
- Address the question clearly and indicate the direction that your argument will take.
- Define key terms/concepts that are in the question, as your understanding of these words will determine the direction of your essay.

Main Body

Para 1
- Each paragraph should address a new point.
- Make it clear what the topic of the paragraph is.

Para 2

Para 3
- Ensure each paragraph refers directly to the question; use the wording of the question if possible.

Para 4
- Use detailed knowledge!
- Support all general statements with specific examples.

Para 5
- Link your paragraphs so that each one is part of a developing argument building up to your conclusion.

Para 6
- Show your knowledge of current historiography.

Conclusion
- Your conclusion must come back to the question.
- Look back at the main thrust of your arguments and evidence in the essay and give a conclusion based on what you have said: this should be a direct answer to the question.

Plan > **Draft** > **Edit**

Creating an essay frame

Essay title: To what extent did events in the final year of World War Two turn wartime allies into Cold War enemies?

Introduction: Always start by identifying/explaining key terms or concepts in the question. You need to set out clearly what the 'events in the final year' of the war were. (End of the war in Europe with Soviet and U.S./British troops meeting at Berlin, Yalta and Potsdam Conferences, the dropping of the atom bomb on Hiroshima, changes of leadership in USA and UK.) You also need to show the direction of your essay and how you are going to respond to the 'To what extent …' part of the question. Here your argument may well be that events in 1945 sowed seeds for conflict, but that it was how the powers responded to events afterwards that actually turned the USA and the USSR into Cold War enemies.

It makes sense with this essay to give each event a separate paragraph. Don't forget to link each event clearly to the question and make sure your opening sentence indicates the theme of each paragraph.

Paragraph 1: *The end of the war in itself meant that that there was no common interest holding the USA and the USSR together and so there was already a strong likelihood of them becoming enemies.* Here you could go on to explain their basic ideological differences, which had already caused much suspicion and tension pre-1945 and the different interests that they had in reconstructing Europe (e.g., Stalin with security and the USA with need for markets).

Paragraph 2: *The Yalta Conference had already shown that the wartime allies had very different ideas on what Europe after the war should look like. This was to sow seeds of conflict for later on.* You could then go on to explain the conflicts over Poland and Eastern Europe

Paragraph 3: *The Potsdam Conference revealed that attitudes had hardened still further between the two sides, making a Cold War conflict more likely.* (Give evidence for this.)

Paragraph 4: *The change of leadership in the United States and United Kingdom was also to have an effect on the relationship between the USA and the USSR. The replacement of Roosevelt with Truman was particularly important in helping to turn the USA and the USSR into Cold War enemies.* (Explain how the attitudes of Truman differed from those of Roosevelt.)

Paragraph 5: *The dropping of the atomic bomb by the USA was very threatening to the Soviets and started the race for nuclear weapons between the USA and the USSR, which helped turn them into enemies.* After you have read the next chapter, you will be able to add to your essay some views by historians about this event.

Paragraphs 6, 7 and 8: As this is a 'to what extent' question, you need to examine an alternative argument. Thus you may want to consider in the next two or three paragraphs if it was really just these events that made the United States and the USSR into Cold War enemies, or if it was events after 1945 that were more important. Always give evidence to support your arguments.

Conclusion: Come back to the question and state your overall conclusion based on the evidence that you have presented in your essay.

More essay titles to try:
- Assess the impact of the Truman Doctrine and the Marshall Plan on the development of the Cold War between 1945 and 1949.
- Assess the significance of the conferences at Yalta and Potsdam on the development of the Cold War up to 1949.
- To what extent was the USA successful in containing Communism in Europe 1947–1949?

4 WHO WAS RESPONSIBLE FOR THE DEVELOPMENT OF THE COLD WAR?

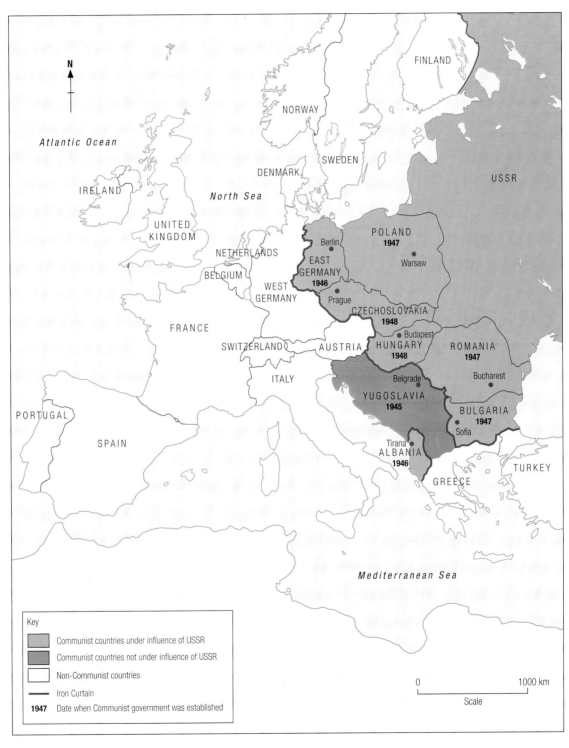

Key

- Communist countries under influence of USSR
- Communist countries not under influence of USSR
- Non-Communist countries
- ── Iron Curtain
- **1947** Date when Communist government was established

0   1000 km

Scale

This map shows the East–West divide after 1949.

Cold War historiography

This chapter examines different historians' viewpoints on why the Cold War developed after World War Two. This **historiography** is specifically focused on the origins of the Cold War. Throughout the other chapters there is more specific historiography on each theme/case study within the Cold War era.

The Orthodox view

The historical position known as the Orthodox or traditional view generally holds that the Soviet Union was responsible for the Cold War. It states that the Soviets were inevitably expansionist, due to their suspicion of the West, and in accordance with their Marxist theory, which advocated the need to spread revolution throughout the world. Thus, Stalin violated the Yalta and Potsdam agreements, occupied and imposed Soviet control in Eastern Europe and 'plotted' to spread Communism throughout the world with Moscow at its centre. The United States, therefore, had to act defensively, from the Truman Doctrine and the Marshall Plan to the establishment of NATO.

Political historian Arthur M. Schlesinger gives a clear analysis from the Orthodox perspective:

Marxism-Leninism gave the Russian leaders a view of the world according to which all societies were inexorably destined to proceed along appointed roads by appointed stages until they achieved the classless nirvana. Moreover, given the resistance of the Capitalists to this development, the existence of any non-Communist state was by definition a threat to the Soviet Union. …An analysis of the origins of the Cold War which leaves out these factors – the intransigence of Leninist ideology, the sinister dynamics of a totalitarian society and the madness of Stalin – is obviously incomplete.

Arthur M. Schlesinger, Jr. 'Origins of the Cold War', Foreign Affairs, October 1967, pp.49-50

Other historians who have presented the Orthodox view include W.H. McNeill and H. Feis.

▲ Historian Arthur M. Schlesinger, Jr. (1917–2007).

The Revisionist view

The alternative perspective, which flourished when the consensus over foreign policy in the United States was crumbling during the Vietnam War, held the USA responsible for the Cold War. Revisionists, such as William Appleman Williams, explained the onset of the Cold War in terms of 'dollar diplomacy'. Revisionists see the motives behind U.S. foreign policy as inherently linked to the needs of Capitalism. Thus, containment of Communism was driven by the requirement to secure markets and free trade, and penetrate Eastern Europe. This followed on from the United States' traditional 'open door' policy of the late 19th century.

This stance was taken further by Revisionist historians Gabriel and Joyce Kolko, who view Soviet action as even less relevant to U.S. foreign policy. They see American policy as determined by the nature of its Capitalist system and by fears of recession. Similarly, Thomas Patterson wrote that 'coercion characterized United States reconstruction diplomacy'. Moreover, many Revisionists hold that Stalin himself was a pragmatic leader, and had the Americans been more willing to understand the Soviets' need for security and offer some compromises, Stalin would have also made concessions.

Perhaps the most radical thesis from the Revisionists comes from the Cambridge political economist, Gar Alperovitz. This followed on from an idea put forward by British physicist, P.M.S. Blackett, who wrote that the dropping of nuclear bombs on Hiroshima and Nagasaki was not important as the last military campaign of World War Two, but rather as the first

diplomatic move by the United States in the Cold War. Alperovitz suggests that Japan was already defeated, and that this 'new' weapon of awesome power was used to warn and intimidate the Soviets.

Post-revisionist view

This school of thought does not exactly combine the Orthodox and Revisionist views, but Post-revisionists do stress that neither the USA nor the USSR can be held solely responsible for the origins of the Cold War. One of the key figures of this group was American historian John Lewis Gaddis. He declared in 1983 that there was a growing 'consensus' of opinion that followed the 'Post-revisionist' line of argument.

The Cold War grew out of a complicated interaction of external and internal developments inside both the United States and the Soviet Union. The external situation – circumstances beyond the control of either power – left Americans and Russians facing one another across prostrated Europe at the end of World War Two. Internal influences in the Soviet Union – the search for security, the role of ideology, massive post-war reconstruction needs, the personality of Stalin – together with those in the United States – the need for self-determination, fear of Communism, the illusion of omnipotence fostered by American economic strength and the atomic bomb – made the resulting confrontation a hostile one. Leaders of both superpowers sought peace, but in doing so yielded to considerations, which, while they did not precipitate war, made resolution of differences impossible.

John Lewis Gaddis. **The United States and Origins of the Cold War 1941–1947** *(Columbia University Press, 1972) pp.359–61*

John Lewis Gaddis and Walter LaFeber both agreed at this time that misperceptions played an important part at the beginning of the Cold War. Both superpowers overestimated the strength and threat of the other, and much of the growing tension of the 1940s was a result of a pattern of 'action and reaction'. Both sides were 'improvising', rather than following a well-defined 'plan of action'. Stalin's search for security was not deterred initially by strong lines being drawn, while at the same time the West did not fully recognize the Soviets' motives.

Views of the post-Cold War historians

… as long as Stalin was running the Soviet Union, a Cold War was unavoidable.

John Lewis Gaddis, **We Now Know: Rethinking Cold War History** *(OUP, 1998) p.292*

With the fall of the Soviet Union in 1989–90, many new Soviet sources were made available. Russian historians were also now free to write their own accounts of the Cold War without Communist Party **censorship**. John Lewis Gaddis, who had formerly been a key spokesperson of the 'Post-revisionists', also had access to the new material and the initial writings of the post-Soviet era Russian historians. He used this material to revise his Post-revisionist view, now putting even more focus on the role of Stalin in the origins of the Cold War. He suggests that it was Stalin's policies coupled with the Soviet totalitarian/authoritarian government that drew the West into an escalation of hostility and the protracted **arms race**. Gaddis considered the role of all other key leaders and players in the early stages of the Cold War, and concludes that if Stalin (rather than any of the others, from President Truman to Secretary of State **John Foster Dulles**) is removed from the equation, the Cold War was unlikely to have developed.

What emerges generally from the post-Cold War 'new' historians is that individuals and their actions, rather than the policies of whole governments, are of vital importance in explaining key events in the Cold War. This is particularly obvious in the origins of the Korean War and in the Berlin Crisis of 1961 (see Chapter Five and Chapter Eight).

European and Soviet perspectives

What was the role of the Europeans in the development of the Cold War?

In the 1980s, mainly due to the end of the '30 year rule' period that secured the confidentiality of government records, historians brought Europe and its role in the origins of the Cold War into clearer focus. Many European governments, economically devastated by war, harboured deep anxieties about Soviet expansionism, and this had an important impact on U.S. foreign policy. The British in particular did much to heighten the U.S. awareness/perception of the 'Soviet threat'. Churchill's Iron Curtain speech is an obvious case in point. European contributions suggested that both the Revisionist and the Post-revisionist historians had not satisfactorily considered the complexity of U.S. foreign policy. A Norwegian scholar, Geir Lunestad, in an article in *Diplomatic History*, asserted that the guiding motives for American foreign policy in the early period of the Cold War can only be properly understood by taking into account the influence of external factors, such as European fears and opinions.

What is the Soviet perspective?

The historiography so far considered is all from a 'Western' perspective. Indeed, as a parallel with the Western historians, it is possible to call the Soviet historians who wrote during the Cold War, (due to the censorship and other controls) the 'Soviet Orthodox' group, and those that began to write following the fall of the Soviet Union, who focused on the role of Stalin, the 'Soviet Revisionists'.

During the initial stages of the Cold War itself, the Soviet line held that the Americans were pursuing a policy of aggressive 'dollar imperialism' dictated by the needs of Capitalism. The Soviet Foreign Minister Sergei Molotov himself wrote a book, *Problems of Foreign Policy*, in which he accused the United States of trying to take over Europe economically and put it under the control 'of strong and enriched foreign firms, banks and industrial companies'. Thus, in response to this, Molotov said the Soviets were only attempting to 'find security', to rebuild after the 'Great Patriotic War' (World War Two) and, where and when possible, to aid in the liberation of the exploited working classes of the world.

Since the end of the Cold War and the opening of former Soviet and Eastern European archives, historians on both sides of the Iron Curtain have reconsidered the role of ideology and the search for security in Soviet foreign policy. Many historians believe that the furthering of socialist objectives became tied to the search for security following World War Two. This also meant that in the crucial initial stages of the Cold War the Soviets believed that the triumph of socialism was unavoidable and that the USSR should aid Communist groups around the world to fulfil this aim. Other historians using the Soviet archives see the greatest motive for the USSR's foreign policy as being the fear of renewed German and Japanese aggression, and of aggression from the rest of the Capitalist world.

In line with the post-Cold War historians mentioned earlier, some Eastern European historians, such as Vojtech Mastny, focus on Stalin's role in the origins in the Cold War. This perspective could be called 'Soviet Revisionism'. Mastny sees Stalin's' role as pivotal, and believes that Soviet foreign policy during this period can be explained in terms of 'Stalinism' and Josef Stalin's own specific **modus operandi** of paranoia and suspicion.

ToK Time

Consider how and why historical opinion might have changed over time. Writer Margaret Atwood says 'context is all', so does this mean that 'historical truth' does not really exist?

'Balance of Power' versus ideology: What is the debate?

Some historians perceive the origins of the Cold War to be simply a traditional 'balance of power' conflict. This thesis can be supported by the insightful, if not prophetic, writings of French historian Alexis de Tocqueville, who wrote the following in 1835:

There are at the present time two great nations in the world … I allude to the Russians and the Americans … Their starting point is different, and their courses are not the same; yet each of them seems marked out by the will of Heaven to sway the destinies of half the globe.

Alexis de Tocqueville, Democracy in America *(Washington Square Press, 1964) pp.124 – 125*

De Tocqueville wrote this before Karl Marx's *Das Capital* or the 'Communist Manifesto', and long before the Bolshevik Russian Revolution. So, is it possible that the conflict between the USA and USSR is not really about ideology at all? Walter LaFeber and Louis Halle consider the conflict in similar terms, as both see the USA and the Soviets as expansionist powers. Therefore, the hostility that followed 1945 was a continuation of policies they had respectively pursued since the 19th century. LaFeber writes:

French historian Alexis de Tocqueville (1805–1859).

The two powers did not initially come into conflict because one was Communist and the other Capitalist. Rather, they first confronted one another on the plains of Asia in the late nineteenth century. That meeting climaxed a century in which Americans had expanded westward over half the globe and Russians had moved eastward across Asia.

Walter LaFeber, America, Russia and the Cold War 1945–84, 5th ed *(Knopf, 1985) p.1*

Former U.S. Secretary of State Henry Kissinger, writing in the 1980s, also claimed that the USSR's motives were not based on ideology, but considers them as a continuum of the long history of Tsarist empire building. However, those commentators and historians that see the origins of the Cold War being initiated by the ideological struggle between Capitalism and Communism identify the starting point of the conflict as 1917 with the Bolshevik Revolution. André Fontaine suggests that the aggressive policies of the USSR in foreign policy were dictated by its Communist ideology. Indeed, some Western revisionists would also highlight the ideological nature of U.S. foreign policy as a spur. Ideology in the USA can be seen as increasingly important in the origins of the Cold War, culminating in the McCarthy witch-hunts of the 1950s (see Chapter Five).

STUDENT STUDY SECTION

Essay frame

Essay title: Assess the importance of ideological differences in the outbreak of the Cold War.

Introduction: Establish what the different ideologies were, i.e., the key differences between Capitalism and Communism. Set down a time frame to work within, perhaps 1945–50 (or to 1953 to end with the death of Stalin). Make your main argument clear, i.e., the opposing ideologies of the United States and the USSR were likely to lead to conflict; however, were these differences more important in creating the Cold War than traditional 'empire building' rivalries and other clashes of 'self-interest'? Self-interest could be defined as attempting to establish a 'sphere of influence' and protecting and expanding economic interests.

Paragraph 1: Deal first with the factor identified in the essay title, perhaps like this: *To a certain extent ideology can be seen as the driving force behind the outbreak of the Cold War* … Give examples of historians who argue that Soviet ideology was important. André Fontaine (1968) sees it as a struggle which begins in 1917 with the Bolshevik Revolution and concluded that aggressive Soviet foreign policy to be largely due to Communist ideology. Consider increasingly 'ideological' language used by the Americans in this period. Give examples from Chapters Two and Three that support this hypothesis.

Paragraph 2: Now look at the other side of the argument, perhaps this way: *It can also be argued, however, that 'expansionism' and self-interest were the reasons why the Cold War started* … Give examples of historians who support this view, e.g., the 'prophetic' writings of Alexis de Tocqueville in 1835, who warns of a balance of power confrontation between the two – not an ideological struggle. Also consider Henry Kissinger's writings in the 1980s which claim that the USSR's motives were not based on ideology, but rather on self-interest. Give historical examples to support the hypothesis, e.g., examples of Russian expansionism into the East and U.S. expansionism to the West before 1917. Give examples from Chapters Two and Three that support this hypothesis. You may wish to reconsider some of the examples for ideological expansionism chosen for Paragraph 1 and re-analyse them as self-interest, e.g., the USSR's control of the buffer states after 1945 could be interpreted in both ways.

Paragraph 3: Now address other factors or recent viewpoints on this issue. Historians writing since the collapse of the Soviet Union have brought ideology back to the fore, and see this as very important to the origins of the Cold War. However, their focus is on the ideology of Stalin in particular, and the Stalinist regime. John Lewis Gaddis writes (1997) that underpinning all the USSR's actions was ideology; it was the very justification for their whole system. Gaddis gives examples from domestic policy to highlight this, e.g., the continuation of communes even though they proved economically inefficient. He sees expansion and consolidation of power in Eastern Europe up to 1953 as safeguarding the Communist system and following Stalinist doctrine. This ideology is identified as dictating policy at Yalta and Potsdam, and from the 'Two Camps' speech onwards. Another example would be the treatment of the 'non-Stalinist' Tito. Find other examples to support these ideas from Chapters Two and Three.

Conclusion: Over to you! Remember to follow the 'weight' of the evidence given for each argument and refer explicitly to the question – how important was ideology for the superpowers?

More essay titles to try
Here are some other essay titles in which you could explore the historiographical debate on the origins of the Cold War:

- To what extent were Soviet policies responsible for the outbreak and development of the Cold War between 1945 and 1949?
- 'The Cold War was caused by fear not aggression.' To what extent does this view explain how the Cold War developed between 1945 and 1949?
- In what ways could Stalin be held responsible for the origin and development of the Cold War?
- To what extent was the Cold War caused by Truman's policies?
- How far did mutual distrust and suspicion cause the Cold War?
- To what extent do you agree that the wartime alliance between the USA and the USSR was 'unnatural' and 'bound to fall apart' after they had defeated their common enemies in World War Two?

5 THE COLD WAR GOES GLOBAL: THE KOREAN WAR AND NSC-68

As you read this chapter consider the following essay questions:

- Why did the USA policy of a containment shift to Asia after 1949?
- Why did the Korean War start?
- What was the impact of the Korean War on the Cold War?

Cold War Timeline 1949–1953

1949	Sept	USSR gets the A bomb
	Dec	Communist victory in Chinese Civil War
1950	April	U.S. National Security Council produces NSC-68
	June	North Korea invades South Korea
	Sept	U.S. troops land at Inchon
	Nov	Chinese launch counter-offensive
	Dec	UN troops fall back to 38th parallel
1951	Feb	UN condemns China as aggressor in Korea
	April	Eisenhower dismisses MacArthur
	July	Truce talks start in Korea
	Sept	USA and Japan sign mutual security pact
	Oct	Greece and Turkey join NATO
1952	March	USSR proposes a neutral Germany
	Nov	Eisenhower elected U.S. President
1953	March	Death of Stalin
	July	Military **armistice** to end Korean hostilities signed

U.S. Foreign Policy 1949–1950

With the establishment of NATO in April 1949, the USA was optimistic that the Communists had been contained in Europe, first by the Truman Doctrine and now by NATO.

In fact, NATO was quite a 'cheap' option for the USA, as its power rested on the atomic bomb. The USA, therefore, did not have to invest huge sums of money into developing conventional forces in Western Europe to match the Soviet Red Army. However, it should be noted that the USA had little choice but to rely on its nuclear threat, as after World War Two the USA had **demobilized** its fighting men, whereas the USSR had not. Thus each side had its 'ace card' – land forces for the Soviets and the atomic bomb for the USA.

However, by the autumn of 1949 two key events occurred that shifted the balance of power in favour of the USSR: the Soviet Union got a nuclear bomb of its own and China fell to the Communist forces of Mao Zedong.

North Atlantic Treaty Organization (NATO)

NATO consisted of USA, Canada, Ireland and 13 European states. It was the first peacetime military alliance in U.S. history. Under its terms an attack on one member of NATO was an attack on all. In 1952, Greece and Turkey joined and then in 1955, much to the dismay of the USSR, West Germany joined. The USSR responded by setting up the Warsaw Pact (see Chapter Three, page 34).

The USSR gets the Bomb

As mentioned above, U.S. security and the key basis of NATO's power was the nuclear bomb. In August 1949 this security was shattered when the Soviet Union announced that it had developed its own atomic weapon. The USA had lost its 'ace card'. Not only that, but the USSR had achieved this far more quickly than the Americans had anticipated.

China falls to the Communists

During the Chinese Civil War (1945–1949) the USA had given limited support to the Nationalists under **Chiang Kai-shek**. When the country ultimately fell to the Communist guerrilla forces of Mao Zedong, the **White Paper** report on this clearly stated that the USA could not substantially have altered the outcome. It suggested that Chiang and his forces were simply too unpopular with the Chinese people, and that it had been more a case of Nationalist 'collapse' than Communist 'victory'. The White Paper saw Mao as somewhat 'independent' from Moscow. Secretary of State Dean Acheson expressed the U.S. government's view in 1949:

*The reasons for the failure of the Chinese National Government appear … not to stem from any inadequacy of American aid. Our military observers on the spot have reported that the Nationalist armies did not lose a single battle during the crucial year of 1948 through lack of arms or ammunition. The fact was that the decay which our observers had detected in Chongqing early in the war had fatally sapped the powers of resistance of the **Guomindang**. Its leaders had proved incapable of meeting the crisis confronting them, its troops had lost the will to fight, and its government had lost popular support. The Communists, on the other hand, through a ruthless discipline and fanatical zeal, attempted to sell themselves as guardians and liberators of the people. The Nationalist armies did not have to be defeated; they disintegrated. History has proved again and again that a regime without faith in itself and an army without morale cannot survive the test of battle.*

Thus, in 1949 the American experts in Asia believed that they had done what they could in China.

The Red Scare: McCarthyism and the anti-Communist crusade in America

Anti-Communist feeling was strong in the USA after World War Two, but it reached fever-pitch in the 1950s, encouraged by Senator **Joseph R. McCarthy** of Wisconsin, who alleged that the Soviet Union had a conspiracy to place Communist sympathizers into key positions in American life. McCarthy's accusations led to '**purges**' and **show trials** of those accused of 'un-American' behaviour. Some historians have drawn parallels with the show trials in Stalin's purges of the 1930s. They affected every level of U.S. society – and no group, institution or individual was safe from suspicion. Perhaps the most infamous trial of the period was that of Julius and Ethel Rosenberg, who were convicted of spying for the Soviets, and executed in 1953.

During the 1950s the 'anti-Red' crusade reached its peak. It helped to shape and intensify public opinion against Communism in America. McCarthy and his followers created an atmosphere of near-hysterical suspicion and fear of 'the enemy within', and McCarthy went as far as to call for a purge of 'comsymps' (Communist sympathizers) in the State Department. He claimed that the Truman administration was under Communist influence and that all American liberals were Communist sympathizers.

It was in this atmosphere in February 1950 that Dean Acheson was forced to make a speech appeasing the McCarthyites. Acheson and President Truman had been the focus of an attack by McCarthy for being 'soft on Communism' and Acheson decided to 'reconsider' the findings of the 1949 White Paper on China. He went as far as to claim that China under Mao was '… completely subservient to the Moscow regime'. In other words, his view was the reverse of the impression set down in the White Paper.

Following this, all but two of the State Department advisers on China who had said that the Guomindang was 'not worth saving' lost their jobs. They had fallen foul of the McCarthy purges. As a result, the U.S. government lost valuable experts on Far East foreign affairs.

Under continued pressure, Truman now called for a far-reaching review of U.S. foreign and defence policy in response to the new threats perceived as resulting from the Chinese Communist victory and the USSR's A-bomb. It seemed now that the USA might be engaged in a Cold War on two fronts and against a Soviet Union that was now a nuclear power.

In this new climate, President Truman was not able to recognize the legitimacy of the new Chinese government.

STUDENT STUDY SECTION

Research questions

1 Research in more detail some of the key features and victims of the Red Scare in the USA:
   a The Hollywood Ten
   b HUAC (House of Un-American Activities Committee)
   c Alger Hiss
   d The Rosenbergs
   e Role of the FBI
   f The McCarran Act.

2 Why was McCarthy finally discredited?

Cartoon analysis

McCarthy's attack on so-called Communist sympathizers, and the hysteria that it generated, led to what became known as 'witch hunts'. This term was derived from the religiously inspired witch hunts of the 17th century in Europe and America.

1 Why is the Statue of Liberty shown in the cartoon being burnt at the stake?

2 What point is the cartoonist making about the impact of McCarthyism on American society?

Getting Set for the Great Witch Burning

This cartoon by Velde from the *Milwaukee Journal Sentinel* is a depiction of the American Statue of Liberty.

NSC-68: 'Total Commitment'.

NSC-68 was a report of the U.S. National Security Council produced in 1950. It is seen by many historians, such as LaFeber, as 'one of the key documents of the Cold War'.

NSC-68 warned of how *all* Communist activity *everywhere* could be traced back to Moscow. It went on to say that recent developments had a 'global theme' and that they indicated the growing strength and influence of the USSR. This was the 'monolithic' view of Communism – in other words all Communism fed back to the 'nerve centre' in Moscow.

The report warned of an 'indefinite period of tension and danger'. It advised the U.S. government to be ready to meet each and every challenge promptly. The report suggested an immediate increase in military strength and spending to $35–$50 billion.

The key significance of NSC-68 was that it encouraged military and economic aid to be given to *any* country perceived by the USA to be resisting Communism.

Secret statement in National Security Council Report 68, State and Defense Department, Washington, April 1950:

[We advocate] an immediate and large scale build-up in our military and general strength and that of our allies with the intention of righting the power balance and in the hope that through means other than all-out war we could induce a change in the nature of the socialist system …

The United States … can strike out on a bold and massive program of rebuilding the West's defensive potential to surpass that of the Soviet world, and of meeting each fresh challenge promptly and unequivocally … This means virtual abandonment by the United States of trying to distinguish between national and global security. It also means the end of subordinating security needs to the traditional budgeting restrictions; of asking 'How much security can we afford?' In other words, security must henceforth become the dominant element in the national budget, and other elements must be accommodated to it …

This new concept of the security needs of the nation calls for annual appropriations of the order of $50 billion, or not much below the former wartime levels.

STUDENT STUDY SECTION

Document analysis

Question

Read the above extract from NSC-68. Identify key phrases in this document, which you think would explain why LaFeber believes it to be one of the most important documents of the Cold War. Give reasons for your choices of particular phrases.

Revisionist historians have criticized American perceptions of Soviet intentions expressed in NSC-68. They see these perceptions as being based on a false premise, and as an 'excuse' for U.S. expansionism – the findings had little to do with the 'real' nature of the Soviet threat.

But the question was: would Americans be willing to pay? The recommendations would require a vast increase in expenditure – the American taxpayer would have to foot the bill. As historian William S. Taubman comments, Acheson may have overstated the case in order to persuade the U.S. public to 'put their money where their anti-Communist mouths were'.

The Korean War: the first 'hot war'

President Truman's Democratic Party faced difficult congressional elections in November 1950. Truman wanted to shelve the issues of the recognition of China and of commitment in Asia and the recommendations of NSC-68 until afterwards. However, on 25 June 1950, 90,000 North Korean soldiers launched an invasion into South Korea. Truman had no time now for sober consideration as to whether 'total commitment' on a global scale was a wise policy to follow. The North Korean attack was seen as a clear example of Soviet expansionism. Again, it is possible to see here the United States' belief in a monolithic Communist bloc; the North Koreans were assumed to be acting on the orders of Stalin. There was a fear that failure to take action would undermine the credibility of the USA in its determination to resist Communism and would encourage a '**domino effect**' in neighbouring states. As Truman put it:

If we let Korea down, the Soviets will keep right on going and swallow up one piece of Asia after another … If we were to let Asia go, the Near East would collapse and no telling what would happen in Europe … Korea is like the Greece of the Far East. If we are tough enough now, if we stand up to them like we did in Greece three years ago, they won't take any more steps.

This idea that Communism would quickly spread from one country to another became known later as the domino effect (see Chapter Six). The U.S. response in Korea was thus dictated by the same policy it had used in Europe: containment.

After initially sending aid to South Korea, the USA sponsored a resolution in the United Nations calling for military action against North Korea. Truman saw this as an important test of the UN. If the UN ignored the North Korean invasion, it would be following the same mistakes of its predecessor the League of Nations, that is, not standing up to aggressor states. As the USSR was boycotting the Security Council in protest at the refusal of the USA to allow Communist China a seat on the Council, this resolution was passed on 27 June 1950. On 1 July, U.S. troops arrived in Korea, soon to be joined by 15 other nations under a UN commander – American General Douglas MacArthur. Thus the USA once again found itself at war and this, as Acheson later explained, 'removed the recommendations of NSC-68 from the realm of theory and made them immediate budget issues.'

STUDENT STUDY SECTION

Review question

Look back over the chapter so far. What a) international considerations and b) domestic considerations would have had an influence on Truman's decision to become involved in the Korean War?

The course of the war

There were several dramatic changes in the course of the war over the first few months, followed by a stalemate situation which lasted until the armistice in 1953:

- The initial push by the North Koreans took them deep into South Korea, leaving only a corner of the peninsula out of their control. South Korean and American troops were pushed back into this small area around Pusan.
- General MacArthur led the UN forces in an amphibious landing at Inchon in order to bypass the Korean troops and cut them off. Within a month he had retaken Seoul and driven the North Koreans back to the **38th parallel**.

- Encouraged by this success, the United States then redefined its war aims and, rather than just concentrating on 'containment', now decided on a policy of 'rollback'. This would mean liberating the North Koreans from Communist rule and reuniting Korea. UN forces crossed the 38th parallel into North Korean territory and began a rapid advance northwards, capturing Pyongyang, the capital of the North, in October.
- The march towards the Yalu River, however, made China concerned about its own security. On 27 November 1950, a force of 200,000 Chinese joined 150,000 North Koreans and sent the UN troops into a rapid retreat. Pyongyang was recaptured in December and by the end of 1950, the North Koreans and their allies had retaken all land up to the 38th parallel. There were heavy American casualties in the bitter cold, and many were taken prisoner.
- A stalemate then developed around the 38th parallel.
- Truman now realized that the United States needed to go back to the original aim of containing Communism above the 38th Parallel. MacArthur disagreed, claiming, 'Here in Asia is where the Communist conspirators have elected to make their play for global conquest. Here we fight Europe's war with arms while the diplomats there still fight it with words'. He was subsequently relieved of his command.
- Peace talks started in 1951 with a focus on the **repatriation** of prisoners of war (POWs).
- The war continued for another two years, during which time fighting continued, causing serious casualties (over 40 per cent of American casualties were in this period). The United States put pressure on China by threatening to use the atom bomb.
- A military armistice was finally signed at Panmunjom in July 1953.

These maps show Phase 1 and Phase 2 of the Korean War.

▼

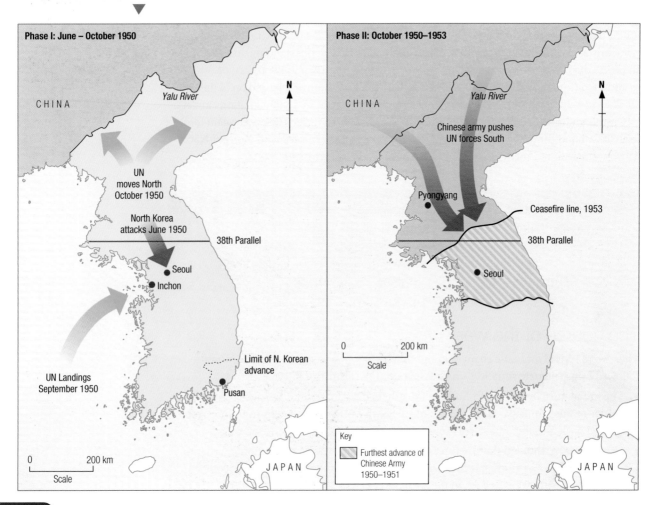

A shell explodes among U.S. troops during a Korean War engagement.

 General Douglas MacArthur (1880–1964)

MacArthur had fought in World War One and received 13 medals for bravery. He became Chief of Staff of the U.S. Army in 1930, and during World War Two he was the commander of the war against the Japanese – responsible for the successful island-hopping strategy that pushed the Japanese back from their island strongholds. Following the surrender of the Japanese, he was put in control of rebuilding Japan and developing a new constitution (see Chapter Six). At the age of 70 he was then put in charge of the UN forces in Korea. However, although he was successful in pushing back the North Koreans, he was dismissed by Truman in 1951 because of his public calls for the use of the atomic bomb against China. He returned to the USA to be greeted as a hero by the American public, but he was unsuccessful in his bid to be nominated as a presidential candidate in 1952.

STUDENT STUDY SECTION

Cartoon analysis

Questions

1 What is meant by the reference to using a 'roundish one'?

2 What is the problem with using only a 'squarish one'?

This American cartoon by Herblock appeared in the *Washington Post* newspaper in 1951.

Why did North Korea attack South Korea in 1950?

This first 'hot war' of the Cold War era, which had such far-reaching consequences, was not one that the USA had expected to fight at any stage before 1950. Why then did it take place?

STUDENT STUDY SECTION

Research questions

1 Study a map of Asia. Why can it be said that Korea occupies a key strategic position?
2 Which countries fought for this land at the end of the 19th century?

Background to the conflict

The Council of Foreign Ministers

The Council of Foreign Ministers was an organization agreed upon at the Potsdam Conference in 1945 towards the end of World War Two. It consisted of the foreign ministers of the UK, USSR, China, France and the United States and had the job of drawing up peace treaties with various countries, sorting out territorial questions and making a peace settlement for Germany. At the later Moscow Conference it also dealt with how Japan and Korea were to be governed.

Japan had officially annexed Korea in 1910 and was still in occupation of Korea when World War Two ended. Korean nationalists, who had led a revolution in 1945 and who included many Communists, were not allowed to decide the fate of Korea in 1945 and it was agreed by the USA and the USSR that the two superpowers would take joint responsibility for repatriating the Japanese forces there. The 38th parallel line of latitude was taken as the dividing point, with the USSR occupying Korea north of the line and the USA occupying Korea south of the line.

This was originally intended to be a temporary arrangement and at the Council of Foreign Ministers' Moscow Conference in December 1945 the United States and the Soviet Union agreed on the creation of a Korean provisional government, followed by a short period of international trusteeship or supervision, leading eventually to independence.

This was difficult to achieve, however, because:

- As the Cold War developed, the USA and the USSR became less willing to co-operate.
- Despite the Moscow Agreement, separate administrations emerged on either side of the 38th parallel. In the South, the U.S. military government put forward as leader the elderly Synghman Rhee, a rebel who had fought against the Japanese and spent much of his life in exile. The Soviets supported the Communists and backed a faction headed by Kim Il Sung, a young Russian-trained Korean Communist who had been a guerrilla fighter against the Japanese. Although the two men were very different, they had much in common: both were Korean nationalists, both wanted to end the division of Korea and each saw himself as the leader of a united Korea.

In the increasingly tense atmosphere of the Cold War, the division of Korea was confirmed in 1947. The Americans persuaded the UN to establish a commission to supervise Korean elections. This commission was refused entry into the North, but observed a separate election in the South in May 1948. Although most Koreans opposed partition, the Republic of Korea (ROK) was set up in the South under Synghman Rhee. It was an undemocratic and strongly anti-Communist administration, which was recognized as legitimate by the UN General Assembly. In response, the Democratic People's Republic of Korea (DPRK) was founded in the North under Kim Il Sung in September 1948 and was immediately recognized by the Communist bloc. 'The Cold War had thus institutionalized a Korean civil war in two hostile states, each claiming to represent all Koreans' (Callum MacDonald in *Korea: The War Before Vietnam*, Free Press, 1987).

Review question

What similarities and what differences are there in the way in which both Germany and Korea became divided into two separate countries?

Although the USA supported Synghman Rhee with economic and military aid, they did not intend to station troops there, and the U.S. military had left South Korea by mid-1949. Soviet troops left the North in 1948. The United States made it clear that they still saw Europe as the most important area in the Cold War, but decided to maintain a line of offshore strong points stretching from Japan to the Philippines rather than involve themselves in expensive military commitments on the mainland. This was made clear in Dean Acheson's 'perimeter' speech of January 1950, in which both South Korea and Taiwan were publicly excluded from the American defensive perimeter in the Western Pacific.

Why did the superpowers get involved?

So, having both withdrawn their troops, why did the superpowers become involved in a war on this peninsula? The thinking of orthodox historians followed the U.S. views of 1950: that this was an attack initiated and led by Stalin. Revisionist historians later claimed that Stalin had no role in the invasion, and that the North was possibly responding to attacks from the South. Historian Bruce Cummings, writing in 1981, stated that Soviet control over the DPRK was 'flimsy' and that Kim Il Sung could have acted independently of the Soviets since the DPRK was by no means solely reliant on Soviet arms. Fortunately, the opening of the Soviet archives after 1990 make it much easier to unravel the controversial causes of this war and to clarify the roles of Kim Il Sung and of Stalin.

What was the role of Kim Il Sung in starting the war?

Kim Il Sung's role is key to explaining this war. It is clear that both Synghman Rhee and Kim Il Sung wanted to unify the country. Thus a civil war would have existed here in any case, regardless of the involvement of the superpowers. However, neither side could unify the country on its own, and thus the involvement of the Soviets in support of Kim Il Sung or the Americans in support of Synghman Rhee was essential for success. Kim Il Sung put a huge amount of effort into persuading Stalin that he should back an attack on the South. Stalin initially had no interest in these plans and Kim Il Sung obtained Stalin's approval only after persistent appeals. Thus it is clear that the impetus for war came from Pyongyang and not from Moscow. The Truman administration's assumption in June 1950, and of many scholars writing since then, that the war was Stalin's initiative is therefore false, though his support for Kim Il Sung was key in allowing the war to go ahead.

What was the role of Stalin in starting the war?

Although initially unwilling to agree to Kim Il Sung's plans for a war against the South, the evidence shows that Stalin gave his approval at the beginning of 1950. There are several possible reasons for this change of mind:

- Stalin may have been more hopeful about the chances of world revolution. The fact that the Communists had won the Chinese Civil War, that the Soviets now had the atomic bomb and that the West was facing economic difficulties might have convinced Stalin that now was the time to push forward with spreading Soviet influence in Asia.

- The United States' role in Japan could have provided an impetus to gain influence specifically in Korea. Stalin knew that the United States had changed its policy in Japan and was now turning Japan into a strong anti-Communist base (see Chapter Six, pages 58–9); if he could gain control of South Korea, this could secure the Soviet position in north-east Asia.

- Historian John Lewis Gaddis points out Stalin's opportunism as another possible factor – his tendency to advance in situations where he thought he could do so without provoking too strong a response. Acheson's perimeter speech could have provided Stalin with a 'tempting opportunity'.

Although changing his mind about supporting the attack, Stalin nevertheless remained cautious. He warned 'the Korean friends' not to 'expect great assistance and support from the Soviet Union, because it had more important challenges to meet than the Korean problem'. He also made it clear that Kim Il Sung would have to gain the approval of Mao Zedong. 'If you get kicked in the teeth, I will not lift a finger. You have to ask Mao for all the help'. Nevertheless, Stalin's support was key to enabling the invasion to take place, and Soviet commanders were involved in all aspects of the preparation and execution of the attack.

What was the role of Mao Zedong in the outbreak of the war?

When Kim Il Sung visited the People's Republic of China, Mao was initially sceptical about the success of the invasion, but gave his approval because Kim fostered the impression that Stalin was more enthusiastic than he actually was, and also Mao was at this time planning an invasion of Taiwan. He needed Soviet support for this and worried that if he expressed reservations about the invasion, Stalin might also show concern about the results of an attack on Taiwan. Having given his approval, he asked Kim if he needed troops stationed on the Korean border in case the Americans intervened, but Kim said that this would not be necessary. Mao then seems to have paid little attention to the actual preparations that were going on in North Korea.

When the attack on the South came, it surprised not only Mao, but also the South Koreans and the Americans. Planning to win the war quickly, the North carried out a massive tank attack, and it was the nature of this attack that caused the United States to take such swift and dramatic action.

STUDENT STUDY SECTION

Discussion question

John Lewis Gaddis suggests that the Korean War could be called 'A Comedy of Errors'. What misconceptions guided the thinking of Truman, Stalin and Mao during the planning and course of the Korean War?

Results of the Korean War
Actions of the United States

Fearing that this attack would be followed by further Soviet aggression elsewhere in the world, the USA carried out the following measures:

- NSC-68's recommendation to triple the defence budget was implemented.
- U.S. land forces in Europe were greatly strengthened.
- NATO was strengthened. Greece and Turkey were brought into NATO and military bases were set up in Turkey (which had a border with the USSR).
- The need for West Germany to become armed and integrated into NATO was given top priority.

Many of these measures had already been under consideration, and the effect of the Korean War was to accelerate these U.S. policies.

In Asia, the United States also took several important steps against what it saw as the threats of Communism (see also Chapter Six):

- The Treaty of San Francisco with Japan was signed in 1952. This enabled the United States to maintain military bases in Japan. The United States now also focused on building up Japan economically to make it a bulwark against Communism.
- Taiwan had to be defended as well. Already at the start of the Korean War, the U.S. Seventh Fleet had been sent to the Taiwan Straits to defend the island against possible Communist invasion. Following the Korean War, the USA supported Taiwan's Chiang Kai-shek with military and economic aid and continued to recognize Taiwan as the only official Chinese state until as late as 1971.
- China was now isolated by the United States. It was condemned by the UN as an aggressor and prevented from taking a seat in the UN Security Council.
- The USA also became committed to supporting other regimes in Asia that it believed were resisting Communism. This eventually led to US involvement in the Philippines and in Vietnam.
- SEATO (South-East Asia Treaty Organization) was formed as an anti-Communist containment bloc in the Asian area.

What did the Korean War and the subsequent actions of the USA mean for other countries?

For Korea: The cost in human lives and property was vast. There was also no hope now of reunification. This was no longer a local issue, but a Cold War issue and the ceasefire line turned into a heavily armed Cold War frontier. North Korea has subsequently remained under Communist rule. South Korea became a model capitalist success story with heavy American and Japanese investment.

For China: Although now isolated by the USA, China's reputation grew greatly and it became a major power in the region. It preserved its own revolution, took on the USA and successfully 'saved' North Korea. This increased Mao Zedong's reputation at home and strengthened the Chinese revolution. However, it also meant that valuable resources at home were diverted away from recovery to the war effort, and in addition that China's aim of uniting Taiwan and China was now far more difficult. Stalin's reluctance throughout the war to help Mao with any substantial military commitments also meant that from now on Mao would be less likely to rely on Soviet help and would be less bothered about following Moscow's lead. (See Chapter Eleven.)

For the USSR: Although the USSR had kept out of direct conflict with the USA, the results of the Korean War were not good for the Soviet Union. The USA's decision to triple its defence budget, rearm West Germany, maintain troops in Europe and fight Communism in Asia meant that the Soviet Union was now embroiled in an even more intense and broader Cold War standoff than had existed in 1950.

For South-East Asia: The USA's perception of all Communist movements as being part of a 'monolithic' movement, and its commitment to intervene wherever it saw the threat of Communism on the move, meant that South-East Asia became involved in the Cold War. It was now harder for nationalist movements in the region to triumph in the post-colonial era and many of these groups were forced into increasing dependence on the USSR or China. However, it was only in Vietnam that the USA, the USSR and China became directly involved in the fighting.

The effects of the Korean War on the Cold War

The development of the military-industrial complex

The huge increase in spending triggered by NSC-68 had important effects inside the United States. It gave a boost to the arms production industries through greater opportunities to get government contracts. Many politicians, including Eisenhower, worried about the growing political and economic strength of this sector of industry – or the military-industrial complex as it became known.

The Korean War caused the globalization of the Cold War. The USA and USSR now found themselves embroiled in conflicts in Asia as well as Europe, and these conflicts would soon spread to other parts of the developing world. It also led to the militarization of the Cold War. To maintain the now increased military commitments, U.S. defence spending increased dramatically, running at around 10 per cent of American **GNP** in the 1950s. In Europe, there was also increased military spending, which helped to boost the economic prosperity of both regions. In the Soviet Union, the Red Army increased from 2.8 million troops in 1950 to almost 5.8 million by 1955. Stalin's successors, however, cut military spending sharply after 1955, though continuing the development of nuclear armaments.

STUDENT STUDY SECTION

Review activities

1 Annotate a map of the world to show the impact of the Korean War *or*

2 Draw a mind map/spider diagram to show the results of the Korean War.

Document analysis

Throughout this book, you will see many activities which are designed to help you develop the document analysis skills you will need for Paper One. The questions on Paper One will be looking to test your skills in:

- interpreting historical sources
- cross-referencing historical sources
- assessing sources for their value and limitations
- using sources in conjunction with your own knowledge in a historical explanation.

Interpreting historical sources

On the document paper, you will need to show an understanding of a range of different types of historical documents, e.g., statistics, cartoons, photographs or written sources.

You will need to be able to show that you understand what the *inference* or the *message* of the source is, and in order to do this well, you will need to use your contextual historical knowledge, e.g., your knowledge of the person who created the source or the historical events going on at the time the source was produced. Sometimes there may be several points being made in the source; you need to 'read between the lines' to understand the more subtle message the source conveys.

Cross-referencing historical sources

Cross-referencing questions sometimes ask you to look for similarities between two sources, sometimes the differences between two sources and sometimes both similarities and differences. Therefore, make sure you always read the question carefully. You need to show that you can handle more than one source at a time, so avoid paraphrasing each source and then waiting for the conclusion to explain the differences/similarities; switch between the sources throughout your answer. For each point of similarity or difference, include a brief quote or specific reference from each source to back up your argument.

Assessing sources for their value and limitations

This involves focusing on the origin and the purpose of the source in order to assess how useful it might be to the historian.

Origin

When using and interpreting sources you need to look first at the nature of the source, i.e., what kind of source it is – a photograph, diary, memoir, speech, cartoon or letter. The type of source will have an influence on how useful it is, e.g., a personal letter can be very useful because the person writing it will usually be giving private views.

You also need to look at where or whom a source comes from, and when it was produced. Your knowledge of the person or organization that produced the source will help you assess the source's usefulness, e.g., is the source written by someone who is likely to have known what was going on?

Purpose

Here you are looking at why the source was produced, written or drawn, and the audience it was intended for.

Was it produced for propaganda purposes? Was it produced to make a person support one particular viewpoint? Was it produced for private, personal purposes? Was it produced to inform people?

Always come back to the question. It is no good stating what the purpose and origin of a source is if you do not then apply this to answering the question. Use your conclusions about the origin and purpose of the source to answer the question that has been set.

If a question is asking for both value and limitations of a source, always start by looking for the value of the source and then move on to the limitations.

Don't forget that even if a source has many limitations, it can still be valuable to a historian. It just depends on what question the historian is asking. For example, a propaganda speech by Stalin is not very useful for explaining the true situation in the Soviet Union. However, it can be useful for showing us the nature of Soviet propaganda and the type of information that the Soviet Union wanted the Soviet people or the West to hear.

Questions

See if you can find an example of some of the following historical documents in relation to the Korean War. Assess why each type of document might be useful for a historian studying the nature of this war and how it was fought. What might be the limitations of each of these documents?

a Private letters/diaries

b Poems/novels

c Cartoons

d Newspaper articles

e Government records

f Speeches by politicians

g Memoirs

h Drawings/paintings

i Photographs

j Statistics

k Eyewitness accounts

Document analysis: the Korean War

Document A

Dear brothers and sisters!

Great danger threatens our motherland and its people. What is needed to liquidate this menace? In this war which is being waged against the Synghman Rhee clique, the Korean people must defend the Korean Democratic People's Republic and its constitution, they must liquidate the unpatriotic fascist puppet regime of Synghman Rhee which has been established in the southern part of the republic; they must liberate the southern part of our motherland from the domination of the Synghman Rhee clique and they must restore the peoples' committees there – the real organs of power. Under the banner of the Korean Democratic People's Republic we must complete the unification of the motherland and create a single, independent, democratic state. The war which we are forced to wage is a just war for the unification and independence of the motherland and for freedom and democracy.

(Broadcast of Kim Il Sung to the nation, 26 June 1950)

Document B

I have ordered United States air and sea forces to give the Korean Government troops cover and support. The attack upon Korea makes it plain beyond all doubt that Communism has passed beyond the use of subversion to conquer independent nations and will now use armed invasion and war. It has defied the orders of the Security Council. Accordingly I have ordered the Seventh Fleet to prevent any attack on Formosa [Taiwan] … I am calling on the Chinese Government on Formosa to cease all air and sea operations against the mainland … A return to the rule of force in international affairs would have far-reaching effects. The United States will continue to uphold the rule of law.

(Statement by U.S. President Truman, 27 June 1950)

Questions

● **Examiner's hint:**
For Document Question 1, make sure you include quotes from Document A to back up your answer.

1 **a** What is the message of Document A?

   b Which phrases emphasize that it is a piece of propaganda?

2 How do Documents A and B differ in the explanation they give of 25 June 1950?

3 What are the value and limitations of using Documents A and B as evidence of why the Korean War started?

ToK Time

Discuss the following questions as a class or in small groups. Feedback ideas and make notes of your key points in your Theory of Knowledge journals.

● Which sources of knowledge – historical texts, websites, newspapers, personal accounts, government documents, diaries or some sources – other do you consider the most trustworthy, and why? (Look back to the question on page 55 that you did on historical documents from the Korean War era.)

● If facts alone cannot prove or disprove something, what else is involved in the 'proof' of a statement or theory?

6 THE USA AND CONTAINMENT IN ASIA

When you have read this chapter, you should attempt the following essay question:

- To what extent was the U.S. policy of containment successful in Asia?

As discussed in Chapter Five, the Korean War confirmed to the USA that fighting Communism was not limited to Europe, but was now a worldwide struggle. Containment, therefore, became a key policy in Asia as the United States sought to hold back the spread of Communism. The domino effect had to be avoided at all costs.

Timeline of Asian containment

1950	Korean War starts
1951	U.S. – Japanese Treaty
1952	U.S. occupation of Japan ends
1953	End of the Korean War
1954	Fall of Dien Bien Phu
	Geneva Accords on French Indochina
	Defence pact between USA and Taiwan
	SEATO is established
1955	First Taiwan Crisis
1958	Second Taiwan Crisis
1963	President Ngo Dinh Diem assassinated
	President John F. Kennedy assassinated
1964	Gulf of Tonkin Incident
	Congress passes Gulf of Tonkin Resolution
1965	U.S. marines land in Vietnam
	Operation Rolling Thunder starts
1968	Tet Offensive
	My Lai Massacre
1969	Paris Peace Talks begin
	President Richard Nixon announces 'Nixon Doctrine' and Vietnamization
1970	Invasion of Cambodia by U.S. and South Vietnamese troops
	Students killed at Kent State University
1972	President Nixon visits China
1973	Paris Peace Agreement signed
	United States withdraws from Vietnam
1975	North Vietnamese troops take over Saigon
	Cambodia falls to Khmer Rouge

In this chapter there are four examples of the United States actively seeking to contain Communism in Asia. How successful were the U.S. efforts in each case?

Case Study 1: Korea

On the surface, Korea (see also Chapter Five) can be seen as a success for the U.S. policy of containment, as Communism was kept north of the 38th parallel. However, as General Douglas MacArthur had gone further than the original aim of pushing the North Koreans back north of the 38th parallel, and had attempted to 'roll-back' Communism, the end result was something of a 'mutilated' success. The Americans had been routed by the Chinese army, and the losses of both UN forces and Korean civilians were huge. The impact on U.S. foreign policy, with NSC-68 coming into force and thus the militarization and globalization of the Cold War, also needs to be considered when assessing if intervention in Korea can be considered a 'success'. By 1953, Communism had clearly been contained in Korea, but at great cost, not just in terms of human and economic losses, but also in terms of the impact on future U.S. policy.

Case Study 2: Japan

The policy of containment was more clearly a success in Japan.

The United States had occupied Japan following Japan's defeat in 1945. General MacArthur was appointed Supreme Commander of the Allied Powers (SCAP), and he was given great powers to devise and execute policies. The American objective was to create a weak and **pacifist** Japan, but this policy was to change radically as the USA decided that Japan was a vital strategic area in Asia for its policy of containment.

MacArthur's initial tasks were to demilitarize the country, bring war criminals to trial and then devise a new **constitution**. When completed, this included a **Bill of Rights** and a clause 'renouncing war forever'. Japan's royal family survived these changes, but the emperor's role was reduced from demi-god to being merely a focus of the people's unity. The emphasis of this new constitution was very much on the rights of the individual, as one of the fundamental beliefs of SCAP was that the most effective way of 'curing' the Japanese of their militarism was by creating a fully democratic society. 2500 political prisoners were released from prison – many were Communists – and laws were introduced which were favourable to trade unions and which attempted to break up the hugely powerful elite Japanese families (the *Zaibatsu*).

However, the shift of the focus of the Cold War to Asia in 1950 changed many of MacArthur's original policies. Suddenly there was a need for a strong, anti-Communist ally in Asia to counter-balance the new Communist Chinese state, the People's Republic of China. Japan would be that ally, so it was now essential that Communism within Japan should be wiped out. Japan also needed to be economically and militarily capable of resisting Communist threats from other Asian countries. Japanese economic recovery and independence became the most important objective of SCAP. As a result, some trade unions were banned from striking and restrictions were placed on Communists, while the old values of duty and loyalty regained their importance. The *Zaibatsu* were also allowed to continue. This was known as the 'reverse course'. A 'red purge' began which eliminated thousands of left-wing officials from government and union positions.

The most notable retreat from the idealism of the early occupation was the revised thinking about Japan's defence. It no longer made sense for the United States to seek a weak and pacifist Japan. Therefore, shortly after the outbreak of the Korean War in June 1950, Japan was permitted to establish a 75,000-strong paramilitary force called the 'self-defence force'. American military influence also continued after the end of the occupation in 1952. Together with the Treaty of San Francisco, the American–Japanese Security Treaty was signed, leaving Japan, in effect, a military protectorate of the USA. The treaty provided for the retention of American bases and allowed the United States to use the American forces stationed there in any way that would contribute to the 'maintenance of international peace and security in the Far East'. It prohibited Japan from granting military bases to any other power without American consent.

Was containment a success in Japan?

The United States achieved its aims of making Japan its bulwark against Communism in the Far East. Japan's economy developed rapidly and, following the so-called 'economic miracle', Japan emerged as a great economic power under the control of a conservative government that succeeded in forging a strong national consensus in favour of economic growth as Japan's priority. Thus there was never any threat of Communism spreading to Japan. However, historians have challenged how far this was due to the policies of the USA or the efforts of the Japanese themselves. The attitude of the Japanese people, their government's policies and their approach to hard work were perhaps at least as important as the policies of SCAP.

It should also be noted that the United States would have liked Japan to become much more of a bulwark against Communism. The USA wanted Japan to establish a large military force and to join a regional defence alliance. The Japanese government resisted these demands. The government knew that the U.S. presence in Japan would deter a Soviet attack and it could meanwhile put priority on pursuing Japan's economic miracle. With the USA picking up their 'defence bill', the Japanese had money to invest in their economic development.

Case Study 3: Taiwan

Containment in Taiwan was also seen as a success. U.S. policy towards Taiwan (Formosa) changed with the outbreak of the Korean War. Before this time, the USA had no formal plans to help the Nationalists resist an invasion from Communist China. However, when North Korea attacked South Korea, President Truman immediately ordered the U.S. Seventh Fleet to the Taiwan Straits to keep peace between the Nationalist and Communist Chinese. From this point on, the United States recognized Taiwan as the only official Chinese state (this was to remain the situation until 1971) and gave substantial economic and military aid to the island in order to contain Chinese Communism.

President Eisenhower withdrew the Seventh Fleet in 1953 to 'unleash' Taiwan's Nationalist leader, Chiang Kai-shek, and allow him to attack mainland China. Nationalists raided the coast of China, which was used as an excuse by the Chinese to bombard the islands of Quemoy and Matsu and invade the Tachen Islands (see map on page 136). In response, Congress passed the Formosa Resolution, which allowed President Eisenhower to take whatever military action he thought was necessary to defend Taiwan. Eisenhower told China that if it took over Taiwan, the United States would use nuclear weapons against a Chinese mainland target. These were Eisenhower's policies of 'massive retaliation' and 'Brinkmanship' in action (see Chapter Seven). The American president also got the USSR to put pressure on China, and it finally backed down.

When China then bombarded Quemoy and Matsu in 1958, the Seventh Fleet was ordered into the Taiwan Straits and the United States again threatened use of nuclear weapons. China again backed down, though it is worth noting that the United States was unhappy about getting dragged into yet another conflict to protect Taiwan, just as the USSR was unhappy that Mao was taking such risks.

Was containment a success in Taiwan?

Despite the dangers of these crises over Quemoy and Matsu, Brinkmanship seemed to have won the day, and Taiwan continued to maintain its independence with American support. (See Chapter Twelve, pp. 135–6 for more discussion on U.S. action in relation to Taiwan.)

Case Study 4: an in-depth study of the USA and containment in Vietnam

The most striking failure of the U.S. policy of containment was in Vietnam, where the North Vietnamese Communists were not contained. After a decade of military involvement, the loss of hundreds of thousands of American lives, billions of dollars and the damaging division of U.S. public opinion, the Americans pulled out of Vietnam in 1973. Their fear of other Asian countries 'falling like dominoes' if Communism was not contained seemed to be realized with the fall of Cambodia and Laos to Communist forces in the same year.

This map of Indochina shows the division of Vietnam after the Geneva Accords, and the Ho Chi Minh Trail.

How did the United States become involved?

Indochina (Vietnam, Cambodia and Laos) was a French colony that had been occupied during World War Two by the Japanese. During this time a nationalist movement had grown, and most Vietnamese had no desire to let Vietnam return to the rule of the French after 1945. The most important nationalist was a Communist called Ho Chi Minh, who led a movement called the Vietminh that was very active against the Japanese. When the Japanese were defeated in 1945, Ho declared the independence of the Democratic Republic of Vietnam.

The French, however, had no intention of allowing Vietnam to have its independence and hostilities broke out between the French and the Vietminh in 1946. Although President Roosevelt had pressured France to relinquish its hold over Vietnam, American opinion towards Ho and the Vietminh hardened once Truman was president. This was due to the developing international situation in Europe and, after 1949, Asia. As the Cold War intensified in both areas, Ho's Communist, rather than nationalist, credentials were emphasized and the assumption grew that he was being directed from Moscow.

In March 1950, military aid was sent to help France defeat the Vietminh. This aid was continued by Eisenhower, who gave the following reasoning for his government's actions in April 1954:

You have the specific value of a locality in its production of materials that the world needs. You have the possibility that many human beings pass under a dictatorship that is inimical to the free world. You have the broader considerations that might follow what you would call the 'falling domino' principle ... You have a row of dominoes set up, you knock over the first one, and what will happen to the last one is the certainty that it will go over very quickly.

The Geneva Conference of 1954
From April to July 1954 a conference was held in Geneva in Switzerland in an attempt to end hostilities and create peace in Indonesia. Many countries attended the conference. The declaration which became known as the Geneva Accords freed Indochina from French colonial control.

Thus, the idea of countries turning to Communism like dominoes falling over became entrenched in U.S. government thinking. The domino effect identified Vietnam as the key domino that must not be allowed to fall if Laos, Cambodia, Thailand, Burma, Malaya, Indonesia, and even possibly Singapore and Japan, were to remain safe from Communism.

Although the United States was funding 80 per cent of the war by 1954, President Eisenhower made the decision not to directly intervene, and in 1954 the French were finally defeated at the battle of Dien Bien Phu. That year at Geneva in Switzerland, a peace agreement (the Geneva Accords) was drawn up which decided that:

- The French would withdraw from Indochina.
- There would be a temporary division of Vietnam at the 17th parallel. Ho Chi Minh would control the north of the country.
- There would be 'free elections' to unite Vietnam in 1956.
- There were to be no foreign bases.
- Laos and Cambodia would be recognized as independent states.

Significantly, the USA did not sign the Geneva Accords. In response to the agreement, they attempted to strengthen the area south of the 17th parallel, supporting a non-Communist government that would be able to resist an invasion from the north. To offset the results of the Geneva Accords they also established SEATO (the South-East Asia Treaty Organization). This was signed by Australia, Britain, France, New Zealand, Pakistan, the Philippines and Thailand. These countries agreed to meet together if there was an armed attack on one of them and, if agreement was unanimous, to take action. In defiance of the Geneva Accords, which said that Laos and Cambodia should remain neutral, SEATO included South Vietnam, Laos and Cambodia as its 'protected areas'. It thus became a legal basis for future U.S. action in Vietnam.

The man that the United States backed to lead the government in the South was Ngo Dinh Diem, a Catholic who had been educated in the USA. In October 1955, Diem proclaimed the establishment of the Republic of Vietnam (also known as South Vietnam) with himself as president. U.S. aid worth millions of dollars was sent to Diem, and the United States also began its military involvement in the South with its commencement of training of the South Vietnamese army. By 1960 almost 1000 Americans were serving in South Vietnam as military 'advisers'.

Although the United States pressed Diem to carry out reform in the South, Diem turned out to be a ruthless leader who, along with his brother Ngo Dinh Nhu, the chief of police, crushed opposition brutally. Land reforms were not forthcoming, and the Catholic faith was promoted, despite the fact that most Vietnamese were Buddhists. Soon it became clear that a brutal family dictatorship was emerging in South Vietnam.

In 1956 Diem, with U.S. support, refused to hold elections. He claimed that he did not feel bound by the agreements of the Geneva Accords, as he did not believe that the Communists could be trusted to hold fair elections. In reality Diem and the Americans were afraid that the elections would have resulted in a united, Communist Vietnam. It has been estimated that Ho Chi Minh would have won about 80 per cent of the vote had elections been allowed to go ahead.

With elections not an option, military opposition to Diem became the only alternative in the South. Groups of Communists (referred to by the South Vietnamese government and the USA as the 'Vietcong' or VC) formed themselves into military units with a political arm known as the National Liberation Front (NLF). North Vietnam supported the VC, as did much of the local population in the South, who had become disillusioned with Diem's government.

The USA became increasingly concerned with its ally Diem, and doubted his ability to maintain its preferred option of the 'two Vietnams' policy.

Ho Chi Minh
Ho Chi Minh (1890–1969) became a Communist during his stay in Paris between 1917 and 1923, where he also campaigned unsuccessfully for Vietnamese independence at the Versailles Peace Conference of 1919. He then worked as a Comintern agent in Asia before founding the Indochina Communist Party in 1930. During World War Two, he formed a resistance movement – the Vietminh – against the Japanese and received secret support from the USA. Following the defeat of the Japanese in 1945, he declared the Democratic Republic of Vietnam in Hanoi, but then had to lead his Vietminh forces against first the French and then the Americans. He became the symbol of nationalism, continuing to inspire the Vietnamese in their resistance against the Americans even after his death in 1969. The former capital of South Vietnam, Saigon, is now named Ho Chi Minh City in his honour.

How did President Kennedy widen the conflict?

After his election as president in November 1960, **John F. Kennedy's** policy towards containing Communism was 'flexible response'. This meant his administration expanded the available means of fighting against Communism. This expansion included the following:

- Increasing the number of U.S. military advisers in the South (there were 17,000 'advisers' in Vietnam by the time of Kennedy's death).
- Starting **counter-insurgency** operations against Communist guerrillas in the South. This included **'search and destroy' missions** against the Vietcong and the spraying of **defoliants**, such as Agent Orange, in order to destroy the jungle that gave them cover. The United States also supported the Strategic Hamlets Program, which consisted of the resettlement of villagers into fortified villages where they could be kept 'safe' from the Communists.
- Introducing a new U.S. military counter-insurgency force, the 'Green Berets', trained in guerrilla fighting.
- Encouraging Diem to introduce social and political reforms.

None of these measures succeeded in limiting the growing success of the Vietcong attacks on the South. Indeed, measures such as the Strategic Hamlets Program and the spraying of Agent Orange only alienated the local peasant population further. Meanwhile, rather than winning support by carrying out a reform programme, Diem's unpopular actions continued to generate mass discontent that reached a head in 1963 with a crisis over his anti-Buddhist policies. When laws were passed banning the celebration of the Buddha's birthday, the Buddhists organized mass protests. These included rallies, hunger strikes and even **self-immolations**. This unrest caused an international reaction, especially when the response of South Vietnam's First Lady, Madam Nhu (Diem's sister-in-law), was 'Let them burn and we shall clap our hands'. Kennedy's government now started to cut off its aid to Diem's regime but, by the end of 1963, Diem and his brother had both been killed in a coup which was known about in advance by U.S. intelligence services. However, getting rid of Diem did not improve the situation, and indeed further served to increase the U.S. commitment to subsequent Saigon governments. General William C. Westmoreland believed that Diem's assassination 'morally locked us into Vietnam'.

Thich Qung Duc's self-immolation in Saigon in June 1963. This Buddhist monk was 73 when he set himself on fire in protest at anti-Buddhism laws.

Strategic hamlets or 'agrovilles'
Strategic hamlets were new villages built by Diem into which peasants could be placed to 'protect' them from Communist infiltration. They were surrounded by barbed wire and only helped to alienate the peasants who felt imprisoned and who resented having to leave their ancestral lands. This initiative failed to keep villagers from joining the Communists.

STUDENT STUDY SECTION

Discussion questions

President Kennedy resisted sending combat soldiers to Vietnam and on a couple of occasions indicated misgivings about U.S. involvement in this war. Nevertheless, by the time that Kennedy was assassinated, the USA was much more deeply and directly involved in fighting the war in Vietnam.

1 In what ways did Kennedy broaden the USA's commitment to Vietnam?

2 Could the USA still have pulled out of Vietnam in 1963?

Why did President Johnson continue the Vietnam War? Was it Johnson's war?

Vice-President **Lyndon Baines Johnson** became president after Kennedy was assassinated in November 1963. He inherited a situation in which there was no longer a stable government in the South of Vietnam and one in which the strength of the Communists in the South was increasing. He also inherited Kennedy's advisers. These factors pointed towards the likelihood of Johnson continuing the war. Johnson was also as determined as his predecessors to win the 'war against Communism' and prevent the domino effect.

Given the deteriorating situation in South Vietnam by 1964, Johnson needed to be able to increase U.S. commitment to the war; however, he also needed justification for this in order to obtain the support of the U.S. public and Congress. The 'excuse' for the United States to step up its activities in Vietnam came with the so-called 'Gulf of Tonkin incident'. On the night of 2 August 1964, the American naval destroyer *Maddox* was fired on by North Vietnamese patrol boats while it was patrolling and gathering intelligence in the Gulf of Tonkin off the North Vietnamese coast. Two days later, on 4 August 1964, the U.S. destroyers *Maddox* and *Turner Joy* were also allegedly fired on. Ship radar apparently showed that they were under attack, but there was much confusion, and no physical evidence of an assault was found. Nevertheless, Johnson called this attack 'open aggression on the high seas' and as a result the United States immediately bombed North Vietnamese installations. The next day, Johnson addressed the U.S. Congress and asked it to pass the Gulf of Tonkin Resolution, which authorized the President to 'take all necessary measures to repel any armed attack against the forces of the United States and to prevent further aggression'. For the next six years, the Gulf of Tonkin Resolution was used as the legal basis for the war in Vietnam.

Once the Gulf of Tonkin Resolution had been passed, the USA responded to the situation in Vietnam by:

- Launching a sustained campaign of bombing North Vietnam, which was known as Operation Rolling Thunder.
- Sending 100,000 ground forces to South Vietnam in 1965. Led by General Westmoreland, U.S. soldiers carried out 'search and destroy' missions. By 1968, there were 520,000 troops in Vietnam.

Bombing of targets in the South also took place in order to provide support for ground troops and to attack the enemy supply routes and bases. Large numbers of rockets, bombs and **napalm** were dropped on South Vietnam, with devastating effects on the local population.

STUDENT STUDY SECTION

Research questions

Researching the following questions will help your understanding of the type of warfare that went on in Vietnam on both sides, and its effectiveness:

1 What were the characteristics of U.S. strategy?

2 What problems did U.S. soldiers face in their fight against the VC?

3 What impact did the bombing campaign have on North Vietnam?

4 What were the characteristics of the guerrilla war fought by the VC against the Americans?

5 Why were the VC successful?

6 How effective was the South Vietnamese army (ARVN)?

Document analysis

The contest in Vietnam is part of wider pattern of aggressive purpose …

Why are we in South Vietnam? We are there because we have a promise to keep. Since 1954 every American president has offered support to the people of South Vietnam. We have helped to build, and we have helped to defend. Thus over many years, we have made a national pledge to help South Vietnam defend its independence. And I intend to keep that promise.

To dishonor the pledge, to abandon this small and brave nation to its enemy, and to the terror that must follow, would be an unforgivable wrong.

We are also there to strengthen world order. Around the globe from Berlin to Thailand are people whose well-being rests, in part, on the belief that they can count on us if they are attacked. To leave Vietnam to its fate would shake the confidence of all these people in the value of American commitment, the value of America's word. The result would be increased unrest and instability and even wider war.

We are also there because there are great stakes in the balance. Let no one think for a moment that to retreat from Vietnam would bring an end to conflict. The battle would be renewed in one country and then another. The central lesson of our time is that the appetite for aggression is never satisfied. To withdraw from one battlefield means only to prepare for the next. We must say in South East Asia as we did in Europe, in the words of the Bible: 'Hitherto shalt thou come, but no further'.

President Johnson in U.S. Department of State Bulletin, 26 April 1965

Questions

1 What reasons does President Johnson give to justify U.S. involvement in Vietnam?

2 What evidence is there in this document that the fighting in Vietnam is part of the wider Cold War conflict?

Now read the next extract, which was written by an American historian, William Chafe, more than ten years after the Vietnam War ended:

Without question, the central precondition for American involvement in Vietnam was the set of assumptions that underlay and shaped the entire history of the Cold War. Once committed to the view that the communist world was one, and systematically involved in a worldwide conspiracy to subvert freedom, any effort in other countries that could be interpreted as hostile to the United States automatically became defined as that worldwide conspiracy … containment … became a diffuse, universal rationale for resisting change in the international status quo. Given such a definition of the world, and the moralistic rhetoric that accompanied it, distinctions between countries and issues became blurred, and it was America's 'moral' obligation to defend 'freedom' anywhere it was threatened, regardless of how dictatorial, tyrannical or repressive the regimes on 'our' side acted …

From William Chafe, The Unfinished Journey, 5th ed. (Oxford University Press, 2002)

Questions

3 What are Chafe's criticisms of the United States' approach to the situation in Vietnam?

4 Which parts of Johnson's speech would provide evidence for Chafe's criticisms?

● **Examiner's hint:**
Question 4 is to test your cross-referencing skills; look back at page 55 for hints on how to approach this type of question.

The Great Society and the 'credibility gap'

The war that Johnson really wanted to fight was actually at home, a war against poverty and social injustice. He called his programme the 'Great Society' and it involved improving civil rights, eradicating poverty, increasing access to health and education, and creating a cleaner environment. This encouraged the development of the 'credibility gap'. The credibility gap was the difference in reality between what the Johnson administration told Congress and what was actually happening. 'I was determined,' he recalled later, 'to keep the [Vietnam] war from shattering that dream, which meant that I had no choice but to keep my foreign policy in the wings … I knew Congress as well as I know Lady Bird [his wife], and I knew that the day it exploded into a major debate on the war, that day would be the beginning of the end of the Great Society'.

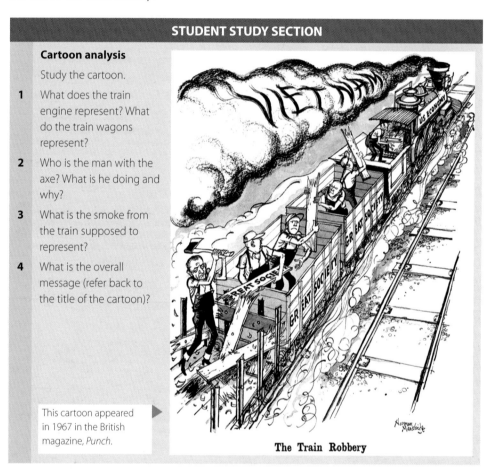

STUDENT STUDY SECTION

Cartoon analysis

Study the cartoon.

1 What does the train engine represent? What do the train wagons represent?

2 Who is the man with the axe? What is he doing and why?

3 What is the smoke from the train supposed to represent?

4 What is the overall message (refer back to the title of the cartoon)?

This cartoon appeared in 1967 in the British magazine, *Punch*.

The Train Robbery

The Tet Offensive

By 1968, the war had reached a turning point. General Westmoreland's policy of 'attrition' had not succeeded in defeating the NLF and at home an anti-war movement was gaining support, fuelled by the growing number of U.S. casualties. Nevertheless, Johnson told the public at the end of 1967 that there was 'light at the end of the tunnel', that is, the United States was starting to win the war. Then, in the early morning of the lunar new year (Tet, a holiday in Vietnam) on 31 January 1968, 70,000 Communists launched a surprise attack. It was the sheer scale of the assault that was most shocking. The Communists attacked more than 100 cities in the South, including Saigon. It took eleven days for the U.S. and ARVN forces to regain control of Saigon. Even more intense was the battle for the beautiful city of Hué; half the city was destroyed and 5800 civilians were killed. The Communists were gradually pushed back from all the other cities after the use of massive firepower against them. This so-called Tet Offensive was a military failure for the Vietcong. The popular uprising in the South they had hoped to trigger did not happen. They failed to hold on to any of the cities gained at the outset of the offensive and it is estimated that they had casualties of over 40,000.

South Vietnam Police Chief Colonel Ngyen Ngoc Loan executes a Vietcong suspect without trial.

However, public opinion in the United States now turned decisively against the war. The American public was sickened by what it saw on television. During what was the first 'televised' war, people were able to watch images in their own homes of the U.S. embassy being attacked by the VC, and they also saw the South Vietnamese Police Chief execute a VC prisoner in the street. All this seemed to indicate to the American public that they were not only not winning the war, but that they were also supporting a regime which flouted basic human rights.

Anti-war protests in the United States reached a new peak. The aftermath of the Tet Offensive resulted in a significant change of strategy for the USA. Bombing of the North was halted and peace talks were initiated. On 31 March 1968 President Johnson addressed on television a stunned U.S. audience, announcing that he would not be standing for re-election the coming November.

ToK Time

Why did the *images* of the Tet Offensive – the storming of the U.S. embassy, the battles in Hué and the summary execution of a Communist prisoner – seem to have more credibility and impact on the American public's view of the war in Vietnam than what they were *told* was going on by the U.S. military and U.S. government?

How far is our perception of 'truth' controlled by language?

As a class discuss images from the Vietnam War, and compare and contrast them with government statements (these could be Vietnamese as well as American) and military press reports from the time. Which of these has more 'truth' about the war and the events in Vietnam?

STUDENT STUDY SECTION

Discussion questions

1 How did the character of the Vietnam War change under President Johnson?

2 Do you agree that the war became Johnson's war? (You may want to set up a formal class debate on this question.)

3 Alternatively, do you agree more with the 'Quagmire Theory'? (that successive presidents took one step after another, thinking each step would be the one to solve the Vietnam problem, but in reality getting deeper and deeper into the quagmire, or muddy marsh)

Did President Nixon achieve 'peace with honour'?

Richard Nixon was elected president of the United States in November 1968. He wanted American withdrawal from the war, but he was not prepared to accept peace at any price. Rather he wanted 'peace with honour'. There was no way that the United States could merely withdraw from South Vietnam or seem to have been defeated. Nixon wanted a settlement which would guarantee the South a reasonable chance of survival. This was to take another four years during which time 300,000 Vietnamese and 20,000 Americans died.

To achieve 'peace with honour', Nixon selected Henry Kissinger as his key foreign policy adviser. Kissinger was prepared to use force to get the North to reach a peace agreement. A 'covert' 14-month bombing campaign was begun along the **Ho Chi Minh Trail** (see map, page 60) – inside neutral Cambodia. This did not force the North to agree to peace terms. Nixon also introduced a policy of 'Vietnamization' – the gradual withdrawal of U.S. troops and handing the war over to the South Vietnamese government – and so from 1969 to 1973 U.S. troop numbers were steadily scaled down. In June 1969, he issued the Nixon Doctrine, which represented a move away from the policies followed in Asia since Truman. It stated that nations were responsible for their own defence:

The nations of Asia can and must increasingly shoulder the responsibility for achieving peace and progress in the area with whatever cooperation we can provide. Asian countries must seek their own destiny for if domination by the aggressor can destroy the freedom of a nation, too much dependence on a protector can eventually erode its dignity. But it is not just a matter of dignity, for dependence on foreign aid destroys the incentive to mobilize domestic resources – human, financial and material – in which the absence of which no government is capable of dealing effectively with its problems and adversaries.

STUDENT STUDY SECTION

Document analysis

Refer back to Johnson's speech on page 65 justifying involvement in Vietnam.

1. What arguments given in the Nixon Doctrine contradict Johnson's arguments for involvement?

2. What does this show about the impact of Vietnam on American global Cold War policy?

Research topic

Victims of the My Lai massacre.

Revelations about a brutal massacre by U.S. soldiers of unarmed old men, women and children in the village of My Lai began to surface in 1969. The resulting trial of Lieutenant William L. Calley added fuel to the anti-war protests and raised deep moral questions about the mass killing of civilians.

1　What happened at My Lai, and what effects did it have on American public opinion?

2　What does this massacre suggest about the attitudes and morale of American troops on the ground in Vietnam?

The Paris Peace Talks

At the peace talks which officially opened in Paris on 13 May 1972 and dragged on until January 1973, Henry Kissinger negotiated with the North Vietnamese, who were also determined to achieve 'peace with honour'. Neither side was willing to compromise, the North demanding that it have representation in the government of the South, and all sides continuing to try to win an advantage at the negotiating table by achieving an upper hand on the battlefield. For the Americans this meant using airpower to put pressure on the Communists – even bombing targets in the North that had previously been considered too sensitive. Another strategy used by Nixon and Kissinger was that of pursuing 'détente' with the Soviet Union and China (see Chapters Eleven and Twelve). One of the aims of trying to develop better relations with the Soviets and the Chinese was to get them to put pressure on North Vietnam to agree to the peace settlement.

Finally, a peace settlement was signed on 27 January 1973. All American troops would withdraw from Vietnam and both North and South would respect the dividing line of the 17th parallel. The last American troops withdrew from Vietnam two weeks after the signing of this peace agreement. However, peace did not come to Vietnam. The North took the initiative and by April 1975, it had taken Saigon.

By the end of 1975, Vietnam, Cambodia and Laos had all fallen to the forces of Communism. Containment had failed – the dominoes of Indochina had fallen.

Vietnam War Moratorium Day, 15 October 1969
As public opinion in the United States turned against the Vietnam War, what had been sporadic demonstrations by hippies and left-wing activists spread to students, the middle-aged and the middle class. Then, on 15 October 1969, across the United States anti-war demonstrations involving over two million people took place. Most wore distinctive black armbands to show their support and to pay tribute to the nearly 45,000 Americans killed in the conflict.

STUDENT STUDY SECTION

Review and discussion questions

1　Why did Nixon need to end the Vietnam War?

2　What did he mean by 'peace with honour'?

3　What strategies did he use to achieve his aim?

4　Did Nixon achieve 'peace with honour'?

Was Vietnam a failure of the American policy of containment? Historians' views

The image of dominoes falling, first used by President Eisenhower in 1953, became a reality. It certainly seems obvious that the Vietnam War failed categorically to contain Communism in Indochina. Many historians of the Cold War hold this view. Indeed, as a case study, and in isolation, the Vietnam War is America's biggest and most overt failure. In its attempt to stop the 'cancer of Communism' spreading from the North across the 17th parallel into the South in Vietnam, it had indirectly fostered the growth of Communist regimes in Cambodia and Laos.

However, some historians have seen that in a broader context the Vietnam War was not a total failure for the United States in terms of containment of Communism. Jim Rohwer in his book *Asia Rising* (Simon and Schuster, 1998) writes that 'the broader aims of America's effort in Vietnam were to keep the capitalist semi-democracies of Southeast Asia from falling to communism' and that Vietnam allowed other countries in the region, such as Malaysia, Thailand and Singapore – all of whom faced Communist threats – the breathing space they needed. 'In other words … America … accomplished in a spectacular way the broader aims of Asian stability and prosperity that the intervention was intended to serve'. Indeed, in support of this thesis, the former Singapore premier, Lee Kuan Yew, noted in his book, *The Singapore Story*:

America's action [in Vietnam] *enabled non-Communist Southeast Asia to put their own houses in order. By 1975 they were in better shape to stand up to the Communists. Had there been no US intervention, the will of these countries to resist them would have melted and Southeast Asia would most likely have gone Communist. The prosperous emerging market economies of ASEAN were nurtured during the Vietnam War years.*

From Lee Kuan Yew's The Singapore Story *(Prentice Hall, 1999)*

STUDENT STUDY SECTION

Cartoon analysis

1 Explain the meaning of each of the 'myths' in the cartoon. (A bloodbath is what was supposed to happen if the North invaded the South. Nixon said in an interview with the American Society of Newspaper Editors in 1971 that 'if the United States were to fail in Vietnam, if the Communists were to take over, the bloodbath that would follow would be a blot on this Nation's history from which we would find it very difficult to return'.)

2 What do all of these 'myths' have in common with regard to U.S. policy in Vietnam?

3 Why has the cartoonist put all the 'myths' in a retirement home?

4 What is the overall message of the cartoon?

This cartoon by Marlette appeared in 1975 in the U.S. newspaper, the *Charlotte Observer*.

'Hi, everybody! Look who's here!'

Review activity

Plot a timeline of key events relevant to the Cold War in Asia from 1945 to 1975. Use a different colour to represent each different Asian country. Add to this 'bullet points' of information explaining when and why the United States became involved, and the outcome of involvement.

Review question

Research why U.S. involvement in Vietnam helped to destabilize the governments of Laos and Cambodia. What impact did the Communist takeover in Cambodia by the Khmer Rouge have on the people of Cambodia? What was the impact of the war on Laos?

Conclusions on the U.S. policy of containment in Asia

Up to 1949, it can be said that the U.S. policy of containment in Europe had been successful. Territorially Communism had made no gains and the one obvious attempt at Soviet expansion after 1947 had been stopped by the Berlin airlift of 1948. The Marshall Plan had helped to revive European economies and stop the threat of Communist parties gaining control in countries such as Italy and France. Containment in Asia, however, as Vietnam shows, was less successful. This was partly due to the fact that Communism in Asia was much more diverse. Unlike in Europe, it was often linked to strong nationalist movements. Mao Zedong and Ho Chi Minh had so much support in their countries because of local circumstances and their struggles for independence. Although the United States was trying to fight against Soviet imperialism, it actually ended up fighting against local movements and nationalist feeling. This explains why the USA could never be as successful in containing these revolutionary movements as they had been in Europe.

STUDENT STUDY SECTION

Working on your essay introduction

After having worked through this chapter, it should now be possible to attempt the essay set at the beginning of the chapter: To what extent was the U.S. policy of containment successful in Asia?

One of the key parts of an essay is the introduction. Refer back to the essay planning grid at the end of Chapter Three and check what should be included in a good introduction. Then have a look at the introductions below and discuss which you think is the best one and why. How could each one be improved?

Introduction 1: In 1947, the United States adopted a policy of containment in the belief that the Soviet Union would keep trying to extend its power unless stopped. The policy of containment was applied in Europe and was successful in stopping Communism from spreading. When China became Communist in 1949, and with the 'Red Scare' putting pressure on his government at home, President Truman decided to extend this policy of containment to Asia. There were several places where the policy of containment was applied – in Korea, in Vietnam, in Japan and in Taiwan. Although the USA can be said to have been successful in containing Communism in Korea, Taiwan and Japan, it failed dramatically in Vietnam.

Introduction 2: The United States faced several threats in Asia in the 1950s and 1960s. China had become Communist in 1949, and then North Korea attacked South Korea in 1950. The island of Formosa (Taiwan) was threatened by mainland China, and Japan was also in danger. The USA believed that it had to deal with these threats. How successful was it?

Introduction 3: Containment became the cornerstone of U.S. policy in 1947 when President Truman issued the Truman Doctrine. This set down the belief that the USA should help any government that was trying to resist Communism, and it led to economic aid in Europe with the Marshall Plan and also a direct confrontation with the Soviets over Berlin in 1948. With China becoming Communist in 1949, the US saw all Communism as a monolithic threat which had to be dealt with in any part of the world. The new ideas for defence were set out in NSC-68, and when North Korea attacked South Korea in 1950, the United States, with UN backing, put containment into action in Asia by sending forces to resist the North Koreans. Following this event, the USA then attempted to contain Communism by building up Japan, protecting Taiwan and fighting Communist forces in Vietnam.

Also try this essay question

What part did the Vietnam War play in the development of the Cold War?

When you have read this chapter you should attempt the following essay question:
• To what extent was there a thaw in the Cold War after 1953?

Timeline of U.S.–Soviet relations 1953–1962

1953	Eisenhower **inaugurated** as U.S. President
	Death of Stalin, who is succeeded by Malenkov and Khrushchev
	Korean armistice
	U.S. Secretary of State Dulles announces 'massive retaliation' policy
1955	Geneva Summit
	Austrian State Treaty ends four-power occupation of Austria
1956	Khrushchev denounces Stalin and promotes 'peaceful co-existence' policy
	Polish workers revolt
	Suez crisis
	Soviets crush Hungarian rising
1957	USSR announces Sputnik satellite success
1958	Khrushchev issues ultimatum to West over Berlin
1959	Khrushchev visits USA and meets Eisenhower at Camp David
1960	U-2 spy plane shot down and Paris Summit collapses
	Kennedy elected U.S. President
1961	Khrushchev and Kennedy meet at Vienna Summit
	Yuri Gagarin is the first man to make an earth-orbiting space flight
1962	Cuban Missile Crisis

Between 1945 and 1950, developments in the Cold War had been affected by events in Europe. After 1950, the course of the Cold War was influenced by other factors, including:

• events in Asia (see Chapters Five and Six)
• the nuclear arms race (See Chapter Ten)
• changes in leadership in the United States and USSR, and a move to establish better relations between East and West. These particular changes will be examined in this chapter.

Eisenhower and Dulles in the United States: roll-back, Brinkmanship and the New Look

Republican Dwight D. Eisenhower was elected U.S. president in 1952. Nicknamed 'Ike', he had a distinguished military background having commanded the Allied armies in Normandy in 1944. After the end of World War Two he served as U.S. Army Chief of Staff and Commander-in-Chief of NATO.

◀ Dwight D. Eisenhower, U.S. president from 1953 to 1960.

Eisenhower's background meant that he was unlikely to be criticized as being 'soft on Communism'. In fact both he and his Secretary of State, John Foster Dulles, were strongly anti-Communist. Dulles was vociferous in his condemnation of the Soviet system:

Soviet Communism believes that human beings are nothing more than … superior animals … and that the best kind of a world is that world which is organized as a well managed farm is organized, where certain animals are taken out to pasture, and they are fed and brought back and milked, and they are given a barn as shelter over their heads … I do not see how, as long as Soviet Communism holds those views … there can be any permanent reconciliation … This is an irreconcilable conflict.

U.S. Senate, 83rd Congress, 1st Session, on the nomination of Dulles, 15 January 1953

In the 1952 presidential election campaign, Dulles had also talked about 'roll-back', by which he meant liberating countries currently held by the Soviets in Eastern Europe, but in reality this never happened. No attempt was ever made under Eisenhower to free countries from Soviet control. Although the United States quietly encouraged rebellions in Eastern Europe in 1953 and 1956 (see Chapter Sixteen), it did not use these opportunities to extend the U.S. sphere of influence.

Rather than carrying out roll-back, under Eisenhower the U.S. administration developed a policy of containment it called the 'New Look'. This meant preventing the extension of Soviet Communism outside of the areas where it was already established, in the belief that without any opportunity to expand, the Soviet system would collapse in on itself. Eisenhower put his containment policy into practice by:

- Setting up alliances to encircle the Soviet Union, for example, SEATO.

- Using military power to protect vulnerable areas, for example, West Berlin.

- Assisting forces fighting Communism, for example, Diem's government in South Vietnam.

- Using the CIA (Central Intelligence Agency) for **covert** operations more extensively than had been done before (see the box on page 74).

- Initiating an increased reliance on nuclear weapons. A national security document in 1953 stated 'The U.S will consider nuclear weapons to be available for use as other munitions.' Conventional weapons would thus play a smaller role in defence.

- Brinkmanship. This involved threats of massive retaliation as an instrument of containment. It entailed going to the brink and threatening nuclear war to intimidate the aggressor into backing down.

Dulles explained the policy of Brinkmanship in 1952 in an interview in *Life* magazine:

You have to take chances for peace, just as you must take chances in war. Some say that we were brought to the verge of war. Of course we were brought to the verge of war. The ability to get to the verge without getting into the war is the necessary art. If you cannot master it, you inevitably get into wars. If you try to run away from it, if you are scared to go to the brink, you are lost.

Despite the aggressive nature of Brinkmanship, Eisenhower was also keenly aware of the dangers of nuclear weapons and prepared to negotiate with the Soviet Union. Thus there were U.S.–Soviet Summits in 1955 and 1959.

The activities of the CIA

The CIA (Central Intelligence Agency) was set up in 1947 by the U.S. government as an intelligence-collecting body, and it undertook extensive covert anti-Communist activities. Historian John Lewis Gaddis wrote of it:

*As the Eisenhower administration took office, the CIA was regularly attempting to infiltrate spies, **saboteurs**, and resistance leaders into the Soviet Union, Eastern Europe and China. It was financing ostensibly independent radio stations broadcasting to those countries, as well as labor unions, academic conferences, scholarly journals, and student organizations - some of them inside the United States.*

From John Lewis Gaddis, *The Cold War* (Penguin, 2005), pp.163–4.

The CIA was also involved in the overthrow of governments it considered too left-wing. In 1953 it helped to overthrow the government of Mohammed Mossadegh in Iran and in 1954 it played a role in overthrowing Jacobo Arbenz Guzmán in Guatemala.

STUDENT STUDY SECTION

Cartoon analysis

Cartoon by Herblock published in the *Washington Post* in 1956. ▶

"Don't Be Afraid—I Can Always Pull You Back"

1 How is Secretary of State Dulles portrayed in this cartoon? Who is he pushing to The Brink? Why does this character look reluctant?

2 What do you think the cartoonist's attitude is towards the idea of Brinkmanship?

3 Find an example from the previous two chapters of where Dulles can be said to have successfully used Brinkmanship.

Review questions

1 How did the new administration's attitude to defence differ from the proposals set out in the Truman administration's NSC-68?

2 How was Eisenhower's New Look a) different from and b) similar to the ideas and policies on containment put forward by Truman?

Khrushchev and co-existence

The fact that U.S.–Soviet summits took place during the 1950s was due not only to Eisenhower's willingness to negotiate, but also due to the attitudes of the new leadership in the Soviet Union.

Following the death of Josef Stalin in 1953, and the subsequent removal of Stalin's secret-police chief, Lavrenti Pavlovich Beria, Soviet foreign policy came under the control of George Malenkov who, with **Nikita Khrushchev** and Nicolai Bulganin, formed a collective leadership. Malenkov formulated the idea of a 'New Course' with the West. This was later picked up by Khrushchev who, having won the struggle for leadership, renamed it 'peaceful co-existence'.

This was a move away from the Leninist doctrine of the inevitability of war. 'Peaceful co-existence' meant that capitalism and Communism should accept the continuing existence of one another, rather than using force to destroy each other. Just as the Americans believed that, deprived of opportunities for expansion, Communism would collapse, Khrushchev declared that in any case capitalism would die out due to its own inherent weaknesses. Thus there was no need to risk nuclear war.

Nikita Khrushchev, Soviet leader from 1953 to 1964.

What other factors encouraged a change in international relations?

It was not just Eisenhower and Khrushchev who were keen to avoid a nuclear war. Other world leaders, such as Winston Churchill, also supported the idea of more communication between East and West in order to avoid a **nuclear holocaust**.

Economic factors also played a role in pushing the two superpowers into a friendlier relationship. In the USSR, approximately one third of the economy was directed towards the military, while consumer goods were scarce and living standards very low. The economy of the United States was in much better shape than that of the Soviet Union, but 12 per cent of the **GNP** was still spent on the military. If improved relations could lead to a decrease in military spending, this would be good news for the economies of both countries.

Also, by 1954 the Korean War had ended, removing a major source of conflict between the United States and the Soviet Union.

STUDENT STUDY SECTION

Review question

The changed international situation after 1953 has led historians to call this period a 'thaw' in the Cold War. Identify the factors that set the scene for improved relations – or a 'thaw' – between the superpowers after 1953.

East–West relations in the 1950s: the reality

An example of improved U.S.–Soviet relations after 1953 was agreement over Austria. In April 1955, the Soviet Union proposed a formal peace treaty with Austria. The **Austrian State Treaty** ended the four-power occupation of Austria and created an independent and neutral country. Following on from this, the Geneva Summit took place in July 1955. This was the first meeting of the heads of government of the major powers since 1945. However, little of substance was achieved at this meeting and proposals concerning the arms race and the issue of Germany got nowhere. The table below shows the proposals and responses made by the United States and the Soviet Union at this time:

Soviet Proposals:	U.S. Reaction:
• Mutual disbandment of NATO and the Warsaw Pact • Withdrawal of all foreign troops from Europe followed by the drawing up of a European Security Treaty • Free elections to be carried out for a reunified German government	Hostile. These ideas were unacceptable to the West European governments, and no agreement was reached on any of these proposals.
U.S. Proposals:	Soviet Reaction:
• An 'Open Skies' proposal. This meant each side would exchange plans of military installations and allow aerial surveillance of each other's installations.	Hostile. The Soviets did not even bother to make a formal reply. They dismissed it as 'nothing more than a bold espionage plot' and Khrushchev said it would be 'like seeing into our bedrooms'. However, the United States went ahead and used the U-2 **reconnaissance** plane (see page 79).

Was the Geneva Summit a failure?

Despite the failure to achieve any concrete progress on Germany or disarmament, the Geneva Summit nevertheless was a breakthrough, in that discussions were carried out in an atmosphere of cordiality. The Summit also led to better relations in terms of trade exhibitions, exchanging of certain scientific information and cultural exchanges. Thus the phrase 'spirit of Geneva' was given to the events surrounding 1955.

Why did East–West tension increase again after 1955?

In February 1956, Khrushchev gave his de-Stalinization speech, which led to challenges to Soviet rule throughout the Eastern bloc (see Chapter Sixteen, page 199). At the same time as Khrushchev faced problems in Hungary, the West was involved in the Suez Crisis (see Chapter Fourteen, pages 172–4). Both of these crises helped to dissipate the good feeling achieved at Geneva. The Suez Crisis also raised fears of growing Soviet influence in the Middle East, and this led to the Eisenhower Doctrine in January 1957. This clearly stated that the United States would assist any country in the Middle East to fight against Communism.

STUDENT STUDY SECTION

The Eisenhower Doctrine: document analysis

There is a general recognition in the Middle East, as elsewhere, that the United States does not seek either political or economic domination over any other people. Our desire is a world environment of freedom, not servitude. On the other hand many, if not all, of the nations of the Middle East are aware of the danger that stems from International Communism and welcome closer co-operation with the United States to realize for themselves the United Nations' goals of independence, economic well-being and spiritual growth. If the Middle East is to continue its geographic role of uniting rather than separating East and West, if its vast economic resources are to serve the well-being of the peoples there, as well as that of others ... then the United States must make more evident its willingness to support the independence of the freedom-loving nations of the area ...

The action which I propose would have the following features.

It would first of all authorize the United States to co-operate with and assist any nation or group of nations in the general area of the Middle East in the development of economic strength dedicated to the maintenance of national independence.

It would, in the second place, authorize the Executive to undertake in the same region programs of military assistance and co-operation with any nation or group of nations, which desires such aid.

It would in the third place, authorize such assistance and co-operation to include the employment of the armed forces of the United States to secure and protect the territorial integrity and political independence of such nations requesting such aid, against overt armed aggression from any nation controlled by International Communism.

From President Dwight D. Eisenhower, 'Special Message to Congress, 5 January 1957', Department of State Bulletin XXXVI, 21 January 1957

Question

What message did this Doctrine send to a) the Soviet Union and b) Arab states about American intentions in the Middle East?

The technology race

In addition to this mounting tension between East and West, the Americans now became increasingly worried about a Soviet threat against the United States. On 4 October 1957 the Soviets launched the world's first artificial satellite – Sputnik – 'travelling companion', to be followed a month later by Sputnik II. This sent the Americans into a state of panic as they became convinced of Soviet superiority in missile technology. This impression was reinforced by Khrushchev, who made the most of the situation:

The Sputniks prove that socialism has won the competition between socialist and capitalist countries … that the economy, science, culture and the creative genius of the people in all spheres of life develop better and faster under socialism.

Khrushchev used every opportunity to insist that he could wipe out any American or European city:

He would even specify how many missiles and warheads each target might require. But he also tried to be nice about it: at one point, while bullying an American visitor, Hubert Humphrey [a senator from Minnesota, who later became vice-president], he paused to ask where his guest was from. When Humphrey pointed out Minneapolis on the map, Khrushchev circled it with a big blue pencil. 'That's so I don't forget to order them to spare the city when the rockets fly,' he explained amiably.

As reported in John Lewis Gaddis, The Cold War, (Penguin 2005) p.70

The missile gap

The U.S. Congress and the media promoted the idea of a 'missile gap'. This scenario was confirmed by the Gaither Report – the findings of a top-secret investigating committee. The report recommended:
- a vast increase in offensive defence power, especially missile development
- a build-up of conventional forces capable of fighting a limited war
- a massive building programme of **fallout shelters** to protect U.S. citizens from nuclear attack.

In actual fact, U.S. Air Force U-2 spy planes flying over the Soviet Union had revealed that, despite Khrushchev's threats, there was no missile gap – the Soviet Union did not have more missiles than the USA. Despite this, Eisenhower had to do something to alleviate public anxiety, and so he supported the establishment of the National Aeronautics and Space Administration (NASA) in 1958 to promote missile development and space exploration. He also provided federal aid to promote science education in schools.

The space race
The 'space race' was another feature of the Cold War which provided plenty of propaganda opportunities on both sides. Not only was it a race for seeing who could be the first to get into space, it was also linked to missile technology, and thus the arms race. Following the success of Sputnik I and II, the United States launched Explorer I. However, the Soviets successfully put the first man into space when Yuri Gagarin orbited the earth in 1961. One month later the first American, Alan Shepard, flew into space. On 20 July 1969, after expenditure of $25 billion, the U.S. National Aeronautics and Space Administration (NASA) successfully landed American astronaut Neil Armstrong on the moon. It was an enormous propaganda coup.

Cartoon analysis

Cartoon by Herblock published in the *Washington Post* in 1957.

'Dear Boy, Where Have You Been Keeping Yourself?'

ToK Time

- To what extent do you believe that science, and scientific development, is driven by politics and governments?
- How far is scientific knowledge 'objective' rather than 'subjective'?
- What similarities and differences are there between the scientific methods you use in your Group 4 subjects and the methods used by a historian? Are there links in the ways of knowing that both areas of knowledge use?
- You could attempt to draw a 'visual' representation of the similarities and differences between the 'Historical Method' and the 'Scientific Method' in your ToK journals, for example, a Venn diagram.

Question

What is the cartoon suggesting about the American attitudes to science before and after Sputnik?

How did events of 1958–1960 affect East–West relations?

By 1958 Eisenhower was confident about U.S. nuclear superiority and, therefore, could contemplate initiating a ban on atmospheric testing of nuclear weapons. The United States stopped this form of testing in October 1958 and was immediately followed by the Soviet Union. It was hoped that this might lead to a formal test-ban treaty. However, Khrushchev heightened East–West tensions at this time by issuing an ultimatum to the West to leave Berlin within six months (see Chapter Eight). In the face of Western determination to stand firm, Khrushchev had to back down. By the early months of 1959, the Berlin Crisis had subsided and talks began about another summit meeting. Khrushchev accepted an invitation to visit the United States in September 1959 – making him the first Soviet leader to visit the USA – and arranged with President Eisenhower for a summit meeting in Paris, scheduled for May 1960.

Cartoon analysis

This Herblock cartoon shows Eisenhower and Khrushchev together in 1959 in the United States.

Question

Why do you think the cartoonist has shown both leaders crossing their fingers?

The U-2 incident

Again, although the meeting between Eisenhower and Khrushchev in the United States produced few concrete results, the talks were a success in terms of generating a positive atmosphere, which led people to talk of the 'spirit of Camp David' (Eisenhower's presidential retreat in Maryland). This optimism was short-lived, however, as a few days before the summit meeting convened in Paris, the Soviets announced that an American plane had been shot down over the Soviet Union on 1 May 1960. The Americans tried to claim it was only a weather plane, which had gone off course, but the Soviets were able to reveal that the aircraft was a high altitude, photo-reconnaissance plane. Even more damaging, the pilot, Gary Powers, who had been captured, confessed to the 'spy' nature of his task. Eisenhower then admitted the truth about the U-2 spy planes and took personal responsibility for the incident.

At the Paris Summit, Eisenhower refused to apologize for the U-2 incident – or to condemn U-2 flights – saying that aerial surveillance was 'a distasteful, but vital necessity'. Khrushchev then cancelled Eisenhower's planned visit to the Soviet Union and the meeting broke up with no further progress being made on a settlement for Berlin or a test-ban treaty. By 1962, any 'thaw' that might have been achieved was shown to be quite definitely at an end when the USA and the USSR had their most intense and dangerous conflict yet over Cuba (see Chapter Nine).

Gary Powers, the captured U-2 pilot.

STUDENT STUDY SECTION

Review questions

1 What issues/events prevented any lasting Cold War 'thaw' during this period?

2 Explain the meaning of the following: co-existence, massive retaliation, New Look.

3 Who or what was each of the following, and how did each one affect East–West relations during the 1950s?

a the Suez Crisis   **e** Sputnik

b the Eisenhower Doctrine   **f** the Gaither Report

c the Hungarian Uprising   **g** the U-2 incident

d the Geneva Summit

N.B. For some of these, you may need to do extra research. See also Chapter Sixteen.

Essay practice

Structuring the main body of an essay

Here again is the question posed at the beginning of this chapter:

- *To what extent was there a thaw in the Cold War after 1953?*

Introduction: Look back at the work you did on introductions in the previous chapter and at the guidelines in Chapter Three. What would be your starting point with the introduction for this essay?

Main body of the essay: As explained in the essay flow chart in Chapter Three, you need to have a clear opening sentence to start each paragraph. This sentence must make it obvious what the point of the paragraph is going to be, and it must clearly link back to the question. The rest of the paragraph should then provide evidence to support your opening statement.

Task 1

Look at the statements below. They can be grouped into three paragraphs to form the main body of the essay. Decide which statements fit better as:

- opening statements for one of the paragraphs of this essay

- evidence in the main body of the paragraphs.

> The war in Korea was brought to a close.
> There were positive steps towards a reduction of tension and thus a 'thaw' after 1953.
> The USA continued to see the USSR as a threat in such areas as Asia.
> Tension increased dramatically in the late 1950s due to a series of incidents, which make it clear that there was in fact no fundamental change in relationship between the superpowers.
> Austria was finally unified.
> The shooting down of the U-2 spy plane ended any good relations that had been built up during Khrushchev's visit to the United States.
> Nothing concrete was achieved at the Geneva Summit regarding the arms race or the German question.
> There is much evidence that there was still tension between the USA and the USSR after 1953.
> Sputnik raised new fears of superior Soviet technology and of a 'missile gap'.
> Khrushchev raised tensions over Berlin with an ultimatum to the West to leave.
> There was co-operation in cultural and economic areas following the 'spirit of Geneva'.
> Cuba brought the Soviet Union and the United States close to a direct nuclear confrontation.

Task 2

In which order would you place the paragraphs? What other evidence might you add in each paragraph?

Write a conclusion that supports the arguments that are in the main body of the essay.

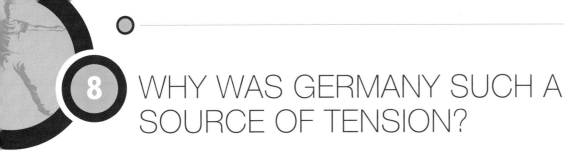

WHY WAS GERMANY SUCH A SOURCE OF TENSION?

Before reading this chapter, refer back to Chapters Two and Three and consider the following essay questions:

- What factors made Germany such an important country for both the West and the Soviet Union?
- What were the steps by which the (a) economic (b) political and (c) military division of Germany took place after 1945?
- What factors prevented an agreement on Germany taking place?
- How can events in Germany be seen to support the (a) Orthodox (b) Revisionist and (c) Post-revisionist historical interpretations of the origins of the Cold War?

Timeline of events affecting the post-war development of Germany 1945-1961

1945	Yalta Conference
	Potsdam Conference
1948	Marshall Aid agreed to by Congress
	Berlin Blockade
1949	NATO established
	Federal Republic of Germany established (FRG – West Germany)
	German Democratic Republic established (GDR – East Germany)
	USSR proposes neutralized Germany
1953	East German uprising
1955	West Germany admitted to NATO and permitted to rearm
	Germany discussed at Geneva Summit – no agreement
1958	Khrushchev demands German peace treaty and demilitarized West Berlin
1960	Khrushchev reissues ultimatum over Berlin
1961	Berlin Wall is built

... underlying all the questions that separated the Great Powers in the first 16 years of the Cold War was Germany.

From Colin Bown and Peter J. Mooney, Cold War to Détente 1945-1980 *(Heinemann Educational, 1981) p.66*

The two Germanys

As you have read in Chapters Two and Three, Germany had, by 1949, become two countries. It was this division of Germany that did much to fuel the Cold War in the years up to 1961. Significant differences existed between West Germany and East Germany in the economic and political spheres.

Economic differences between West Germany and East Germany

Economically, West Germany was larger than East Germany with a larger population and greater industrial output. It had also received Marshall Aid. In fact, West Germany in the 1950s and 1960s experienced what became known as the 'economic miracle' and, accordingly, the standard of living of most West Germans rapidly increased. Meanwhile in East Germany, leader Walter Ulbricht's post-1949 programme of forced collectivization of farms and of socialization was disastrous for the economy. With the hardships and drop in living standards that this entailed, many East Germans fled to the West via Berlin.

Political differences between West Germany and East Germany

Politically, West Germany had democracy. In East Germany there had been no free elections since 1946 and, by the 1950s, it was a rigidly Stalinist, authoritarian state. Discontent with the situation in East Germany manifested itself in the riots of 1953. Workers in East Berlin and elsewhere in the East rose up in revolt. The riots were quickly put down with the help of Soviet tanks. This was the first major rebellion within the Soviet sphere of influence. (See Chapter Sixteen, page 198.)

As a result of these differences, there were no further efforts by either side to reunite as one country. Changing the situation seemed more risky than maintaining the status quo. However, the potential for conflict remained, and particularly in the increasingly untenable situation of Berlin, which Khrushchev described as 'a fishbone in East Germany's gullet'.

Why did the Berlin Crisis develop?

Khrushchev and the crisis of 1958

After the Berlin Blockade (see Chapter Three), Berlin remained divided under joint American–British–French–Soviet occupation and the economic and political inequalities of the two Germanys could be clearly seen in the differences between West Berlin and East Berlin. West Berlin appeared to be a glittering, dynamic example of what capitalism could achieve. This factor, along with the political freedoms and open lifestyle of the West Berliners, encouraged East Germans to escape from the hardships of the East to the prosperity and freedom of the West through the open frontier in Berlin. All East Berliners had to do was to travel from East Berlin to West Berlin, which could be done by train or subway, and from there emigration to West Germany was easy.

This exodus of mainly young and skilled East Germans – which was encouraged by the West – meant that between 1945 and 1961 about one-sixth of the whole German population took the opportunity to move to the West via Berlin. In addition, the divided city of Berlin allowed the West to maintain a unique propaganda and espionage base 186 kilometres (110 miles) deep into East German territory.

In 1958, Khrushchev proposed a peace treaty that would recognize the existence of the two Germanys. On 27 November 1958, he then demanded that Berlin should be demilitarized, Western troops withdrawn and Berlin changed into a 'free city'. If the West did not agree to these changes within six months, Khrushchev threatened that he would turn over control of access routes to the Western sectors of Berlin to the GDR (East Germany). This was clever diplomacy; it would allow the GDR to interfere at will with traffic using land corridors from the FRG (West Germany). The Western allies would then have to negotiate with the GDR, which would force them to recognize the existence and sovereignty of the GDR. It was a dangerous situation. The West could not contemplate losing face over Berlin or giving up its propaganda and intelligence base, but to resist Khrushchev could mean the possibility of war.

Why was Khrushchev prepared to precipitate this Cold War crisis? Evidence from the Soviet archives points to the fact that the most important influences on Khrushchev's policy making at this time were:

- Soviet fear of West Germany acquiring nuclear weapons
- concern over the failing East German economy
- pressure from Walter Ulbricht, leader of the GDR.

In the face of Western outrage at his proposal, Khrushchev dropped his ultimatum. He was successful, however, in forcing the Allies to discuss the German question. In February 1959, they agreed that a foreign ministers' conference should meet in Geneva in the summer. At Geneva both sides put forward proposals for German unity, but no agreement was secured. Khrushchev then met in the United States with Eisenhower in September 1959, but again no agreement was reached. A follow-up summit to be held in Paris in May 1960 was called off at the last minute after the shooting down over the Soviet Union of an American U-2 spy plane (see Chapter Seven, page 79).

As the numbers of refugees fleeing from East Germany via Berlin continued to grow, Ulbricht grew increasingly frustrated with Khrushchev's failure to solve this problem. He wanted Khrushchev to sort out the Berlin problem immediately and not in the context of a broader German peace settlement with the West.

Khrushchev, however, hoped that he would have more luck in getting concessions over Berlin with the new American president, John F. Kennedy.

Kennedy and flexible response

John F. Kennedy was elected president in 1960. His approach to containment was a policy of 'flexible response', as we have seen in his approach to Vietnam (see pages 62–3). In terms of his wider Cold War policy, it involved:

- more spending on conventional forces
- enlarging the nuclear arsenal
- continuing with CIA covert work
- giving economic aid to developing countries to help them resist Communism
- continuing negotiations with the Soviet Union.

Therefore, Kennedy broadened the range of options for resisting Communism, as it seemed to his administration that the Communist threat was much more diverse than it had been previously. Not only was it more geographically diverse, but Communist forces now were giving assistance to revolutionary movements in the developing world. With flexible response, Kennedy was moving away from Eisenhower's policy of 'massive retaliation' or, as he put it, 'We intend to have a wider choice than humiliation or all-out nuclear war'.

John F. Kennedy, U.S. president from 1961 to 1963.

STUDENT STUDY SECTION

Review question

Compare Eisenhower's 'New Look' with Kennedy's 'flexible response'. What aspects of their containment policies are similar? What aspects are different?

Khrushchev, Ulbricht and the crisis of 1960–1961

President Kennedy first met Nikita Khrushchev at the Vienna Summit of 1961. Khrushchev believed that he might be able to exploit Kennedy's relative inexperience in foreign affairs. He also had an advantage in that Kennedy had just suffered the embarrassment of the failure of the Bay of Pigs invasion (see Chapter Nine, page 94).

Khrushchev, therefore, decided to renew his ultimatum on Berlin. However, Kennedy, in his determination to appear tough with the Soviets, was not prepared to give any concessions to the them. Calling Berlin '… an island of freedom in a Communist sea …' and '… a beacon of hope behind the Iron Curtain …', he announced in a television broadcast that 'We cannot and will not permit the Soviets to drive us out of Berlin, either gradually or by force'. He also responded with an increase in military spending and a civil defence programme to build more nuclear fallout shelters.

ToK Time

How do political leaders attempt to maintain their 'credibility'? Which is more important for this – using reason, morality or emotion when addressing the public?

A 19-year-old East German guard escaping to West Berlin on 15 August 1961 two days after the border was sealed.

The Wall

With the tension growing over the situation in Berlin, the number of refugees moving from East to West increased. On 12 August 1961 alone, 40,000 refugees fled to the West. Given Kennedy's response and the growing crisis in East Germany, Khrushchev bowed to Ulbricht's pressure and agreed to the closure of the East German border in Berlin. On the morning of 13 August 1961, barbed wire was erected between East and West Berlin. This was followed by a more permanent concrete wall.

East Berlin children watching the building of the wall, with concrete blocks. It had an average height of 3.6 metres (11¾ feet).

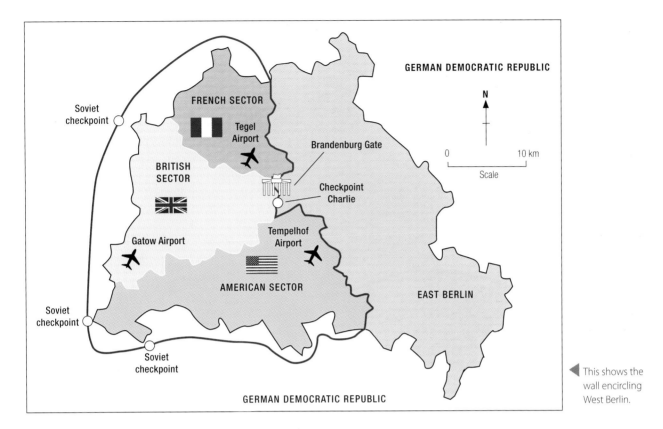

What did the building of the Wall mean ...

... for Khrushchev?

For Khrushchev, the Berlin Wall was a defeat in the sense that it was a visible admission that the Communist propaganda message had failed: the Soviets had to create a barrier to keep the people in the East. However, it meant that he was able to regain control over the situation and free himself from the continuing pressure from Walter Ulbricht and the danger that Ulbricht might act independently. Once the Wall was built, Khrushchev went back on his promise to Ulbricht and did not sign a separate peace treaty with the GDR that would have given East Germany control over the access routes to Berlin.

... for Ulbricht?

Although Ulbricht did not get his peace treaty, the closed border in Berlin, combined with Soviet assistance, helped him to consolidate Communist control in the GDR.

... for the citizens of Berlin?

For the citizens of Berlin, the erection of the Wall was a horrifying experience. Families and friends were immediately cut off from each other with no hope of reunion. They continued to be on the front line of the Cold War.

... for the Cold War?

In terms of the Cold War, however, the building of the Berlin Wall had the effect of settling the question of Germany and removing it as a key issue in Cold War negotiations. The Americans complained vigorously about the Wall – at one point U.S. tanks confronted Soviet tanks at Checkpoint Charlie (the official border post between the two Berlins) for several hours – but the USA was actually relieved that a war over Berlin had been averted. The focus of the Cold War moved from Europe, although it is important to note that for the Soviet Union the situation of U.S. missile bases in Turkey on the eastern fringe of Europe remained an important issue.

The symbolism of the Wall

Between 1961 and 1989, the Berlin Wall stood as a powerful symbol of the division between East and West. Indeed, it seemed as if the idea of an 'Iron Curtain', as put forward by Winston Churchill during his Fulton speech in 1946, had become a reality – in the form of a concrete wall. Following the building of the Wall, President Kennedy visited West Berlin and gave his emotive and highly publicized '*Ich bin ein Berliner*' speech:

Two thousand years ago the proudest boast in the world was 'civis Romanus sum' [I am a Roman citizen]. *Today, in the world of freedom, the proudest boast is Ich bin ein Berliner* [I am a Berliner].

There are many people in the world who do not understand what is the great issue between the free world and Communism. Let them come to Berlin. And there are some who say in Europe and elsewhere that we can work with the Communists. Let them come to Berlin.

Freedom has many difficulties and democracy is not perfect: but we have never had to put up a wall to keep our people in. I know of no city which has been besieged for 18 years and still lives with the vitality, force, hope and determination of this city of West Berlin. While the wall is the most obvious and vivid demonstration of the failures of the Communist system, we take no satisfaction in it, for it is an offence not only against history but against humanity …

In 18 years of peace and good faith this generation of Germans has earned the right to be free, including the right to unite their family and nation in lasting peace with the goodwill of all people. When the day finally comes when this city will be joined as one in this great continent of Europe, the people of West Berlin can take great satisfaction in the fact that they were in the front line for almost two decades.

From a speech given in West Berlin by President John F. Kennedy on 26 June 1963

East German border guards remove the body of 18-year-old Peter Fechter, shot dead trying to escape into West Berlin in September 1962.

STUDENT STUDY SECTION

Document analysis

- In what ways does Kennedy use the building of the Wall as a propaganda weapon against the USSR? Quote directly from his speech, above, to support your arguments.

Over the next three decades hundreds of people were killed attempting to defect to the West. East German border guards were instructed to shoot to kill. There were also many spectacular and ingenious escapes.

When the collapse of the Soviet Union began in 1989, it was again the Wall – or rather the rapid and eager dismantling of it by the people of Berlin – which was the most vivid symbol of political reality: the Cold War was over.

Crowds dismantling the Berlin Wall in 1989.

STUDENT STUDY SECTION

Document analysis: cross-referencing skills

Read these sources, look back at the Student Study Section at the end of Chapter Five and then answer the following question. There is a sample answer at the end of this section.

Question

How do these documents compare in their analysis of the results of the building of the Berlin Wall?

Document A

The Berlin crisis has been a dreadful moment, but this was followed in Europe by a prolonged period of stability, if not calm. The Soviet Union was not unhappy with the outcome … [There was] a sense of Soviet satisfaction. A problem had been solved. For the 190 people who were to die in the attempt to escape across the Wall, it was solved with grim finality. For the seventeen millions left in the German Democratic Republic, as East Germany called itself, their citizenship was now uncomfortably close to imprisonment. The continent's political permafrost settled deeper … Europe settled down into its two armed camps …

From Martin Walker, *The Cold War* (Vintage Press, 1994) p.159

Document B

The Berlin Wall was an ideological defeat of colossal proportions for the Soviet Union and world Communism. The Wall became a symbol of the Cold War, concrete evidence of the inability of East Germany to win the loyalty of its inhabitants. It was also seen as hard proof that Soviet-style socialism was losing its economic competition with Capitalism. Although the Wall ended the mass emigration that had been destabilizing East Germany and also led to a period of prolonged stability in Europe, no one at the time knew that this would be the outcome. When a crisis arose in October 1962 over Soviet missiles in Cuba, the initial U.S. reaction was that the Soviets had put the missiles there as a way of forcing the West out of Berlin.

David Painter, *The Cold War: An International History* (Routledge, 1999) p.53

Document C

In August 1961 the Soviet Union was humbled as the Berlin Wall was constructed to save East Germany from ignominious economic collapse. Peaceful coexistence had failed to attract Western concessions, particularly a settlement of divided Germany, and as the Wall was raised peaceful coexistence collapsed.

Bradley Lightbody, *The Cold War* (Routledge, 1999)

Sample answer

Documents A, B and C all agree that the Berlin Wall resulted in a 'hardening' of the Cold War. Document A directly states this, 'the political permafrost settled deeper', whereas B implies this by stating that the Wall became a 'symbol of the Cold War' and indirectly led to the 'Soviet missiles in Cuba.' Document C comments that all hopes for peaceful coexistence collapsed. However, Documents A and B also show that, although the 'permafrost' deepened, the Wall led to a period of stability and a solution to the German problem. Document B, though, makes the point that at the time, 'no one … knew … that this would be the outcome.'

There is a direct contradiction between the sources concerning the impact of the Wall on the Soviets. Documents B and C agree that the Berlin Wall was a failure for the Soviet Union, showing that it was 'losing its economic competition with Capitalism.' Document C says that it 'humbled' the USSR, and also Khrushchev's policy of coexistence had been shown to fail. Document A, however, states that the 'Soviet Union was not unhappy with the outcome' and the Wall was in fact 'accompanied by a sense of Soviet satisfaction.' Document A also shows what B and C omit, the result for the East Germans, which is that 'their citizenship was now uncomfortably close to imprisonment.'

● **Examiner's hint:**
Notice that in this sample answer the documents are cross-referenced *throughout* each paragraph. Also, relevant quotes are included to support key points.

Essay questions on Germany and the Cold War

Essay frame

When and why was Germany the focus of Cold War hostility in the 16 years after World War Two?

This is a difficult essay because of the amount of information that needs to be covered. Notice the 'when' and the 'why'. Both have to be dealt with, and the analysis will be in the 'why' bit so don't miss it out! An essay like this needs careful planning. It would be possible to write an entire essay just on the Berlin blockade, but this question demands that other issues are covered, and that too much time and space is not spent on only one aspect.

Here are some hints for a possible approach to the content and structure. You will still need to develop your own opening sentences for each paragraph. Look back at Chapters Three and Seven for reminders on how to do this.

Introduction: Importance of Germany concerning strategic position in Europe. Brief overview of main decisions concerning division of Germany made at Yalta and Potsdam. Outline of main tension points to be covered and identification of the main arguments: tension was caused because of differences of aims for Germany, also events in Germany itself and increasingly because of wider developments in the Cold War.

Paragraph 1: When? Breakdown of agreements made at Yalta and Potsdam: 'Our first break with Soviet policy in Germany came over reparations', General Lucius Clay in 1946. Why? Agreements unworkable, difference of economic aims for Germany (see Chapters Two and Three).

Paragraph 2: When? 1948 Berlin Blockade. Why? Different political aims that East and West have for Germany by 1948 trigger this crisis, but the wider events of the Cold War are key to explain the actions of the West. Stalin's actions in Eastern Europe (Czech coup 1948) convince West that they must resist Stalin, also policy of containment.

Paragraph 3: When? 1955 West Germany enters NATO. Why? This is an issue because of USSR's fear of an armed Germany on borders. Retaliates with creation of Warsaw Pact.

Paragraph 4: When? Events 1958–1961. Why? Inequalities between East Germany and West Germany and issue of Berlin. Look back at Khrushchev's aims and influence of Ulbricht. Aims of the West and Kennedy – determined not to back down.

Conclusion: Note the effect of the building of the Wall in removing Germany as a source of tension. Don't forget to come back to the question, but don't summarize everything that you have said in the main body of the essay. Identify the key reason that comes out of your essay as to why Germany was a source of tension during this period. Possibly point to the shift in the focus of tension from Germany in general to Berlin in particular.

Other essay questions on Germany:

Attempt to plan or write these up.

1   For what reasons and with what results was Germany a centre of Cold War tension between 1945 and 1961?

2   Assess the role of Germany in the origin and development of the Cold War.

3   How far was Germany the cause of USA/USSR disagreements between 1943 and 1961?

THE CUBAN MISSILE CRISIS: COULD IT HAVE LED TO NUCLEAR WAR?

Throughout this chapter, consider the following essay questions:
- How effectively did both Kennedy and Khrushchev handle the Cuban Missile Crisis?
- What impact did this crisis have on the Cold War?
- Has the danger of this crisis been overstated?

The Cuban Missile Crisis was perhaps the most dramatic Cold War confrontation between the USSR and the USA. During the 13 days of the crisis, the United States and the Soviet Union came close to a direct military showdown for the first and only time during the Cold War. Both leaders were under intense **domestic** pressure to prove themselves, and their individual personalities and perceptions were critical in the development and resolution of the crisis.

The timeline below shows how the USA and the USSR reacted to the sequence of events that followed the 1959 takeover of the government of Cuba by Fidel Castro and his fellow revolutionaries.

Policies of Cuba	Date	Actions of USA	Actions of USSR
	1959		
Castro seizes power	**Jan 1**		
Batista's supporters executed	**Jan 7**	USA recognizes Cuban goverment	
Castro visits USA to discuss package of U.S. aid for his industrialization programme	**April**		
USA will only give money if Cuba follows guidelines of International Monetary Fund (IMF)			
Request for loan from Organization of American States (OAS) also turned down			
Agrarian Reform Law (which appropriates land and bans land ownership by foreigners) introduced	**May**	Convinced that Cuba is Communist: hostility increases	
	1960 **Feb**		First Deputy Minister of USSR visits Cuba. Five-year Treaty signed: USSR to buy 5 million tons of sugar and to give $100 million credit to buy industrial machinery and material. Secretly agrees to send arms.
First shipment of arms from USSR arrives in Cuba	**March**	Eisenhower orders CIA to train exiles for a future attack on Cuba	
Castro seizes Texaco and Esso oil refineries after they refuse to accept Russian oil	**June**		
	July	Eisenhower reduces Cuban sugar quota by 700,000 tons	Soviets agree to buy the surplus sugar
	August	USA presents a document to OAS charging Cuba with introducing Communism into Western sphere. Not supported by OAS	
Castro expropriates U.S. industrial property and nationalizes banks			

Policies of Cuba	Date	Actions of USA	Actions of USSR
Cuba expropriates 166 more U.S. companies in reply to embargo	Oct 7	Kennedy in election speech calls Cuba 'a Communist menace'	
	Oct 19	USA proclaims embargo on Cuba except for foodstuffs and medicine	New sugar quota signed
	Nov	USA suspends sugar quota for 1961	
	Dec		
	1961		
Castro orders U.S. embassy to cut its staff to 11	Jan 2	Eisenhower breaks off diplomatic relations	
Castro announces that his regime is a socialist regime	April 14		
	April 15	Air strike against Cuba	
	April 17	Bay of Pigs landing	
Cubans victorious over counter-revolutionaries	April 19		
	Nov 30	Operation Mongoose put into operation	
Castro declares himself to be a Marxist-Leninist	Dec 2	Castro's speech greeted with enthusiasm; believe that Castro has now revealed what they knew all along	No comment on Castro's speech
	1962		
	Feb	U.S. trade embargo – except for certain foodstuffs and medicine Cuba expelled from OAS	
Economic situation now in crisis; signs trade agreement with China	May		
Sugar production is 2 million tons lower than in 1961	June		New trade agreement with Cuba
	Oct 14	U.S. U-2 planes photograph missile sites under construction	
	Oct 16	ExComm set up	
	Oct 22	President Kennedy publicly announces the establishment of Cuban quarantine	
	Oct 24		Soviet warships turn back
	Oct 26		Khrushchev sends first telegram U-2 plane shot down
	Oct 27	Robert Kennedy and Anatoly Dobrynin meet	Khrushchev sends second telegram
	Oct 28		Khrushchev agrees to withdraw missiles
Castro refuses to allow UN inspectors into Cuba	Nov	Democrats maintain control in mid-term elections	

Background to the Cuban Missile Crisis

Why was the United States opposed to Castro's revolution?

The origins of the Cuban Missile Crisis can be traced back to the overthrow of the pro-USA Cuban government of General Fulgencio Batista by Fidel Castro in 1959. Cuba lies only 145 kilometres (90 miles) from the coast of Florida. For this reason, the USA considered the island of Cuba to be within its sphere of influence, and it was determined that any government in Cuba should reflect and protect U.S. interests, which were considerable. In the economic arena, the U.S. companies controlled most of the financial, railway, electricity, telegraph and sugar industries. The Platt Agreement signed between Cuba and the United States in 1902 had given the USA the right to establish a naval base at Guantanamo Bay (the base which still exists today). It also stipulated that the U.S. would 'exercise the right to intervene for the preservation of Cuban independence' and for 'the maintenance of a government adequate for the protection of life, property and individual liberty.' It was clear that the U.S. administration intended to decide what constituted Cuban independence and when a government was or was not 'adequate'.

▶ This map shows the geographical position of Cuba in relation to the United States.

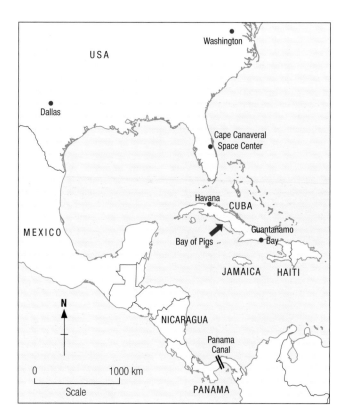

Castro takes power

On 7 January 1959, realizing that Batista had lost the support of most Cubans, the United States reluctantly recognized the new government of Fidel Castro, which had taken power after fighting a guerrilla war campaign for seven years. The United States still hoped to control events in Cuba through its economic interests and the presence of a large pro-U.S. middle class. Initially Castro insisted that he was not a Communist, asserting, 'This is not Communism or Marxism, but representative democracy and social justice in a well-planned economy'. In April 1959, he visited the United States in the hope of getting economic assistance for the far-reaching reforms he believed Cuba needed.

However, Castro's revolutionary reforms involved **nationalization** of U.S. economic interests, and most pro-U.S. Cubans chose to move to the United States rather than to stay and resist. The U.S. government tried to moderate Castro's reforms by refusing him economic assistance unless he followed guidelines set out by the International Monetary Fund (IMF). The Organization of American States (OAS) refused to give Castro financial aid for economic development, and so Castro turned to the Soviet Union, which offered economic aid in February 1960 (see timeline on page 90). This direct involvement of the Soviet Union with a Caribbean state was an immediate challenge to the USA, coming as it did to a country right on its doorstep.

Who was Fidel Castro?

Fidel Castro was born into a wealthy land-owning family. He attended a Jesuit school and then graduated as a lawyer from Havana University. He took on the legal cases of poor people, and he became very aware of the inequalities in Cuban society. Like all Cubans, he particularly resented the domination of Americans in every aspect of Cuban life. In 1947, Castro joined the Cuban People's Party, which campaigned against poverty and injustice. However, although the Cuban People's Party was expected to win the 1952 election (Castro was a candidate), it was not given the opportunity due to a military **coup** led by General Fulgencio Batista which took over Cuba's government. Castro then decided that revolution was the only option for gaining power in Cuba and led an attack on the Moncada Army Barracks. This ended in disaster, but Castro was fortunate to survive, and he used his trial to make a speech about the problems of Cuba. This later was written up as a book entitled *History Will Absolve Me*. The international recognition and personal popularity that followed his courtroom speech meant that he was released from prison. Castro then planned an attack with other rebels (known as July 26 Movement after the date of the attack on the Moncada Barracks) against the Cuban military **junta**. They based themselves in the Sierra Maestra Mountains where they fought a guerrilla war against Batista's regime. This eventually was successful, and Fidel Castro marched into the Cuban capital, Havana, on 9 January 1959 as the country's new leader.

STUDENT STUDY SECTION

Review and discussion questions

Study the timeline on pages 90–1, then answer the following questions:

1 What actions taken by Castro would have convinced the United States that he was a Communist?

2 What actions taken by Castro indicate that in fact he may not have been a Communist in 1959?

3 What evidence is there to support the view that the United States helped push Castro into a relationship with the Soviet Union?

Research activity

In order to understand the nature of Castro's revolution, research the following aspects of his struggle:

- What military tactics did Castro use?
- How did his army behave towards the local population?
- What political and economic policies did the Cuban military regime follow with the local population?
- How do Castro's guerrilla tactics compare with those of other guerrilla armies, such as the Vietminh?
- What other groups in Cuban society contributed to the final success of Castro?

How did the United States deal with the 'threat' of Castro?

The United States decided to deal with this threatening situation in two ways:

- economically, by proclaiming an embargo on all exports to Cuba except for foodstuffs and medicine
- militarily, by organizing an invasion force of Cuban exiles to overthrow Castro.

The first plan, as can be seen from the timeline, failed in that it drove Castro to sign more economic agreements with the Soviet Union. The second plan, the invasion, ended in a humiliation for the U.S. government.

Why was the Bay of Pigs invasion a failure?

In March 1960, President Eisenhower approved a CIA plan to overthrow Castro's government. Part of this plan involved training Cuban refugees for an invasion of Cuba at the Bay of Pigs. President Kennedy inherited the plan and gave it his approval. However, the invasion was a failure, ending in the capture of 1214 of the original 1400 invaders. These prisoners were later released in return for $53 million worth of food and machines paid for by voluntary groups in the United States.

This was a severe humiliation for Kennedy and his administration. He was blamed by all parties for the failure of this venture and was condemned internationally for allowing it to have taken place. However, it is now clear that the reasons for the failure of the Bay of Pigs invasion was more the fault of the CIA. It underestimated the strength of popular support for Castro within Cuba. It had counted on a popular uprising against Castro, which never materialized, and indeed the whole episode strengthened popular support for his regime. In addition, the actual invasion plans were severely flawed with the soldier-exiles suffering from shortage of ammunition and lack of air cover. Castro's air force was much more effective than had been originally supposed. Despite the CIA's assurances to the contrary, the exiles could not survive without the cover from the U.S. Air Force and this was something that President Kennedy could not sanction if he was to publicly distance himself from the plot.

This photograph show the growing friendship between Castro and Khrushchev.

What were the results of the failure of the Bay of Pigs invasion?

For Kennedy, the failure of the invasion was humiliating and meant a loss of prestige within the United States and in the rest of the world. It also set back Kennedy's attempts to identify the USA with **anti-colonialism**. Castro's support within Cuba increased and his position was strengthened: 'What is hidden behind the Yankees' hatred of the Cuban Revolution … a small country of only seven million people, economically underdeveloped, without financial or military means to threaten the security or economy of any other country? What explains it is fear. Not fear of the Cuban revolution, but fear of the Latin American Revolution'.

The Soviet Union and Khrushchev were also given ammunition to use in criticizing the United States. Other Latin American governments and peoples were outraged and the episode revived fears of U.S. imperialism in the area.

The failure of the Bay of Pigs invasion also strengthened Cuba's ties with the USSR. After the failed attack, Castro declared himself to be a Marxist-Leninist and concluded a defensive alliance with the Soviet Union. Thus, the USA was unable to prevent the flow of Soviet advisers and weapons into Cuba.

The USA continued its efforts to reverse the Cuban revolution through covert action (Operation Mongoose), which involved the sabotage of economic targets, such as sugar plantations and petroleum installations, assassination plots against Castro and other Cuban leaders, and the diplomatic isolation of Cuba. For example, Cuba was expelled from the Organization of American States (OAS) in 1962. The USA also put military pressure on Cuba by carrying out training exercises near Puerto Rico.

The Cuban Missile Crisis
Why did Khrushchev put missiles in Cuba?

In 1962, Khrushchev made the decision to put intermediate range ballistic missiles (IRBMs) into Cuba. This was a highly provocative act and was bound to cause a reaction from the USA. So, why did Khrushchev make this move?

Khrushchev wrote in his memoirs that the reason was to protect Cuba and also because 'it was high time America learned what it feels like to have her own land and her own people threatened'. The United States had missiles in Turkey, which bordered on the Soviet Union, and putting missiles a similar distance away from the United States was seen as a way of redressing the balance.

Equally important, Khrushchev aimed to seize a propaganda advantage after the humiliation of the Berlin Wall (see Chapter Eight) and to acquire a bargaining chip against the stationing of U.S. nuclear missiles in Europe.

By swiftly and secretly installing missiles in Cuba, an island only ninety miles away from the United States, the Russians would have stolen a march on the Americans. It was a gamble with extremely high stakes, but if it had paid off, the Soviets would have immensely improved their prestige in the eyes of the world, not least in Latin America, and by doing so would also have increased their bargaining power in Cold War offensives, for example Berlin.

From Robert Beggs, **Flashpoints: The Cuban Missile Crisis** *(Longman, 1977) p.91*

John Lewis Gaddis, however, believes that Khrushchev put the missiles into Cuba mainly because he feared another invasion of Cuba. Khrushchev may have seen the Bay of Pigs

The CIA and Castro
The CIA carried out numerous assassination attempts against Castro. Stories about plots against Castro include exploding cigars, poison in milkshakes, training an ex-girlfriend to shoot him, and, as confirmed in recently published CIA documents, hiring the Mafia to kill Castro. However, Fidel Castro has gone on to survive ten U.S. presidents.

invasion not as a sign of Kennedy's weakness, but rather of his determination to crush the Cuban revolution. Should the U.S. government succeed in this aim, it would be a defeat for Communism worldwide. The fact that the United States had missiles in Turkey, so near to the heart of the Soviet Union, provided a justification for installing missiles in Cuba to protect the island. This viewpoint is supported by the Soviet historians Zubok and Pleshakov, who believe that Khrushchev was primarily concerned with preserving revolutionary Cuba and, thereby, Soviet **hegemony** and the spread of Communism (Zubok and Pleshakov, 'Khrushchev and Kennedy: The Taming of the Cold War', in *The Cold War*, eds. Larrs and Annlane, Blackwell, 2001).

Why was the presence of missiles so intolerable to the United States?

On 14 October 1962, Kennedy was presented with photos from a U-2 spy plane that showed evidence that launch pads were being constructed by the Soviets for 64 IRBMs.

Aerial photograph of missile sites in Cuba, issued by the United States Embassy in London on 23 October 1962.

It is important to note that in fact the positioning of the missiles in Cuba did not really affect the worldwide nuclear balance. However, it did increase the Soviet **first strike** capability, and it meant that warning time for missiles fired at the United States would be far less than for missiles fired from within the Soviet Union (see map). More important, perhaps, is the fact that to the U.S. public it certainly seemed that the balance of power had changed. 'Offensive missiles in Cuba have a very different psychological and political effect in this hemisphere than missiles in the USSR pointed at us', President Kennedy pointed out at a meeting with his advisers.

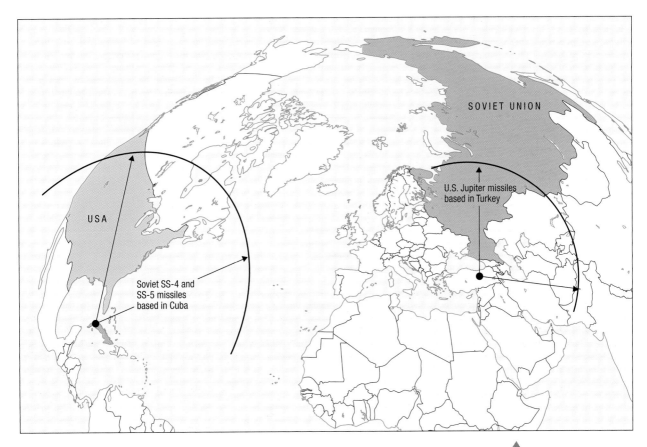

USA

Soviet SS-4 and
SS-5 missiles
based in Cuba

U.S. Jupiter missiles
based in Turkey

This map shows the position
and range of missiles based
in Cuba compared to those
based in Turkey.

Therefore, President Kennedy faced a crisis. The prestige of the USA and also of Kennedy himself was again at stake. Cuba was not just 90 miles away from the USA, but it was also the place where the disastrous and – for Kennedy – humiliating Bay of Pigs episode had taken place. Another factor for Kennedy was the impending Congressional elections, which were to take place in early November. For the Democratic Party to face elections with missiles installed in Cuba would be a disaster for the Kennedy administration. So the president had to take action, but how could he resolve the crisis without precipitating a dangerous and world-threatening head-on collision with the USSR?

How was the crisis resolved?

President Kennedy summoned a crisis management team, the Executive Committee (ExComm) to deal with the threat of missiles in Cuba. This began what has become known as 'The Thirteen Days'. Kennedy rejected calls from the military for an immediate air strike followed by an invasion of Cuba (General Curtis LeMay actually called for the total elimination of Cuba) and ordered instead a naval blockade of the island. The president made the American position public by going on television to announce the establishment of the '**quarantine**' around Cuba to prevent the delivery of any nuclear warheads to the island. Khrushchev ignored the quarantine, and Soviet ships containing missiles headed for Cuba. However, on 24 October, six Soviet ships turned back towards the Soviet Union. At this point Dean Rusk, the U.S. Secretary of State, commented, 'We're eyeball to eyeball and I think the other fellow just blinked'. Nevertheless, the crisis continued as the missile sites still remained on Cuba.

On 26 October, Khrushchev sent a telegram to Kennedy saying that the Soviet Union would remove the missiles in return for a U.S. pledge not to invade Cuba. At this point, he was convinced that the United States was on the verge of attacking Cuba:

… We and you ought not to pull on the ends of the rope in which you have tied the knot of war, because the more the two of us pull, the tighter the knot will be tied. And then it will be necessary to cut that knot, and what that will mean is not for me to explain to you, because you yourself understand perfectly of what terrible forces our countries dispose. … I have participated in two wars and know that war ends when it is rolled through cities and villages everywhere sowing death and destruction. For such is the logic of war; if people do not display wisdom they will clash like blind moles.

In a letter from Khrushchev to Kennedy dated 26 October 1962, quoted by the Secretary of Defense Robert McNamara in the television documentary, **The Fog of War**.

However, before Kennedy could respond to this telegram, Khrushchev sent a second, more demanding letter to the U.S. government insisting on the inclusion of the removal of Turkish missiles in any deal over Cuba. The crisis escalated after a U.S. U-2 plane was shot down over Cuba. This had been done by military leaders in Cuba without authorization by the Soviet Union and seemed a sign that events could easily spiral out of control. The shooting down increased pressure on Kennedy to take military action against Cuba. The consequences of this would have been extremely serious as, unknown to the Americans at the time, nuclear short-range missiles were already on Cuba and ready for use by the Cubans.

Kennedy continued to see military action as a last resort and, on the advice of Llewellyn (Tommy) Thompson, who had been U.S. ambassador to the Soviet Union, he decided to accept Khrushchev's first offer and ignore the second. At the same time, however, Kennedy's brother and then Attorney General, Robert Kennedy, met with Anatoly Dobrynin, the Soviet ambassador in Washington, D.C., to agree that the United States would remove missiles from Turkey.

On 28 October, Khrushchev cabled President Kennedy and agreed to remove all missiles from Cuba in return for U.S. assurance that it would not invade Cuba. There was no reference to U.S. removal of missiles from Turkey – this part of the deal remained secret.

How effective was Kennedy's handling of the Cuban Missile Crisis?

The Orthodox view

The traditional interpretation of President Kennedy's role in the missile crisis has stressed that this was Kennedy's finest hour, that he successfully used nuclear brinkmanship to preserve world peace. The writings of Robert Kennedy, Theodore C. Sorensen and Richard E. Neustadt all put forward the following arguments in support of this view:
- Kennedy was right to respond to this crisis in a firm and forceful way, as the missiles represented a Soviet threat to alter the balance of power either in actuality or in appearance.
- The idea of imposing a quarantine (blockade) exerted maximum pressure on the Soviet Union while incurring the minimum risk of war.
- Kennedy himself always remained calm and in control of the situation. He resisted pressure for action from the military, he was statesmanlike and did not attempt to humiliate Khrushchev.
- The results of the crisis helped to preserve the balance of power and world peace.

The Revisionist view

The Revisionist interpretation of Kennedy's role in the missile crisis stresses that Kennedy unnecessarily raised the Cuban episode to the level of crisis and confrontation and thus subjected the world to the danger of nuclear war. Roger Hagman, David Horowitz and I.F. Stone put forward the following arguments in support of this view:

- The missiles did not affect the nuclear balance and the USA was under no greater threat. This was rather a political problem that could have been resolved by political means.
- The imposition of the blockade and the fact that Kennedy made the crisis public turned it into an unnecessarily dangerous situation.
- Kennedy was only interested in personal and national prestige. The forthcoming November elections meant that the President wanted the situation solved quickly, so he could not wait for lengthy negotiations.
- The aftermath of the crisis was not victory but arrogance, which led the United States to increase its activity in Vietnam.

What if the Russians had refused to back down and remove their missiles from Cuba? What if they had called our bluff and war had begun, and escalated? How would the historians of mankind, if a fragment survived, have regarded the events of October? … Since this is the kind of bluff that can easily be played once too often, and that his successors may feel urged to imitate, it would be well to think it over carefully before canonizing Kennedy as an apostle of peace.

From an article by I.F. Stone on John F. Kennedy written after Kennedy's assassination.

New interpretations

Recent evidence seems to support the view that Kennedy did indeed act in a statesmanlike way, was prepared to compromise and was not motivated by self-interest. The tape recordings of ExComm meetings at the time show Kennedy repeatedly pushing for compromise and point to the fact that he was keenly aware of the dangers of nuclear war. He deceived ExComm by having the secret agreement to remove missiles from Turkey, and it was revealed in 1987 that he had another option up his sleeve: if all else failed, the United Nations Secretary General was to suggest a Turkey–Cuba trade-off that Kennedy would then accept.

What conclusions can be reached about Khrushchev's actions?

Khrushchev was able to claim a victory over the missile crisis. He argued that Kennedy had now promised not to invade Cuba, so the continued existence of a socialist Cuba in the Soviet sphere of influence was guaranteed. This is clearly significant, especially if you take Gaddis's view that this was the main reason that Khrushchev put missiles on Cuba in the first place. Khrushchev must also be given credit for being prepared to back down in the face of nuclear war, especially when many saw his handling of the crisis as a humiliation for the Soviet Union. However, the Soviet military were particularly angry. They were already unhappy about Khrushchev's military cuts, and they now had to accept a hasty withdrawal from Cuba, as well as the ultimate humiliation of having U.S. officials count the missiles as they were removed.

Castro was also furious with Khrushchev's handling of the affair. He was not consulted about the final deal concerning the missiles or over his agreement with Kennedy to withdraw the Soviet IL-28 bombers and Soviet troops which had been sent to help the Cuban army. He was also left with the U.S. base at Guantanamo Bay, while U.S. missiles were removed from Turkey in 1963.

Khrushchev had to work hard in the ensuing months to rebuild his relations with Castro and the Cuban regime and prevent a Sino-Cuban alliance developing (see Chapter Eleven). Russian historians Zubok and Pleshakov wrote that during this crisis Khrushchev, 'acted in the chillingly "realist" manner of Stalin: walking over the egos and bodies of those who had helped in the implementation of his grandiose designs, but then just happened to be in the way of retreat.'(Zubok and Pleshakov, 'Khrushchev and Kennedy: The Taming of the Cold War', in *The Cold War*, eds. Larrs and Annlane, Blackwell, 2001, p.130)

What was Castro's role in the crisis?

It is clear now that Castro played a greater role in the development of this crisis than has previously been realized. Particularly significant is the period of time around 24–26 October. Castro was determined to make the most of the situation, and he claims that he would not have hesitated to use the nuclear weapons which were already in Cuba should the United States have attempted a land invasion. This is despite the fact that it would have led to the destruction of the island. The shooting down of the U-2 plane indicates the difficulties that Khrushchev and Kennedy had in keeping control of the situation on the ground as it developed.

What were the results of the crisis …

… for the USA?

Kennedy's personal prestige increased. It shocked the United States into realizing the fragility of its own security, and increased the U.S. focus on building up military strength.

… for the USSR?

Despite his claims of victory, the crisis was a humiliation for Khrushchev and contributed to his fall from power in 1964. The USSR did not itself suffer from this humiliation and continued as a superpower for the next three decades.

… for Cuba?

Castro remained in power with the threat of a U.S. invasion removed. However, Cuba became determined not to become a pawn in the East–West struggle, and pursued a foreign policy independent of Moscow (see Chapter Fifteen). Havana became a centre of revolutionary activity, educating and training activists and spreading revolution in Africa and Central America, although the Castro regime did continue to rely on the USSR for economic aid and arms.

… for China?

China saw the resolution of the crisis and the USSR's unwillingness to challenge the United States as final proof that the USSR had ceased to be a revolutionary state. Its relationship with the USSR continued to deteriorate from this point, and China opted to continue developing nuclear weapons independently (see Chapter Eleven).

… for the wider international situation?

The Orthodox view is that the world was made a more secure place because:
- A hotline was established between the USSR and USA to make immediate telephone communication easier.

- Both sides realized the danger of nuclear war. Two important treaties were signed following the crisis: the Test-ban Treaty of August 1964, which forbade nuclear tests in the atmosphere, space or underwater (not signed by France and China) and the Nuclear Non-Proliferation Treaty of 1968, which prevented signatories from transferring weapons or knowledge of how to make them to non-nuclear powers.

Recent interpretations point out that the arms treaties did not in fact prevent the arms race, which intensified after the Cuban Missile Crisis even if it was conducted within an increasingly precise set of rules. Nevertheless, the world was more secure after the missile crisis in that there was more stability: neither side would now issue challenges to the other side's **sphere of influence**.

STUDENT STUDY SECTION

Research questions

1 One of the results of the Cuban Missile Crisis is that Cuba decided to be more independent of the USSR. It became involved in revolutionary activity in Latin America and also in Africa. Research Cuba's actions, and its success or failure in spreading revolution, in one of these areas, for example, Angola.

2 Che Guevara became an icon of socialist revolutionaries. Research Che's role in the Cuban revolution and then his actions in spreading revolution after 1965 outside of Cuba.

Essay question

Consider the following essay title and then look at the essay frame that follows:
'The danger of the Cuban missile crisis has been seriously exaggerated.' To what extent do you agree?

Essay frame

Introduction: Remember to clarify any key words in the title and to show you understand what the question is asking. Here you need to explain what the 'danger' of the missile crisis was and to set out briefly the areas of debate that you will be discussing in your essay.

Part 1 of essay: You will have to set out both sides of the argument. In the first paragraph discuss ways in which there was a real danger. Points you could consider are:
- actions of Kennedy and Khrushchev
- pressures on Kennedy and Khrushchev
- aims of Castro
- perceptions of people who were there at the time
- difficulty that Kennedy and Khrushchev had controlling events on the ground, for example, the shooting down of the American U-2.

Consider when and how you will bring in the view of historians. The Orthodox historians believed the danger to be very real and that Kennedy saved the crisis by his astute management of the crisis. Consider also the view of the Revisionist historians, who argue that Kennedy actually increased the danger by his reckless actions.

Part 2 of essay: You now need to look at the other side, that is, the view that the danger was exaggerated. What evidence can you find for this? Would Kennedy or Khrushchev really have been prepared to push the nuclear button given the consequences, particularly Khrushchev, who knew that the Americans had nuclear superiority over the USSR at this time?

Part 3 of essay: What is the most recent view? Recent analysis would argue that the danger was even more real than supposed at the time. Look back in the chapter to find evidence for this.

Conclusion: This is up to you! Remember to come back to the question and answer it directly.

● **Examiner's hint:**
After writing your essay, go back and highlight the first sentence for each paragraph. Can you tell from reading the first sentence what the point of the paragraph is going to be? This is vital if the examiner is to follow clearly the direction of your argument.

Document analysis

Document A

President Kennedy dedicated himself to making it clear to Khrushchev by word and deed … that the United States had limited objectives and that we had no intention of accomplishing those objectives by adversely affecting the national security of the Soviet Union or by humiliating her …

During our crisis he kept stressing the fact that we would indeed have war if we placed the Soviet Union in a position she believed would adversely affect national security or such public humiliation that she lost the respect of her own people and countries around the globe. The missiles in Cuba, we felt, vitally concerned our national security, but not that of the Soviet Union.

This fact was ultimately recognized by Khrushchev, and this recognition, I believe brought about this change in what, up to that time, had been a very adamant position. The President believed from the start that the Soviet Chairman was a rational, intelligent man, who if given sufficient time and shown our determination, would alter his position. But there was always the chance of error, or mistake, miscalculation, or misunderstanding, and President Kennedy was committed to do everything possible to lessen that chance on our side.

From Robert Kennedy, *Thirteen Days. A Memoir of the Cuban Missile Crisis* (Norton, 1973) p.96

Document B

The fate of Cuba and the maintenance of Soviet prestige in that part of the world preoccupied me … We had to establish a tangible and effective deterrent to American interference in the Caribbean. But what exactly? The logical answer was missiles. We knew that American missiles were aimed against us in Turkey and Italy, to say nothing of West Germany …

I had the idea of installing missiles with nuclear warheads in Cuba without letting the United States find out if they were there until it was too late to do anything about them …

I want to make one thing absolutely clear: when we put our ballistic missiles in Cuba, we had no desire to start a war. On the contrary, our principal aim was to deter America from starting a war …

The climax came after five or six days when our Ambassador to Washington, Anatoly Dobrynin, reported that the President's brother, Robert Kennedy, had come to see him on an unofficial visit. Dobrynin's report went something like this:

'Robert Kennedy looked exhausted … He said that he had not been home for six days and nights. "The President is in a grave situation", Robert Kennedy said, "and he does not know how to get out of it. We are under very severe stress … from our military to use force against Cuba … We want to ask you, Mr Dobrynin, to pass President Kennedy's message to Chairman Khrushchev through unofficial channels. President Kennedy implores Chairman Khrushchev to accept his offer and to take into consideration the peculiarities of the American system … If the situation continues much longer, the President is not sure that the military will not overthrow him and seize power. The American army could get out of control'".

I hadn't overlooked this possibility. I knew that Kennedy was a young President and that the security of the United States was indeed threatened …

We sent the Americans a note saying that we agreed to remove our missiles and bombers on the condition that the President give us his assurance that there would be no invasion of Cuba by the forces of the United States or anybody else. Finally Kennedy gave in and agreed to make a statement giving us such an assurance …

It had been, to say the least, an interesting and challenging situation. The two most powerful nations in the world had been squared off against each other, each with its finger on the button … It was a great victory for us, though … The Caribbean crisis was a triumph of Soviet foreign policy and a personal triumph in my own career … We achieved, I would say, a spectacular success without having to fire a single shot!

From Nikita Khrushchev's memoirs, *Khrushchev Remembers*, (Andrew Nurnberg Associates, 1977)

Questions

Now answer the following questions using the above documents:

1. What impression does Robert Kennedy give of President Kennedy's handling of the crisis?

2. What does Khrushchev say about: (a) the reasons why he put missiles on Cuba (b) the reasons why he agreed to remove the missiles and (c) the outcome of the crisis?

3. Are there any areas over which the two sources disagree?

4. What are the value and limitations for historians of using these sources (both being memoirs by key players) in analysing the Cuban Missile Crisis?

 ToK Time

Discuss the following questions in small groups and feedback to the class:

- Our understanding of events in history often 'changes over time'. At the time of the Cuban Missile Crisis, it was perceived by many that the world was on the brink of a nuclear holocaust. How important is it for historians to find out whether this situation was overstated (exaggerated)?
- Does a re-evaluation of historical events give us a better understanding of significant events and crises today?
- Will what we believe is the 'truth' about an event today have a different interpretation in 10 or 20 years' time?
- To what extent does historical truth change over time, and how might this affect the way we view primary and secondary sources?

● **Examiner's hint:**

Here are some points to consider when evaluating memoirs as historical evidence:

- Why do people write memoirs? What do you think the purpose of Kennedy or Khrushchev might have been in doing this?
- Did the person writing the memoir have first-hand knowledge of the event/ events being described?
- How long after the event/ events being described were the memoirs written?

WHAT WAS THE IMPACT OF THE ARMS RACE ON THE COLD WAR?

When you have read this chapter, attempt the following essay questions:

- How did the arms race affect the development of the Cold War?
- How did the concept of 'deterrence' influence the development of Soviet–American nuclear strategy from the early 1960s?

The major lesson of the Cuban Missile Crisis is this; that the indefinite combination of human fallibility and nuclear weapons will destroy nations.

Robert McNamara in the television documentary Fog of War

The effects of the atom bomb dropped on the Japanese city of Hiroshima at the end of World War Two. At least 75,000 people died instantly. Tens of thousands more died from the effects of radiation in the months and years that followed.

The advent of nuclear weapons with the dropping of the first A-bomb on Hiroshima had a crucial impact on the Cold War. These new and terrifying weapons:

- started an arms race between the major powers, which became an integral part of the Cold War, helping to maintain and continue the hostility between the superpowers
- caused both sides to rethink military strategy and thus the way conflicts were handled during the Cold War
- put huge economic strains on both countries and thus played a role in the ending of the Cold War.

Key terms used in this chapter

Atom bomb or A-bomb: A nuclear bomb, which is launched from a missile or plane
Hydrogen bomb or H-bomb: A thermonuclear bomb (also referred to as nuclear) which is much more powerful than the A-Bomb
Strategic bombers: Planes capable of carrying and delivering nuclear weapons
ICBM: Inter-continental ballistic missiles, which have a range of over 3000 nautical miles and which carry nuclear warheads
SLBM: Submarine-launched ballistic missiles. These missiles with nuclear warheads are carried on submarines.
ABM: Anti-ballistic missiles, which can be used to intercept and destroy nuclear weapons
MIRV: Multiple independently targetable re-entry Vehicle. This device is launched by a missile that allows several warheads to be used, each guided to a different target

How did the nuclear arms race develop during the Cold War?

As you have seen, the decision of President Truman during World War Two to use the A-bomb to end the war in the Pacific has caused much debate. It has been viewed by some historians as the first act of the Cold War (see Chapter Four), and can be seen as the trigger for the nuclear arms race between the USSR and the USA.

The A-bomb was regarded by the USA as a vital counter to the much larger conventional forces of the USSR. However, the Soviet Union was well on its way to developing its own A-bomb, which was tested successfully in 1949, several years before the USA had thought possible. The arms race was on. The United States then stepped up its efforts to develop the hydrogen bomb, which was 1000 times more powerful than the bombs dropped on Hiroshima and Nagasaki. It achieved this in 1952, only to be followed by the USSR a year later.

The 1950s also saw the development of inter-continental ballistic missiles (ICBMs). As was described in Chapter Seven, the U.S. government became concerned that the USSR was moving ahead of it in terms of arms production and missile technology, and, after the launch of Sputnik, the Americans became even more concerned about a perceived 'missile gap'. U-2 flights over the USSR reassured Eisenhower that in fact there was no missile gap. Nevertheless, the United States continued with a massive build-up of ICBMs. This put pressure on the Soviet Union to respond, particularly when the reality of its inferior missile numbers was revealed by President Kennedy. By 1968, the Soviets had also developed ABM defensive missile systems. Meanwhile, the United States' development of MIRVs, which increased the chances of nuclear weapons reaching their intended targets, helped intensify the race, with the USSR instituting its own MIRV programme in 1975.

Timeline of the development of the arms race between the USA and the USSR		
First in race		**Second in race**
USA 1945	atom bomb	1949 USSR
USA 1952	hydrogen bomb	1953 USSR
USSR 1957	ICBM	1958 USA
USSR 1957	first satellite	1958 USA
USSR 1958	early warning radar	1960 USA
USA 1960	SLBM	1968 USSR
USSR 1968	ABM	1972 USA
USA 1970	MIRV	1975 USSR
USSR 1971	Sea Cruise missile launched	1982 USA

The build-up of arms after 1945						
Strategic bombers	**1956**	**1960**	**1965**	**1970**	**1975**	**1979**
USA	560	550	630	405	330	316
USSR	60	175	200	190	140	140
ICBMs	**1960**	**1964**	**1968**	**1970**	**1974**	**1979**
USA	295	835	630	1054	1054	1054
USSR	75	200	800	1300	1587	1398
SLBMs	**1962**	**1965**	**1968**	**1972**	**1975**	**1979**
USA	145	500	656	655	656	656
USSR	45	125	130	497	740	989
Warheads	**1945**	**1955**	**1965**	**1975**	**1985**	
USA	6	3057	31,265	26,675	22,941	
USSR	0	200	6,129	19,443	39,197	

STUDENT STUDY SECTION

Document analysis

Using both the timeline on page 105 and the table of arms race statistics above, what conclusions can you draw about the characteristics of the arms race up to 1985? Give evidence from both documents to support your answer.

Why was the arms race so intense during the Cold War?

The development of the Cold War, and the increasing hostility between East and West, meant that both sides viewed the stockpiling of nuclear weapons as necessary to safeguard their interests. The continuing advances in technology continually made each side feel vulnerable; each felt they had to stay one step ahead of the other. As President Truman said when being advised on the dangers of developing the H-bomb: 'Can they do it? … if so, how can we not?' Secrecy in the 1960s, and the fear of falling behind in the case of the Americans, or the need to catch up in the case of the Soviets, fuelled the race. Therefore, until the 1980s, both sides continued to develop increasingly powerful and sophisticated weapons, as shown in the timeline on page 105.

What strategies were developed for using nuclear weapons?

Both sides had vast numbers of highly destructive nuclear weapons throughout the Cold War period. The question was, could they ever actually be used? Bernard Brodie, a leading American strategist at the time, was quick to see the military significance of nuclear weapons. In his book *The Absolute Weapon* (New York, 1946), he explained that whereas before the invention of nuclear weapons the chief purpose of the military had been to 'win wars', from now on their chief purpose would be to 'avert them'. He claimed that the new weapons could have no other purpose. Thus, military victory in **'total' war** was no longer possible.

Leaders in both the USA and the USSR saw the danger of nuclear weapons. Stalin went so far as to say, 'Atomic bombs can hardly be used without spelling the end of the world' (quoted in Simon Sebag Montefiore, *Stalin: The Court of the Red Tsar*, Knopf, 2004, p.601) and, following an early hydrogen bomb test, President Eisenhower commented that, 'Atomic War will destroy civilization'. Khrushchev was also appalled by the prospect of military use of nuclear weapons, and his policy of 'peaceful co-existence' meant that war with the West was not now inevitable, though this did not stop him threatening it!

Despite the obvious dangers of nuclear weapons, both sides believed that there had to be a strategy that could be devised in which they could be used, otherwise what was the point of having them?

Eisenhower and 'massive retaliation'

Although many of Eisenhower's advisers were working towards the idea of some kind of limited nuclear warfare, Eisenhower himself put forward the idea of 'massive retaliation' – that the United States would fight with every weapon at its disposal if attacked, despite the devastating consequences that this would have. Although this policy was criticized by many, it could be argued that Eisenhower – who was highly conscious of the dangers of war – was trying through this threat of all-out nuclear war to ensure that no such conflict would take place.

Others also realized that the concept of a 'limited nuclear war' was highly problematic. George Kennan in his Reith Lectures for BBC radio in 1957 argued:

It is a thesis which I cannot accept. That it would prove possible, in the event of an atomic war, to arrive at some tacit and workable understanding with an adversary as to the degree of destructiveness of the weapons that would be used and the sort of target to which they could be directed seems to me a very slender and wishful hope indeed.

G.F. Kennan in Russia, the Atom and the West *(OUP, 1958) p.59*

McNamara and 'counterforce'

President Kennedy was determined to widen the options beyond massive retaliation. As has already been discussed (see Chapter Six), he formed a policy of 'flexible response'. Part of this was developing a nuclear strategy which could be fought in a more limited way than the idea of 'massive retaliation'. Kennedy's Secretary of Defense, Robert McNamara developed a 'counterforce strategy' in which the objective would be to destroy the enemy's military forces, but not cities and thus not civilian populations. Clearly there were problems with this strategy:

- the issue of successfully hitting a target accurately at this early stage of missile development
- hitting a military target without affecting a city when so many military facilities were located near to cities
- ensuring that the Soviets also followed the same 'no cities' rule.

The USSR was angered by this new policy as it implied that the United States would make 'pre-emptive strikes' in a crisis situation:

A strategy which contemplates attaining victory through the destruction of the [Soviet] *armed forces* [by nuclear strikes] *cannot stem from the idea of a 'retaliatory' blow; it stems from pre-emptive action and the achievement of surprise.*

V.D. Sokolovsk, 'A Suicidal Strategy', Red Star, *19 July 1962*

Public opinion in the United States also was not favourable to this policy as it seemed to make nuclear war more, not less, likely.

The impact of the Cuban Missile Crisis: Mutually Assured Destruction (MAD)

During the Cuban Missile Crisis, the risk of events spiralling out of control highlighted the problems of a counterforce strategy as described above.

What had appeared to be 'rational' behaviour in Moscow had come across as dangerously 'irrational' behaviour in Washington, and vice versa. If a common rationality could be so elusive in peacetime, what prospects would there be for it in the chaos of a nuclear war? McNamara himself recalls wondering, as he watched the sun set on the most crucial day of the crisis, whether he would survive to see it do so again. He did survive, but his conviction that there could be a limited, controlled, rational nuclear war did not.

John Lewis Gaddis in **The Cold War** *(OUP, 2005) p.80*

So, the idea of targeting military objectives was changed. McNamara now believed that both sides should aim to target cities with the objective of causing the maximum number of casualties possible. The belief here was that if no one – Soviet or American – could survive a nuclear war, then there would not be one.

This became known as 'Mutually Assured Destruction', or MAD, and it went back to the idea first proposed by Brodie in 1946, that the existence of nuclear weapons meant that there could never be a total war between the superpowers. Historian Richard Crockatt sums it up:

By a curious logic, vulnerability, the nightmare prospect envisaged by the Eisenhower administration, had come to be seen as the guarantor of national security, however fragile that might be.

R. Crockatt in **The Fifty Years War** *(Routledge, 1995) p.148*

Both the Soviet Union and the United States came to accept MAD. They continued to build up their nuclear weapons, but at this point both also saw the need for agreements on how to manage them. For this reason, the Cuban Missile Crisis was followed by:
- the Test-ban Treaty, which stopped nuclear weapons testing in the atmosphere in 1968
- the Nuclear Non-Proliferation Treaty in 1968, which required nations possessing nuclear weapons not to pass on relevant information or technology to non-nuclear countries
- the Strategic Arms Limitation Interim Agreement in 1972, which restricted the number of land- and sea-based ballistic missiles.

There was also now tacit agreement on Eisenhower's idea of 'open skies', allowing satellite reconnaissance in order to minimize the possibility of surprise attack. The Anti-ballistic Missile Treaty of 1972 also banned defences against long-range missiles. This was to ensure that MAD remained the key strategy. If defences were allowed, then one or both superpowers might believe that they stood a chance of using nuclear weapons and this would take away the 'stability' that came from MAD (see Chapter Thirteen for more discussion on these arms limitation agreements which form part of the détente process).

The introduction of ABMs destabilized MAD, the balance of terror. We were both so afraid of nuclear armaments. We knew that you wouldn't strike and we wouldn't strike. But now if one side could counter the other's ability to respond, then they had the advantage.

Anatoly Dobrynin, former Soviet Ambassador to the United States, interviewed on CNN about the Cold War

---

It was this understanding, the fact that nuclear weapons could not be used, that helped to keep the Cold War going for so long. The arms race, Gaddis argues 'exchanged destruction for duration'.

The impact of Reagan and Gorbachev

U.S. President **Ronald Reagan** changed this way of thinking – this 'stability' in the area of nuclear relations. Firstly, he stepped up the arms race with the biggest arms build-up in the history of the United States. There were new developments, such as the stealth bomber and the neutron bomb, and, in 1983, Cruise missiles were first shipped to Europe. However, it was the Strategic Defense Initiative (SDI, or 'Star Wars') that upset the Soviet Union the most. This aimed to set up a space-based missile system that could intercept and destroy missiles before they reached the United States. It was criticized by the Soviets, as well as by many of the United States' allies. This was because it would have undermined the 'assured destruction' required for MAD and given the USA a first-strike capability, thus destabilizing the international situation. The Soviets, whose economy was on the verge of collapse, also knew that they could not compete with this new round of nuclear technology expansion. Indeed, some historians believe that it was the threat of SDI that lead directly to the success of arms talks between Soviet leader **Mikhail Gorbachev** and President Reagan (see Chapter Seventeen).

However, equally important was the changed thinking of Gorbachev, the new Soviet premier. He argued that as nuclear war was not possible, security must therefore be gained by political rather than military means, that negotiation and co-operation were as important as the continued build-up of the military. This change in the Soviet mind-set will be discussed further in Chapter Seventeen.

The role of conventional weapons

The fact that nuclear weapons could not be used except as a last resort meant that both sides needed to keep large conventional forces which remained central to military strategy. Indeed the Korean War and the Vietnam War were fought with conventional arms, and highlighted the importance of staying ahead in this area as well. The USSR still retained the lead in conventional forces. By the mid-1970s, the Warsaw Pact countries had nearly twice as many men and three times as many tanks in Europe as their counterparts in NATO.

STUDENT STUDY SECTION

Research questions

1   Why did the Soviets call the neutron bomb the 'Capitalist bomb'?
2   Why were there protests in Europe over the deployment of Cruise missiles? What forms did these protests take?

Review questions

1   Explain the meaning of the following: (a) massive retaliation (b) counterforce (c) Assured Destruction (d) Mutually Assured Destruction (e) SDI.
2   'It's not mad! Mutual Assured Destruction is the foundation of deterrence'. (Robert McNamara speaking on the CNN *Cold War* television series).
    Explain in your own words why McNamara believed that MAD acted as a deterrent to nuclear war. Do you agree with McNamara's view that MAD made the world a safer place? Or, do you believe that 'the lack of superpower war owed much to plain luck'? (Theo Farrell in 'Counting the Costs of the Nuclear Age', *International Affairs*, Vol 75, No 1, p.125)
3   In what ways did the arms race affect the Cold War? (discussion or essay question)

Cartoon analysis: Identifying the message of a cartoon

When analysing the meaning of a cartoon you need to answer several questions:

- Which political figures are shown in the cartoon? Make sure you can recognize the political figures of the time.
- What event/issue is the cartoon is referring to? Look carefully at the date and use your knowledge of the period.
- Are there symbols or other items in the cartoon that have significance?
- Are there any labels or writing on the cartoon that help explain what is going on? What about the title?
- Do you have any knowledge about the cartoonist or the country from which he or she comes that might help to explain his/her point of view?

The following cartoons were all drawn for the Montreal newspaper, *The Gazette*, by a Canadian cartoonist called John Collins, and all are connected with the nuclear arms race.

'International Downhill Race', cartoon by John Collins, 1962.

'Emerging from the Ice Age', cartoon by John Collins, 1963.

'Fifty years of Progress', cartoon by John Collins, 1968.

Questions

1 Annotate each cartoon with arrows to show clearly who or what is being shown in each case. Look carefully – there are several images in each cartoon that will need annotating.

2 Using your contextual knowledge, identify what was happening in the Cold War regarding the arms race at the date the cartoon was drawn.

3 Now, using the information from the last two questions, explain what the message of the cartoon was in each case. Make sure you use the titles of the cartoons in your answers as these are key to helping to understand the messages.

● **Examiner's hint:**

You should begin your answer by stating, 'The main message of the cartoon is … ', so that the examiner can see immediately that you have the key idea. For the first cartoon your opening sentence could read, 'The main message of this cartoon is that the arms race is a race that is very fast (possibly out of control) and very close'. Then go on to explain details in the cartoon that support this message.

Issues to consider when looking at the value of cartoons as source material:

● Cartoons show a point of view about an event or person.
● A cartoonist usually draws a point of view that other people will understand and appreciate and so this makes it useful for showing one current view or perception of what is happening.
● In order to help work out how representative the cartoonist's view is, you can look at the publication in which it is published. If it is published in a newspaper or magazine with a large and or/wide readership, this will make it more useful in showing contemporary perceptions.
● A Soviet cartoon will be useful for showing the nature of Soviet propaganda.

Issues to consider when looking at the limitations of cartoons as source material:

● A cartoon is only one point of view (of either a section of society or a particular country) and might not be the view of the majority of people.
● The situation in the cartoon can be exaggerated in order to make a point.
● You need to consider how much knowledge the cartoonist would have about an event or issue.
● A Soviet cartoon will represent the views of the Soviet leadership only and will be making a propaganda point.

Don't forget to refer directly to the details of the specific cartoon and the cartoonist you are analysing when answering a question on its value and limitations.

How useful do you think John Collins's cartoons are to historians studying attitudes to the arms race?

11 # SINO-SOVIET RELATIONS

Consider the following essay questions as you read this chapter:

- How far were relations between the PRC and the USSR affected by differences over ideology?
- What were the turning point events that kept relations between the Soviet Union and the People's Republic of China hostile for over 20 years?
- Why was there a thaw in **Sino**-Soviet relations at the end of the 1980s?

China becomes a Communist nation

Mao Zedong, the Chairman of the victorious Chinese Communist Party (CCP) proclaimed the People's Republic of China (PRC) in Beijing on 1 October 1949, saying:

Our work will be written down in the history of mankind, and it will clearly demonstrate the fact that the Chinese, who comprise one quarter of humanity, have from now on stood up …

Chairman Mao Zedong

 Chairman Mao proclaiming the People's Republic of China in 1949.

Background

China and Russia had experienced a troubled history, mainly as a result of their shared 4500 mile border. During Russian Tsarist times there was much tension along the border, and in the 19th century China lost territories to Russia, amongst others, while it struggled against Western domination. The failure of the ruling Manchu Dynasty in China to resist Western exploitation ultimately led to its downfall in the nationalist revolution of 1911. The new regime in China quickly got itself into difficulty attempting to consolidate control over the whole of the country. It was unable to cajole the Western powers into giving back the territories and rights that they had taken from the Manchu in what were known as the 'unequal treaties.'

China was impressed and grateful when the new Bolshevik regime, in what was now known as the Union of Soviet Socialist Republics, suggested that it would give up all claims to the former Tsarist empire outside Russia. However, a year later, the Bolsheviks seized Outer Mongolia; at the end of World War Two, the Soviets stripped $2 billion of equipment and machinery from Manchuria.

Civil war in China

Encouraged by the apparent success of the Bolsheviks in the new USSR, the Chinese Communist Party now grew in China. Some of their principal aims for China had similarities with another political group, the Guomindang (GMD), or Nationalist Party. Both wanted to unify China and redress the humiliation it had endured.

The ruling GMD, led by Chiang Kai-shek, came to see the CCP as its key internal political enemy and waged a campaign to wipe it out. This continued throughout the 1930s until an uneasy truce between the GMD and the CCP was agreed on in order for the Chinese to unify against wartime Japanese invaders. When Japan withdrew from China at the end of World War Two in 1945, the GMD and the CCP once again turned on each other, and a brutal civil war ensued. It was not until October 1949 that Mao Zedong, the leader of the Chinese Communist Party, emerged victorious.

Stalin and Mao: 1945–1953

The key differences between the USSR and the Chinese Communists were ideological. Josef Stalin felt that Mao's interpretation of Marxism, using peasants as the basis for revolution, could not be genuine revolutionary Marxism, which should feature workers leading an urban-based class war.

China and the Cold War Timeline
For a full timeline of events relating to China and the Cold War, see Appendix II.

Mao with Stalin in 1949 at the celebrations in Moscow for Stalin's 70th birthday.

From the infancy of Chinese Communism, Mao's contact with Moscow was neither pleasant nor gratifying. His unorthodox method of revolution, based on peasant mobilization in the countryside, was tolerated by Moscow as legitimate only because all other types of Communist insurrection in China had failed. Mao's approach was never endorsed by Stalin as proper for revolutionizing China.

Immanuel Hsu, The Rise of Modern China *(OUP, 1999) p.671*

However, this ideological difference was not the only reason Stalin failed to give support to the CCP in the Chinese civil war. Stalin also:

- feared Mao as a rival for the leadership of the Communist world
- did not want the Cold War to spread to Asia
- knew that Chiang's GMD would recognize Soviet claims to the disputed border territory along frontiers in Manchuria and Xinjiang
- underestimated the CCP and believed the GMD to be the stronger party. He urged the CCP to unite with the GMD, even in the late 1940s when CCP victory was looking inevitable.

Mao became convinced that Stalin wanted a divided and weak China to leave the USSR dominant in Asia. He saw Stalin's policies as rooted in self-interest, rather than true revolutionary doctrine. Mao later said that in 1945 Stalin refused China permission to carry out a revolution and that he had told them, 'Do not have a Civil War: collaborate with Chiang Kai-shek. Otherwise the Republic of China will collapse'. Mao, therefore, believed that Stalin saw him as another **Tito** (see Chapter Sixteen), rather than a true revolutionary.

The Sino-Soviet Treaty of Alliance

Nevertheless, once the CCP had won the civil war, Mao was invited to visit Moscow in 1950. This trip produced the Sino-Soviet Treaty of Alliance, the first treaty between the USSR and China. The USSR became more enthusiastic about the CCP after its victory, and the Soviet press poured praise and admiration on Mao and the new PRC. However, Mao later said of the agreement, 'This was the result of a struggle. Stalin did not wish to sign the treaty; he finally signed it after two months of negotiating.' The U.S. State Department referred to the alliance as 'Moscow making puppets out of the Chinese'. The Treaty offered the PRC the promise of Soviet expertise and low-interest aid:

Each contracting Party undertakes, in the spirit of friendship … to develop and consolidate economic and cultural ties between China and the Soviet Union, to render the other all possible economic assistance.

The Sino-Soviet Treaty of Alliance

However, the Chinese were offended by the rather 'unfriendly' treatment they received. The Soviets had been superior in their dealings with PRC officials and had not bothered to put on any entertainment for their guests, and Mao thought the accommodation given to the Chinese was poor. In fact, Nikita Khrushchev later said of the Treaty, 'It was an insult to the Chinese people. For centuries the French, English and Americans had been exploiting China, now the Soviet Union was moving in'. Indeed, it was soon clear that the USSR wanted to exploit the treaty in its own favour – Soviet aid would be loans and the Chinese would have to repay with interest.

Nevertheless, Soviet planners and engineers initially developed 200 Chinese construction projects in the 1950s. Traditional buildings were pulled down for Soviet-style constructions. Soviet scientific technology was prioritized in China over Western technology. Socialist science was seen as best, even if it was far less effective. The PRC also accepted that Soviet military assistance was necessary, at least until they had their own nuclear programme.

Review question

Why was Stalin reluctant to support Mao and the CCP?

The USSR, the PRC and the Korean War: 1950–1953

When Americans forces, under the UN flag, came close to the Chinese border near the Yalu River, Stalin encouraged the PRC to send troops into Korea. The Soviets gave material assistance to the one million Chinese troops engaged in battle.

Despite this support for PRC intervention in the Korean War, Mao bitterly complained when the Soviets demanded that China pay for all weapons and materials the USSR had supplied.

The cost of Stalin's 'trust' was high: China sent a million 'volunteers' to intervene in the Korean War and had to pay the entire $1.35 billion for the Soviet equipment and supplies necessary for the venture, and Mao lost a son in the war.

Immanuel Hsu, The Rise of Modern China *(OUP, 1999) p.675*

Sino-Soviet Relations after Stalin: 1953–1956

Although Mao had some respect for the Soviet leader, there had been tensions and suspicions in the relationship between Mao and Stalin. It has even been suggested that Stalin deliberately delayed the end of the Korean War in order to exhaust the PRC. Therefore, when Stalin died in 1953, it was possible that relations would improve. A truce was signed in the Korean War soon after Stalin's death and, to a certain degree, there was a relaxation in tension, referred to by historian Michael Lynch as something of a 'honeymoon' period. The new Soviet leaders appeared willing to supply further loans and technology to China, they attempted to make their treaties more equal and facilitate easier credit for the PRC.

Mao, Khrushchev and 'the split': 1956–1964

Despite the chance for improved Sino-Soviet relations during the leadership years of Nikita Khrushchev, three key issues undermined the potential for easing tension between the PRC and the USSR:

- The 'Secret Speech' by Khrushchev in Moscow in October 1956 attacking Stalin's crimes against the party, including comments about the 'Cult of Personality' (see also Chapter Sixteen), which Mao saw as an attack on his own style of leadership.
- The crushing of the Hungarian uprising. Mao saw this and Soviet problems in East Germany and Poland as failures by the USSR to contain **reactionary** forces (see Chapter Sixteen).
- Khrushchev's doctrine of 'peaceful co-existence' with the West (Chapter Seven), implying that global revolution could be achieved by means other than armed struggle. Mao saw this as ideological heresy.

Mao and the PRC considered these issues a clear departure from Marxist doctrine and evidence that the Soviet Union was now dominated by '**revisionists**' (a term used to describe those straying from Marxism). Further evidence in support of this view came in the form of the 1955 Geneva Summit and the Austrian State Treaty of 1955 (see page 75).

STUDENT STUDY SECTION

Document analysis

Document A

*… more than three years after he started pushing Maoism onto the world stage, … Mao gave the order to denounce Khrushchev by name as a 'revisionist'. A public slanging match quickly escalated. For Mao, the **polemic** acted as a sort of international advertising campaign for Maoism …*

Jung Chang and Jon Halliday, *Mao: The Unknown Story* (Random House, 2005)

Document B

Khrushchev and Mao had all the prejudices of nationalists, however much they might be Communists … Mao treated Khrushchev as a superficial upstart, neglecting no opportunity to confound him with petty humiliations, cryptic pronouncements, and veiled provocations. Khrushchev could 'never be sure what Mao meant … I believed in him and he was playing with me'.

John Lewis Gaddis, *The Cold War* (Penguin, 2005) p.141

Questions

1   According to Chang and Halliday in Document A, how does Mao attempt to use to his advantage Khrushchev's departure from Stalinism?

2   What does Gaddis mean in Document B when he says that 'Khrushchev and Mao had all the prejudices of nationalists'?

Conference of Communist Parties, 1957

Mao attended this conference of the world's Communist Parties and, as Michael Lynch points out, this was to be the second and last time he ventured outside China. He had hoped Tito would be in attendance, but the Yugoslav leader did not appear. Mao called on the USSR to abandon 'revisionism'. He declared that international revolution could not be supported by working along side 'class enemies', that is, Western Capitalists. In addition, Mao believed that the USSR was initiating détente with the West to further isolate China.

The Chinese chief spokesperson at the meeting was **Deng Xiaoping**. He was to prove exceptional in putting forward the PRC's ideological stance, and ultimately he was very embarrassing for the Soviets. Deng stated that the proletarian world revolution could only come about through force and that capitalism had to be crushed in violent revolution. He out-argued the leading Soviet theorist, Mikhail Suslov.

This had been a sound international platform to present the PRC as the 'real' leaders of international revolutionary Communism, which is exactly how Mao and the PRC were beginning to see themselves.

ToK Time
How far is it correct to assume that 'different cultures have different truths'? Can this be applied to the different interpretations of Marxist-Leninism adopted by the Soviets and the Communist Chinese?

Khrushchev's visit to Beijing, 1958

Khrushchev attempted to ease the growing tension between the USSR and China by visiting Mao in Beijing. However, right from the start things did not go well, and Mao apparently went out of his way to make Khrushchev feel uncomfortable.

For example, it was the height of the summer heat in Beijing and Khrushchev's hotel had no air conditioning and was plagued by mosquitoes. Mao arranged one round of talks in his swimming pool, which was fine for Mao who was a regular swimmer, but not so easy for Khrushchev who hated swimming. To add insult to an already difficult situation, Khrushchev had to wear a pair of shorts that were rather too tight for him, and had to be helped to float by a rubber ring!

The talks, unsurprisingly, were not productive. Again, Deng used the occasion as an opportunity to attack Soviet policy, stating that:

- the Soviets had betrayed the international Communist movement
- the Soviets were guilty of viewing themselves as the only true 'Marxist-Leninists'
- the Soviets had sent spies posing as technical advisers into China.

Mao Zedong and Nikita Khrushchev in Beijing, 1958.

Taiwan, 1958

As has been explained in Chapter Six, the key issue of the PRC's Nationalist enemies in Taiwan was not resolved. The GMD and their leader Chiang Kai-shek could not be tolerated as an 'independent' state off the mainland by the PRC. It resolutely wanted reunification with Taiwan and was furious about U.S. support for the Nationalists.

The PRC had bombarded islands off Taiwan in the early 1950s (see Chapter Twelve), but had been deterred from further action by U.S. 7th Fleet patrols of the straits between Taiwan and the mainland. In 1958, Mao decided to test the United States' resolve again. Without discussing it with the Soviets, he ordered a build-up of troop manoeuvres in the region, giving the impression that the PRC was preparing for a full-scale attack on Taiwan. The United States responded by preparing for war with the PRC.

However, Mao did not launch an attack. He was unprepared to take on the full might of the U.S. war machine, and he did not have the support of the Soviet Union.

Khrushchev said that he was not prepared to go to war with the United States to 'test the stability' of the Capitalist system, and he accused Mao's regime of being '**Trotskyist**' in pursuing international revolution at any cost. The Soviets also saw this action as evidence of Mao's lack of understanding of political reality, and his tendency towards **fanaticism**.

The effects of the Taiwan crisis were negative for Sino-Soviet relations. The Soviets withdrew their economic advisers and cancelled commercial contracts with the PRC.

STUDENT STUDY SECTION

Document analysis

The second Taiwan Strait crisis was very like the first in 1954–55, which Mao had staged to twist his ally's arm for A-bomb technology … On 23rd August Mao opened up a huge artillery barrage against the tiny island of Quemoy … Washington thought Mao might really be going for Taiwan. No one in the West suspected his true goal: to force the USA to threaten a nuclear war in order to scare his own ally – a ruse unique in the annals of statecraft.

Jung Chang and Jon Halliday, *Mao: The Unknown Story* (Random House, 2005)

Question

What reasons do Chang and Halliday suggest for Mao's initiation of the Second Taiwan Crisis?

Sino-Soviet relations and the 'Great Leap Forward'

What was the Great Leap Forward?

The Great Leap Forward (GLF) was initiated by Mao at a meeting in January 1958. The key idea behind the GLF was to develop rapidly China's agricultural and industrial sectors simultaneously. Mao hoped to harness the energy of the vast population of China and by so doing dispose of the need for Soviet aid. He believed that sheer force of will would get around the necessity of importing heavy machinery. In the process, Mao would also create the 'proletarian class' required by the Marxist model. He anchored the GLF in the development of two key areas – grain and steel production. His predictions were very ambitious, suggesting that China could outproduce the UK in steel in just 15 years.

In order to achieve both increased grain and steel production, Mao promoted the construction of small backyard steel furnaces in every commune and in each urban neighbourhood. Peasants and workers set about attempting to produce steel from scrap metal, stripping their local areas of all potential fuel sources to burn in the furnaces. Suspicious of the academic 'intellectuals', Mao ignored their concerns about the economic value of the poor-quality 'pig iron' that these furnaces produced. China's harvests rotted in the fields as peasants focused on making the worthless metal, often out of basic essentials, such as their own pots and pans.

Despite the fact that Mao had seen for himself that high-quality steel could only be produced in proper factories, he continued with the 'backyard furnaces' plan for most of 1959. It is said that behind Mao's reasoning was a desire not to crush the 'revolutionary spirit' of the peasants and workers.

Public works launched during the GLF were also generally unsuccessful, due to the deliberate lack of experienced and expert leadership. As for the broader agricultural picture, on the communes, some 'revolutionary' techniques were experimented with. For example, there was 'close cropping', where seeds were planted very close together (following the false idea that the same crop would not compete with itself), and also the idea of leaving an area of each field fallow to improve fertility.

Failure and starvation

At the Lushan Conference in July 1959, Marshal Peng Dehuai spoke out against the disastrous impact of the GLF. Mao had Peng removed from his post, and used his denunciation to launch a nationwide campaign against the 'rightists' (right-wing elements). From 1959, China experienced a widespread famine. Even though millions were starving in China, Mao insisted that China continue to export grain – he did not want the humiliation of the outside world knowing the results of his great economic plan. Chinese government sources record horrendous weather conditions affecting China from 1958 to 1962, and there is clear evidence of droughts and floods. But the impact of the GLF exacerbated the problems caused by the weather. As a direct result of the GLF policies, millions of Chinese died. In January 1961, the PRC finally decided to end the GLF revolution. No more grain was exported, and Canadian and Australian grain was imported.

The consequence of the Great Leap Forward was total economic disaster for China. The offical Chinese records state that 14 million Chinese died in the famine, although some Western sources have estimated that around 30 million perished. Mao stepped down as

State Chairman of the PRC in 1959, realizing that he would be held responsible for the disaster that was emerging; he did, however, keep his position as Chairman of the CCP.

Soviets denounce the GLF

In 1959, Soviets called the rapid industrial change aspect of the GLF 'faulty in design and erroneous in practice'. Mao was personally furious at this criticism. His anger became fuelled by humiliation when it was rumoured that the PRC Chief-of-Staff, Marshal Peng, had given information to the Soviets about the widespread starvation caused by the agricultural methods of the GLF. The Soviet government declared that the concepts and applications used were 'unorthodox', and the Soviet official press revelled in the failure, denouncing Mao.

Infuriated, Mao was now determined to strike back at the USSR for undermining the position of the PRC in the eyes of the international Communist community. It would now back any Communist country that dissented from Moscow's lead.

Albania

China got its opportunity to attack the USSR and support a 'dissenting Communist state' over Albania. In 1961, the USSR withdrew aid to Albania. Khrushchev made a speech that year during the Moscow Congress of the Communist Party of the Soviet Union, attacking the Albanian regime for its 'Stalinist' doctrines and backward ways. The PRC observer at the Congress walked out in protest. China interpreted this speech as an attack on their system as well. Soon after, the PRC offered to replace Soviet money and technical assistance to Albania. This conflict over Albania led to the final severance of diplomatic relations between the Soviets and the Chinese Communists after more than ten years of growing hostility.

In their war of words, Khrushchev referred to Mao as the 'Asian Hitler' and a 'living corpse'; Mao called Khrushchev 'a redundant old boot'.

STUDENT STUDY SECTION

Document analysis

Document A

By the mid 1950s there were growing problems in the Sino-Soviet alliance. Soviet advisers had caused some resentment in China when their nationalist susceptibilities were ruffled by perceived arrogance. Soviet insistence on payment for material supplied during the Korean War did not help matters. The key to the growing friction was ideology. De-Stalinization and attacks on the cult of personality went down badly in Beijing, as did Soviet critiques of the Great Leap Forward … Personal relations between the leaders were poor and Mao resented criticism of Molotov and the 'anti-party group' for views that resembled his own.

From Mike Sewell, *The Cold War* (CUP, 2002) p.67

Document B

The relationship to China had been lauded as the ultimate proof of Socialism's applicability to the Third World … With the alliance in tatters, Moscow had to explain what had gone wrong … [it was] explained by the wrongheadedness of the 'Mao-clique' … on the other hand, the combination of immense disappointment and no proper cause for failure led many Soviet leaders to racist explanations: the Soviet effort in China was failing because of the inborn deviousness and selfishness of the Chinese.

From Odd Arne Westad, *The Global Cold War* (CUP, 2007) p.70

Document C

Despite a degree of mismanagement unparalleled in modern history [the GLF] ... *Mao survived as China's 'great helmsman'. What did not survive was the Sino-Soviet alliance which had, as far as Mao was concerned, outlived its usefulness. Khrushchev, fearing the implications, tried desperately to reconstitute it right up to the moment he was deposed in 1964, despite repeated insults, rebuffs and even instances of deliberate sabotage from Mao.*

From John Lewis Gaddis, *The Cold War* (Penguin, 2005) p.142

Question

How similar are the views in Documents A, B and C on what caused the Sino-Soviet split?

Review exercise

Discuss in pairs/small groups how each of the following led to the split between the USSR and the PRC:

1 The Chinese Civil War
2 Stalin's attitude to Mao
3 Korean War
4 Stalin's death
5 Khrushchev's new policies
6 Mao's response to Khrushchev
7 Taiwan
8 The Great Leap Forward
9 Albania

Attempt to prioritize the events in order of importance. From your discussions, was there a 'turning point' event at which time the Sino-Soviet split became inevitable? Which side seems to be more responsible for causing the split – the Soviets or the Chinese? Remember to support your answers with evidence from the chronology of events and, where possible, the viewpoints of historians.

● **Examiner's hint:**
The document question requires you to look at ways in which sources make similar points about the Sino-Soviet split and ways in which they differ. Remember to use brief quotes from the document to support your answer and to have a brief conclusion summing up how consistent the sources are in the views expressed.

The Sino-Indian War, 1962

Another issue that raised tension between the Soviet Union and China was the war with India. In 1962, fighting broke out on the Tibetan border between China and India. The PRC had invaded Tibet in 1950, an area it wished to bring under Chinese control, and indeed an area it viewed as 'Chinese' and therefore a domestic issue. The continuous brutality of the PRC forces in Tibet aroused international condemnation. The Indian government was also sensitive about troops occupying territory close to its border.

It has been suggested by some historians that Mao had been planning a war with India for some time. China did not recognize the boundary between the two countries that had been drawn up during the British colonial period. Mao demanded that the border be renegotiated by China and India themselves. However, India did not believe there was anything to negotiate about. Its view was that the border was established and settled, and thus the two countries were deadlocked over the issue.

Clashes increased along this border, and from May 1962, the PRC began to prepare for war with India. Although outwardly aggressive, Mao was worried about triggering a war. One of his key concerns was that the nuclear test site at Lop Nur in north-west China was in missile range of India, even though it was beyond the American range from Taiwan.

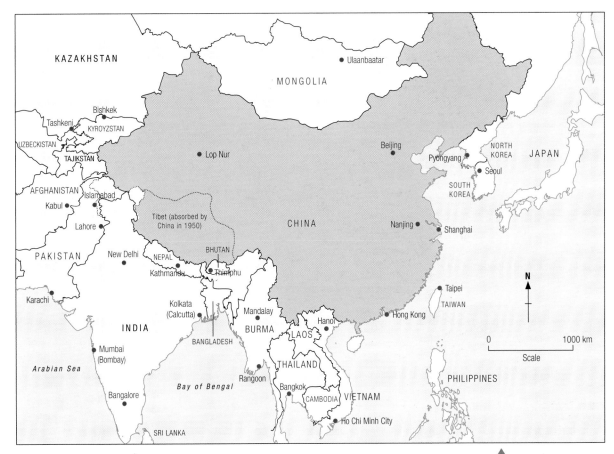

Map of India and China/ showing national borders.

The war proper erupted on 10 October 1962 between the Chinese People's Liberation Army and the Indian military. Part of the fallout from the war was that India allowed American U-2s to fly from bases at Charbatia, from where they were able to photograph China's first A-bomb test. In the war, the Soviets were officially 'neutral'; however they gave India MIG fighters. Therefore, when the Soviet foreign minister offered to act as a mediator, Mao viewed this as outrageous hypocrisy.

The war ended on 20 November 1962. The Chinese had taken the disputed areas and unilaterally declared a ceasefire. Although the PRC had emerged victorious this was tempered by the fact that the Americans had been able to gain sensitive intelligence and possible access to bases in India. The Soviets had aided the enemy in this war and the PRC's relationship as a key member of the non-aligned movement (see Chapter Fifteen) alongside Nehru's India was shattered.

The Cuban Missile Crisis, 1962

Sino-Soviet relations reached new depths of division during the Cuban Missile Crisis (see Chapter Nine for a discussion of the key events). Mao was openly disparaging about Khrushchev's handling of the crisis. He seized on this perceived mismanagement as an opportunity to expose to the Communist world the USSR's lack of commitment to the revolutionary cause. Mao attacked:

- the placement of *detectable* missiles in first place
- the 'capitulation' (backing down)
- the negative impact it would have on the struggle against U.S. imperialism.

In his book, *The Rise of Modern China*, Immanuel Hsu claims that 'Mao considered Khrushchev a coward' over his handling of the Cuban Missile Crisis. It could, of course, be argued that Khrushchev had acted like a 'great statesman', that he had applied his policy of peaceful co-existence and thus averted a nuclear catastrophe. But for Mao and the PRC, the idea of existing peacefully with the non-Communist states went against everything their ideology dictated. It seemed to them that the USSR was betraying the revolution, as well as tolerating the exploitation of pre-revolutionary states by Capitalist powers, such as the United States.

STUDENT STUDY SECTION

Document analysis

Document A

Only after victory in the revolution is it possible and necessary for the proletariat to pursue peaceful co-existence. As for the oppressed peoples and nations, their task is to strive for their own liberation and overthrow the rule of imperialism and its lackeys. They should not practise peaceful co-existence with the imperialists … It is therefore wrong to apply peaceful co-existence to relations between oppressed and oppressor … nations.

A statement made by Mao Zedong in 1963

Document B

In this cartoon by Vicky, published in the UK in November 1962, Mao is calling 'Chicken!' while Kennedy and Khrushchev face each other across a precipice.

Document C

We might ask the Chinese comrades, who offer to build a beautiful future on the ruins of the old world destroyed by thermo-nuclear war: did they consult, on this issue, the working class of countries where imperialism is in power? … What right have you to decide for us questions involving our very existence and our class struggle – we too want socialism, but we want to win it through the class struggle, not by unleashing a world thermo-nuclear war.

The Soviet response to Mao's 1963 statement

Questions

1   Explain the propaganda message in Document A.

2   How does Document B support the views stated in Document A?

3   What are the key points being made by the Soviets in Document C?

4   What are the value and limitation of using Document B as evidence of China's response to the Cuban Missile Crisis? (Refer back to Chapter Ten for a discussion on cartoons as evidence.)

Review exercise

Consider and plan the following essay questions:

1   To what extent was the Sino-Soviet split caused by the relationship between Mao and Stalin?

2   How important was the initiative of 'peaceful co-existence' in the development of Sino-Soviet tension?

Sino-Soviet relations and the Cultural Revolution, 1966–1976

Mao's 'Great Proletarian Cultural Revolution' was launched in May 1966. His declared aim was to intiate a revolution at the very heart of traditional Chinese 'culture'. He wanted to eliminate the creeping return of liberal and **bourgeois** thinking and behaviour. Mao believed that this would re-ignite the revolutionary class struggle that had, so he thought, petered out. Most historians agree that this was really Mao's 'relaunch' of himself after the disasters of the Great Leap Forward had forced him to take something of a back seat.

The main tools of the Cultural Revolution were the young, who were encouraged to denounce their elders, teachers and parents, and send them for 're-education'. This was done with much enthusiasm by Red Guards wielding Mao's 'Little Red Book'. Teachers, writers, intellectuals, musicians, older leaders, in fact all who were viewed as representing 'old thoughts,' were attacked. Power struggles developed at both local and national level.

As there were no clear directives from the Party as to how the 'old culture' should be disposed of, many attacks got out of hand. As many as half a million people died. Meanwhile, Mao was able to get rid of his critics and resume supreme control of the PRC. While the excesses of the young Red Guards continued, Mao declared the Cultural Revolution over in 1969. In the hope that society could return to some sort of order from the **anarchy** and chaos that had been unleashed, many of the young Maoists were then sent to the countryside themselves, to 'learn from the peasants'.

Khrushchev left office in 1964. However, there was to be no reconciliation between the USSR and the PRC. The Soviet leadership continued to attempt to isolate the PRC. When Mao launched the Great Proletarian Cultural Revolution to eliminate 'revisionists' and China descended yet again into internal crisis, and at certain points to near civil war, the Soviets denounced the revolution as total fanaticism, and criticized Mao for creating a state of anarchy.

The Soviets also took the opportunity to attack the PRC on a number of other propaganda fronts during the Cutural Revolution, including the following: accusations:
- trading illegally with the **apartheid** regime in South Africa
- receiving assistance from West Germany on nuclear research
- developing a worldwide opium trade
- sending supplies to U.S. forces in Vietnam.

Mao responded to these 'false' accusations by calling on other Communist countries to follow the Chinese model rather than the 'revisionist' Soviet system.

China, the USSR and nuclear weapons

A continuing theme in Sino-Soviet relations was the dispute over aspects of military power, particularly nuclear weapons. In 1957, it appeared that the USSR had gained superiority over the USA with the launch of the Sputnik satellite (see Chapter Seven). Mao saw this as a tool to engage the USA in Brinkmanship, and to begin to undermine the United States. Unlike the more pragmatic Soviet Union, Mao did not fear nuclear war, as he actually believed it was now an unavoidable part of the revolutionary struggle.

However, Khrushchev had very different views. He wanted to use the apparent technical superiority as leverage to convince the United States to pursue 'co-existence'. This disagreement between the two Communist superpowers on how to engage their Capitalist enemy intensified over the Test-ban Treaty of 1963. The Treaty was an agreement by the

The Little Red Book
The 'Little Red Book' was a small red book of Mao's thoughts and sayings that became an essential accessory during the Cultural Revolution.

Extreme violence of the Cultural Revolution
'Zhongnanhai [where the government leaders lived] had been turned into a torture park. A hundred thousand yelling savages outside, thousands inside the torture halls. The Liu children were compelled to watch Mao's knights drag the half-dead victims onto a stage. Liu and Wang Guangmei were forced into the airplane position. Guards raised Liu up and then dropped him to the floor like a sack of flour. They beat him in the face and head. They kicked and punched him. One soldier yanked Liu by his white hair and pulled his head back while cameras clicked.'
Harrison Salisburg, *The New Emperor* (Harper Collins, 1992).

USSR and Western nuclear powers to stop atmospheric testing of atomic weapons. Again, Mao viewed this as the USSR abandoning its role as revolutionary leader and instead working with the imperialist powers.

Khrushchev responded to the PRC's criticism of attempts at superpower arms control by accusing the Chinese of wanting to see the USSR and Western powers destroy each other, leaving the PRC as the number one power.

Mao had been angered by the Soviet response to the PRC's request for nuclear technology. The basic circular argument between them was:

China: 'If you are our friend, you should want to help us develop our own nuclear programme.'

USSR: 'As you are our friend, you do not need your own nuclear programme as we will look after you.'

The Soviet position was inflexible. If the PRC wanted help from the USSR in nuclear development then it would have to allow the Soviets to control its defence policy. Typically, Mao stated that this approach betrayed the revolutionary ideal and was also patronizing. He asserted that the Soviets did not view other Communist countries as equals.

Timeline of Chinese technical development

1960	Soviet scientists complete withdrawal from China
	China continues with its own research programmes and even uses material from reconstructed shredded documents left by the Soviets
1964	China detonates first atomic bomb
1967	China detonates a hydrogen bomb
1970	China launches its first space satellite

The development of its own nuclear weapons was a huge achievement for China. It not only meant that the PRC would have to be taken seriously as an international power, but it also demonstrated to the USSR that it did not need Soviet support. To push this point the Chinese code-named their first bomb '59/6', which referred to the year and month the Soviet scientists began to pull out of China. Mao explained the positive results of the Soviet departure:

Guided missiles and atom bombs are great achievements. This is the result of Khrushchev's 'help'. By withdrawing the experts, he forced us to take our own road. We should give him a big medal.

Chairman Mao Zedong

Mao appeared not to be as wary of nuclear catastrophe as were the USSR and the USA. Indeed, he suggested that nuclear weapons were a useful tool of diplomacy. He also saw them as the key to China usurping the Soviet Union as leader of the international Communist struggle:

The success of China's hydrogen bomb test has further broken the nuclear monopoly of United States imperialism and Soviet revisionism and dealt a telling blow at their policy of nuclear blackmail. It is very great encouragement … to the revolutionary people of the whole world.

Chairman Mao Zedong

With the launch of the first Chinese space satellite in 1970, the Soviet Union was worried that now the PRC had the potential to develop ICBMs.

Document analysis

Document A

'Mushrooming Cloud' by Herblock, 1965.

Document B

Defying the logic of balancing power within the international system, Mao sought a different kind of equilibrium: a world filled with danger, whether from the United States or the Soviet Union or both, could minimize the risk that rivals within China might challenge his rule.

From John Lewis Gaddis, *The Cold War* (Penguin, 2005) p.142

Questions

1 What is the message of the cartoonist in Document A?

2 What does Document A suggest about China's role in the Cold War at this time?

3 According to Document B, why might Mao want to encourage international hostility towards China?

Discussion point

What arguments could the PRC put forward to defend its right to have its own nuclear weapons programme? Consider how these arguments compare and contrast to those made by countries today who want to develop their own nuclear programmes.

The PRC and Leonid Brezhnev, 1968–1982

During his leadership of the Soviet Union, **Leonid Brezhnev** followed a 'Stalinist' foreign policy, and so there was to be no improvement in Sino-Soviet relations while he was leader.

The invasion of Czechoslovakia, 1968

In the 'Brezhnev Doctrine' (see Chapter Sixteen, page 202) the Soviet Union stated that to maintain order in Eastern Europe, the satellite states had to accept Soviet leadership. When Czechoslovakia attempted to assert some independence, the doctrine was put into practice, and in 1968 Soviet tanks were sent to crush the period of liberalization now known as the 'Prague Spring'. This invasion undermined the USSR's standing with other Communist states, and this correspondingly damaged its attempts to isolate the PRC.

Mao condemned the use of force against Czechoslovakia. This was not only because the Soviet Union was no longer behaving in a 'truly socialist' manner in his eyes, but also because he was worried that Soviet military might and the Brezhnev Doctrine could be turned against China.

STUDENT STUDY SECTION

Document analysis

Document A

A few days ago, the Soviet revisionist leading clique and its followers dispatched massive armed forces to launch a surprise attack on Czechoslovakia and swiftly occupied it, with the Czechoslovak revisionist leading clique openly calling on the people to resist, thus committing enormous crimes against the Czechoslovak people. This is the most obvious and most typical example of fascist power politics played by the Soviet Union … It marks the total bankruptcy of Soviet revisionism.

*The Chinese Government and people strongly condemn the Soviet revisionist leading **clique** and its followers for their crime of aggression – the armed occupation of Czechoslovakia – and firmly support the Czechoslovak people in their heroic struggle of resistance to Soviet military occupation.*

Extract from a speech by Chinese Premier **Zhou En-lai**, 23 August 1968 at Romania's National Day Reception

Document B

*Since Brezhnev came to power, the Soviet revisionist clique has stepped up its **collusion** with US imperialism and its suppression of the revolutionary struggle of the peoples of various countries, intensified its control over and its exploitation of the various east European countries … and intensified its threat of aggression against China. Its dispatch of hundreds of thousands of troops to occupy Czechoslovakia, and its armed provocation against China on our territory are two unacceptable acts staged recently by Soviet revisionism.*

In order to justify its aggression, the Soviet revisionist clique loudly proclaims its so-called theory of 'limited sovereignty' and theory of 'socialist community'. What does all this stuff mean? It means that your own sovereignty is 'limited', while his is unlimited. You won't obey him? He will exercise his 'international dictatorship' over you – dictatorship over the people of other countries, in order to form the 'socialist community' ruled by the new Tsars.

Extract from a speech by Lin Biao to the Ninth Party Congress of the Chinese Communist Party in Beijing, 1 April 1969

Questions

1   What criticisms of the USSR's action in Czechoslovakia are made in Documents A and B?

2   Why might other Communist states agree with the opinions given in these speeches by Zhou En-lai and Lin Biao?

ToK Time
How far is 'opinion' an asset or an obstacle to the work of a historian?

Sino-Soviet border war, 1969

The hostility between the Soviets and the Chinese Communists inevitably came to a head in violent clashes along their mutual border. The PRC denounced the Soviets as 'imperialists', no different from the Tsars of old, as they still had not returned territory taken from the

Chinese in the 19th century. In 1962, border disputes increased to a new level along the Xinjiang frontier and the Amur and Ussuri rivers. Both sides increased the numbers of troops facing one another across the border.

In 1969 the frontier dispute erupted into a proper war. According to the Chinese, the Soviets had violated China's border 4189 times in the period up to 1969. The tension boiled over into actual fighting on 2 March 1969 on Cheng-pao or Damansky Island in the Ussuri River. By August, there was clearly the possibility of all-out war between the two Communist states. If this happened, there was a danger of the conflict turning nuclear. Mao feared a Soviet invasion and possible nuclear strikes, so he ordered that tunnels be dug and supplies stored in preparation for this. Fighting continued sporadically for most of the year.

In the end, there was no escalation to all-out nuclear war. However, the war had brought the world's two most powerful Communist countries to the brink.

Some historians view 1969 as the lowest point in Sino-Soviet relations for a number of reasons:
- serious border incidents threatened to turn into full-scale war
- the PRC and Soviet Union realigned missiles to face one another
- there was an intensification of the rivalry to be the leading Communist nation.

The PRC, the USSR and Indochina

Indochina became a complex focal point for the Sino-Soviet split. China had a strategic interest in Indochina as Vietnam, Cambodia and Laos were on its border. The PRC had been involved in the peace talks that brought an end to the problems in Indochina in 1954 (see Chapter Six). The United States had not wanted the PRC there, and the U.S. Secretary of State, John Foster Dulles, had refused to acknowledge the PRC representative, Zhou En-lai.

The Vietnam War

As explained in Chapter Six, when the United States refused to accept the free elections in Vietnam set down in the 1954 agreement, it was drawn further and further into the civil war that developed through its support for the regime in the south. The PRC was not directly involved in the Vietnam War, but gave moral and diplomatic support to Ho Chi Minh. The Chinese also attacked U.S. involvement as 'naked American imperialism'.

There then developed a struggle between the USSR and the PRC to win the Vietnamese Communists to 'their' side in the ideological split. China accused the USSR of being in league with the USA in Vietnam, and the PRC refused to allow the USSR to use Chinese airports for Soviet airlifts to Vietnam.

Nevertheless, the USSR eventually won this contest by keeping up a steady supply of aid and arms throughout the war. In 1978, relations were formalized in the Soviet-Vietnamese Treaty of Peace and Friendship.

Sino-Soviet clashes over Cambodia and Vietnam

Having lost influence over Vietnam to the Soviets, the Chinese then attempted to form closer ties with Cambodia. Cambodia had become Communist in 1975 under Pol Pot's Khmer Rouge party. In many ways, Pol Pot's regime was modelled on 'Maoism'. However, between 1975 and 1979 the brutality of the regime was horrendous and exceeded anything perpetrated in the Cultural Revolution. Although 2.5 million Cambodians died, Pol Pot was hailed a Maoist hero.

In November 1978, Vietnam signed a military alliance with the USSR. Following a series of clashes on the border, Vietnam invaded Cambodia on 24 December 1978. Its stated aim was **regime change** – to overthrow Pol Pot. The Vietnamese began to expel all Chinese people from the territory they occupied. Many of these exiles became the 'boat people' who were later stranded at sea attempting to find refuge. Pol Pot appealed to the United Nations. China then decided to come to the defence of Pol Pot's regime, arguing that Vietnam's invasion of Cambodia was 'Soviet expansionism'.

Thus, on 17 February 1979, China invaded Vietnam. Its intent was to draw Vietnamese/ Soviet forces out of Cambodia. In response, the Soviets increased their backing for the Vietnamese, and both sides claimed the other as the aggressor. In addition, the Vietnamese/ Soviets also attempted to present their intervention to the United Nations as being on '**humanitarian**' grounds.

There was no quick victory for the Chinese, and the war dragged on into March. Although Vietnam had clearly won the war, the Chinese People's Liberation Army claimed success. In fact, the PLA had suffered heavy casualties and had been forced to withdraw. The war had been a major setback for PRC propaganda against the USSR, as well as for its attempt to confirm its role as leader of the Communist world.

Sino-Soviet rapprochement, 1982–2000

There were a number of key reasons for the relaxation of tensions between the Soviet Union and the PRC during the last two decades of the 20th century:

- Mao Zedong's death in 1976
- the overthrow of the anti-Soviet **Gang of Four** in China
- the adoption by the new PRC leader, Deng Xiaoping, of a more tolerant line in relation to the Soviet Union and the West
- Leonid Brezhnev's death in 1982.

Map of China and its border with the USSR in 1984.

During the comparatively brief Soviet leaderships of Andropov, and then Chernenko, attempts were made to improve relations with China. For example, diplomatic formalities were renewed in 1982 and high-ranking Chinese attended Brezhnev's funeral. But, for most of the 1980s, there were three key issues dividing the PRC and the USSR:

- the Soviet invasion of Afghanistan
- Soviet troops on the border with China
- Soviet support for the Vietnamese occupation of Cambodia.

All moves towards a better relationship during this period came to nothing, primarily because of the Soviet invasion of Afghanistan in 1979. China condemned the invasion as Soviet 'imperial expansionism.' The PRC did not view the invasion as a 'defensive move' as the Soviets claimed, but as an excuse to mass troops on the border with China.

Mikhail Gorbachev and Deng Xiaoping

With Mikhail Gorbachev assuming the Soviet leadership in 1985, and Deng Xiaoping leading the PRC, there was, for the first time in over 20 years, the real chance of improving relations between the two Communist superpowers. Indeed, this was a primary objective for Gorbachev.

In 1986, new trade agreements were drawn up, and procedures for full diplomatic relations restored. In November 1987 Gorbachev asked to meet Deng, but the Chinese refused the request as the Soviets had not managed to get their Vietnamese allies to pull out of Cambodia. However, in May 1988, the PRC and the USSR signed a cultural exchange agreement.

Relations improved further when in 1989 the Soviets began their withdrawal from Afghanistan, and Gorbachev was finally invited to Beijing.

Tiananmen Square, 1989

The PRC's decision to brutally crush the Chinese pro-democracy movement demonstrations in Beijing's Tiananmen Square in 1989 highlighted the fundamental differences that had developed by this time between the regime in Communist China and Gorbachev's Soviet Union.

Gorbachev had initiated far-reaching reforms in the USSR and, for the first time since the death of Stalin, a Soviet leader had begun to dismantle Stalin's structural legacy (see Chapter Seventeen). **Perestroika** addressed economic restructuring, and **glasnost** suggested more political freedom and reform.

In China, Deng had also brought about some economic reforms, but there had not been a corresponding policy of political openness. Indeed, Deng believed that economic reform in China was only possible if under the control of the CCP.

Before Gorbachev's visit, on 16 April 1989 students began a peaceful protest for more political freedom, with slogans such as 'Down with bureaucracy!' and 'Long live democracy!' Students in their thousands flooded into the central Tiananmen Square in Beijing. Between 21 and 22 April up to 100,000 people demonstrated. An official PRC newspaper, the *People's Daily*, condemned the students as a 'small bunch of troublemakers' and called the demonstration 'a counter-revolutionary rebellion'.

On 13 May, 3000 students began a hunger strike in Tiananmen Square. This was highly embarrassing for the leaders of the PRC, particularly as Gorbachev was due to arrive two days later. The protesters welcomed Gorbachev as a hero of reform, chanting his name and incorporating *glasnost* and *perestroika* in their slogans.

The tension rose on 19 May when a million people took to the streets to support student hunger strikers. On 20 May **martial law** was declared. Deng refused to compromise with the students. Finally, on 4 June 1989, apparently under direct orders from Deng, troops were sent in to disperse the crowd. The students shouted slogans at the army and some threw rocks. The troops opened fire. It remains unclear exactly how many people died. It is likely that the number is in the thousands. Thousands also fled into hiding and were hunted down and arrested by the authorities.

The PRC officially announced that troops had been forced to defend themselves, and that about 100 civilians were dead and a hundred more wounded. It denied that thousands had been killed.

STUDENT STUDY SECTION

Document analysis

Question

This photograph is one of the most iconic images from the pro-democracy demonstrations in China. Why do you think this image is so powerful?

Cartoon analysis

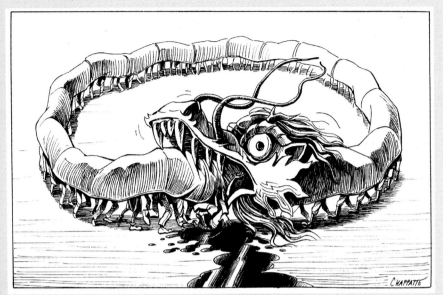

Question

What is the cartoonist's message?

The PRC's brutal crushing of the demonstration was condemned around the world. The following appeared in *Time Australia*, 19 June 1989, allegedly quoting a Chinese worker: 'Tell the United Nations, tell the world what has happened in China. Tell them that the Chinese government is killing the Chinese people.' Despite the violence, there were no crippling sanctions applied to the PRC by the international community, though relations with the USA did suffer (see Chapter Twelve).

The fall of the Soviet Union

When Gorbachev's reforms brought about his downfall, it seemed to Deng and the CCP that their hardline stand against the pro-democracy protests had been the right one. With the new political freedoms came the collapse of Communism in Eastern Europe between 1988 and 1991 (see Chapter Seventeen). This included the ending of the official status of the Communist Party of the Soviet Union in 1990. The following year the USSR was dissolved.

The People's Republic of China no longer had a competitor for the leadership of the Communist world. However, the PRC did not seize the international revolutionary initiative. Rather, the regime looked to enhance China's position as a major world player and continue its economic modernization.

STUDENT STUDY SECTION

Review exercise

Look at the Chinese 'overview' timeline in Appendix II. Identify the 'turning point events' in Sino-Soviet Relations. Then, in your own words, explain why these events caused tension between the PRC and the USSR – you could annotate your own version of the timeline.

Approaches to essay questions

1   *How far were relations between the PRC and the USSR affected by differences over ideology?*
You could adopt a structure that evaluates the effect of ideology on relations between the USSR and the PRC by contrasting it with 'self-interest'.

There is much evidence that the relationship soured into a split due to their differences over ideology, and this can be supported by the evidence of events from your timeline. However, there is also a convincing line of argument that suggests that ideology was really just a cover for a more traditional power struggle between the two countries, which were focused more on nationalist self-interest than specific ideology. Again, you will need to select examples of events from your timeline to support your arguments. Some of the events can be used on both sides of the argument – although you will analyse them differently.

2   *What were the turning-point events that kept relations between the Soviet Union and the People's Republic of China hostile for over 20 years?*

The danger with this essay question is that you end up writing a narrative account, in other words simply retelling the chronological story of events, without attempting to analyse the question. To avoid this, you could adopt a thematic approach, and structure your essay around the following arguments:
- Ideological differences, with examples
- Personality clashes, with examples
- Self-interest, with examples
- Domestic problems, with examples.

This essay would work, but would be given a further dimension if 'external forces' were also discussed. After you have read the next chapter on Sino-American relations, a further theme of 'the role of the USA' could be added.

3   *Why was there a thaw in Sino-Soviet relations at the end of the 1980s?*

After establishing the key causes of hostility between the USSR and the PRC in your introduction, the main body of the essay could then compare and contrast the changes that precipitated Chinese moves towards a 'thaw' with those of the USSR. As with the previous essay, your plan can be improved by adding the role played by the USA, after you read the next chapter.

12 SINO-AMERICAN RELATIONS

In this chapter, consider the following essay questions. Refer to the timeline in Appendix II.
- What were the key causes of Sino-American hostility from 1949 to 1970?
- Why was there a Sino-American détente in the 1970s?

Background

During World War Two the United States had some direct contact with the Chinese Communist Party (CCP), and had given it some material assistance in the fight against the common enemy, Japan. However, most U.S. aid went to Chiang Kai-shek and the Nationalist Guomindang Party (GMD). After the Japanese surrender and withdrawal from China at the end of the war, the CCP and GMD fought each other in the civil war. The Americans pumped material assistance and advice to Chiang's 'anti-Communist' forces, but this did not bring about the Nationalist victory the United States had hoped for. (See Chapter Five for China's role in the globalization of the Cold War.)

When Mao Zedong and the CCP came to power in October 1949, the United States refused to recognize the Communist-controlled People's Republic of China (PRC) as a legitimate state. Instead, they backed Chiang Kai-shek and the Chinese Nationalists who, at the end of the Chinese civil war, had fled to the island of Taiwan, about 100 miles off the coast of mainland China. The Americans then ensured that it was the anti-Communists on Taiwan and *not* the People's Republic of China that was given China's seat at the United Nations.

Taiwan quickly became the key area of dispute between the USA and the PRC. However, there were other important areas of Sino-American tension: Korea, Japan and Tibet. The USA was also concerned over the Chinese development of nuclear weapons.

As Hugh Brogan put it:

The Chinese looked at the Americans through the same sort of telescope as that which the Americans were pointing at them. They too seemed to be a self-confident aggressor power making the first moves in a campaign that, unless unchecked, might lead on to world conquest.

Hugh Brogan in The Pelican History of the United States of America (Penguin, 1986) pp.625–6

These disputes were the focus for the underlying ideological conflict that initially mirrored the divide between the USA and the USSR. However, by the end of the 1960s there was a radical change in policy by both the Americans and the Communist Chinese in their policies towards one another.

The 1950s – increasing tension
Tibet, 1950

In 1950 the Chinese People's Liberation Army (PLA) invaded Tibet. This was not considered by Mao to be an issue of foreign policy, but entirely a domestic concern. After all, the Chinese saw this as part of their consolidation of the CCP's control of the mainland, and reunification of former Chinese territories.

However, this was not how much of the outside world viewed the brutality with which the Tibetans were suppressed. There followed a reign of terror in the region, and the United

China and the Cold War Timeline
For a full timeline of the events relating to China and the Cold War, see Appendix II.

States condemned the People's Republic for what it perceived as expansionism, as well as the horrific bloodshed. The Tibetan spiritual leader, the Dalai Lama, who later fled Tibet, called the actions of the Maoist regime '**cultural genocide**'.

The Korean War, 1950–1953

As has been discussed in Chapter Five, Korea was divided along the 38th parallel at the end of World War Two. The North was under a Communist regime and the South under an anti-Communist government. The North was supported by the Soviets, and the South, initially, had been supported by the Americans.

When the North, under Kim Il Sung, invaded the South in 1950, the U.S. State Department believed that this attack was under the direction of Josef Stalin and Mao Zedong. Indeed, they thought that this was a 'joint venture' by the new Communist bloc in Asia. However, as Michael Lynch comments, 'it is now known that Mao was as much taken by surprise by the North Koreans' move as the Americans were.'

The PRC had not been particularly concerned with the divided Korea. Its continuing focus was on the issues surrounding Taiwan and Tibet. It was also attempting to consolidate control within mainland China itself and to initiate 'revolutionary' reforms.

At the time, the Soviet Union was boycotting the United Nations because of the U.S. refusal to officially recognize the PRC. Therefore, in the vote to send troops into Korea to defend the South, the Soviet Union did not use its veto (see Chapter Five).

Mao condemned American action, but the USA justified its position by claiming that the North had been the 'aggressors'. Mao countered by claiming that the South had been the initial aggressors. Although U.S. forces arrived in South Korea under the UN flag in June 1950, the PRC's Zhou En-lai asserted that the U.S. troops were imperialist invaders.

The Chinese Foreign Ministry issued a public statement to be delivered at the UN by India, indicating its support for North Korea:

The American aggressors have gone too far. After making a five-thousand mile journey across the Pacific they invaded the territories of China and Korea. In the language of the American imperialists that is not aggression on their part, whereas the just struggle of the Chinese in defence of their land and their people is aggression. The world knows who is right and who is wrong …

United Nations Document S/1902, 15 November 1950, pp.2–4

The PRC organized mass demonstrations in China and warned the Americans that it would be forced to intervene if there was any push into the North. There were already thousands of the People's Liberation Army troops fighting with the North Koreans as 'volunteers'.

In October 1950, UN troops under General Douglas MacArthur crossed north over the 38th parallel and the PRC declared war. Over the next three years, millions of Chinese fought in Korea. By the time of the truce in 1953, the PLA had lost nearly a million men.

The impact of the Korean War on Sino-American relations

The Korean War led to open conflict between the USA and the PRC. The **Panmonjun Amnesty** did not bring about any degree of improvement. The Americans had previously been reluctant to guarantee long-term protection for Taiwan, but after the war they pledged themselves to the defence of the island. Also, Mao was now less in awe of the potential military might of the USA.

The key result of this war in terms of Sino-American relations was that the hostility between the People's Republic of China and the United States now became a key factor in international relations.

In addition, the PRC had been considerably weakened by the Korean conflict, both in terms of the loss of life and the economic cost of the war. However, politically, the war may have strengthened the position of the CCP. The fact that the Soviets had made the Chinese pay the entire bill for the cost of supplies helped to rally the Chinese to their own Communist Party, and made them more determined to stand alone. Mao emphasized that it was Chinese, and not Soviet, blood that had been spilled for the 'international Communist cause'.

STUDENT STUDY SECTION

Document analysis

On the Chinese mainland 600 million people are ruled by the Chinese Communist Party. That party came to power by violence, and, so far, has lived by violence. It retains power not by the will of the Chinese people but by massive, forcible repression. It fought the United Nations in Korea; it supported the Communist War in Indo-China; it took Tibet by force. It fomented the Communist Huk rebellion in the Philippines and the Communist insurrection in Malaya. It does not disguise its expansionist ambitions. It is bitterly hateful of the United States, which it considers a principal obstacle in the way of its path of conquest. As regards China, we have abstained from any act to encourage the Communist regime – morally, politically or materially. Thus: We have not extended diplomatic recognition to the Chinese Communist regime. We have opposed seating in the United Nations. We have not traded with Communist China or sanctioned cultural exchanges with it.

U.S. Department of State Bulletin, 15 July 1953

Question

What claims does the U.S. Department of State make about Chinese actions?

Taiwan, 1954 and 1958

The Korean War had altered the American perspective towards Asia and the Communist Chinese, and this included its policy on Taiwan. In early 1950 President Truman stated:

The United States has no desire to obtain special rights or privileges or to establish military bases on Formosa at this time. Nor does it have any intention of utilizing its armed forces to interfere in the present situation. The United States government will not pursue a course which will lead to involvement in the civil strife in China.

President Harry S Truman, 5 January 1950

However, by 1953, Taiwan had become a key territory in the American policy of containment in Asia (see Chapter Six).

This map shows the coast of China with Taiwan, Quemoy and Matsu.

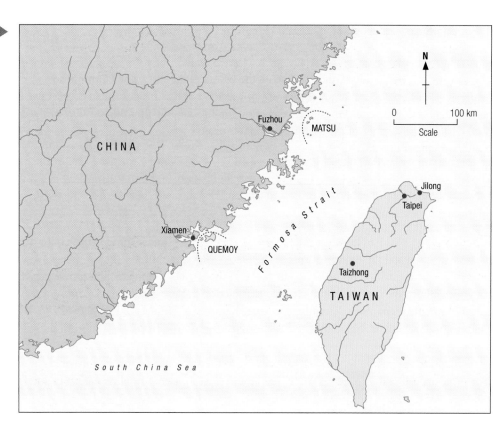

The PRC had not attempted to take Taiwan earlier for a number of reasons:

- Taiwan was well defended and the PRC was not confident it had the air power or the landing craft necessary.
- The U.S. Navy Seventh Fleet, which had been based in the area to secure it for strategic reasons during the Korean War, was now present.
- At the end of the Korean War, the United States stated it would protect Taiwan from aggression.

In 1954, Mao decided to test the commitment of the United States and shelled the islands of Quemoy and Matsu (see map). Eisenhower responded strongly, even suggesting that nuclear weapons would be used against military targets in China if Taiwan was directly threatened.

Why had the United States and Eisenhower responded so forcefully? Firstly, the United States had to show strength to its other allies in the region. It was also confident that the Soviet Union would not go so far as to support the PRC in a war. In addition, John Lewis Gaddis suggests that Nationalist leader Chiang Kai-shek had a role in bringing in the USA:

... when Mao began shelling the offshore islands in September 1954 ... Chiang claimed the psychological effects of losing them would be so severe that his own regime on Taiwan might collapse. Eisenhower and Dulles responded as they had to Rhee: Chiang got a mutual defence treaty that bound the United States to the defence of Taiwan.

John Lewis Gaddis in **The Cold War** *(Penguin, 2005) p.132*

In 1958, Mao began shelling Quemoy and Matsu again, and at the same time there was a build up of PLA troops in the area. U.S. Navy vessels were fired on in the Straits. The USA prepared for war with the PRC. In the end, no full-scale attack on Taiwan came. Mao had stepped back from the brink.

The United States believed that the People's Republic of China was an expansionist state and provided leadership for other revolutionary countries. This view of the PRC's aims linked into the American domino effect theory (see Chapter Six) and thus was perceived as a genuine threat to the security of the West. Therefore, the United States pursued the following policies in relation to the containment of China:

- a U.S. trade embargo with the PRC
- obstruction of PRC entry to the United Nations
- huge economic and military aid to Taiwan
- aid programme for the region
- instigation of a regional containment bloc – SEATO
- bi-lateral defence treaties with Asian states seen as under PRC threat.

The Sino-American Cold War in the 1960s

As was discussed in Chapter Five, McCarthyism had had a significant impact on American policies towards China during the Eisenhower administration. These policies were continued under the apparently more liberal administration of John. F. Kennedy, which maintained the policy of 'containment and isolation' of China.

The U.S. government used the failure of the Great Leap Forward (see Chapter Eleven) to highlight to the public and the rest of the West the excesses of this 'Marxist-driven economic experiment' and the PRC's willingness to sacrifice millions of the Chinese people in pursuit of its Communist ideology.

STUDENT STUDY SECTION

Cartoon analysis

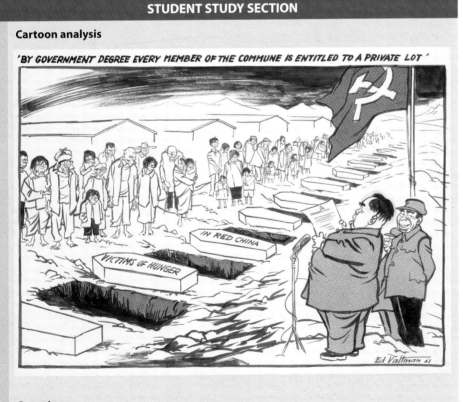

'BY GOVERNMENT DEGREE EVERY MEMBER OF THE COMMUNE IS ENTITLED TO A PRIVATE LOT'

IN RED CHINA

VICTIMS OF HUNGER

Ed Vaultman 61

Cartoon by Edmund Vaultman published in the West in 1961.

Questions

1 What is the message of the cartoonist here?

2 How would this message encourage support for American policy towards China at this time?

The key issues of dispute between the PRC and the United States in the 1960s were:
- Taiwan
- Vietnam
- decolonization movements
- the Chinese Cultural Revolution.

The United States, the PRC and Taiwan

Throughout the 1960s the PRC persisted in its demands for the reunification of Taiwan with the mainland. Indeed, as Margaret Macmillan writes: 'The existence of a separate government and another China was an affront to the Chinese nation and to Chinese nationalism' (*Seize the Hour: When Nixon Met Mao*, John Murray, 2006, p.228).

Although there was no return to the brink of war that had occurred between the USA and the PRC in the 1958 crisis, the issue was of fundamental importance to the Chinese. This was their overriding preoccupation, and no compromises, such as 'two Chinas', were acceptable to them. Any improvement in Sino-American relations could only be possible, in the PRC's view, when Taiwan no longer existed as a separate state.

The United States, Vietnam and the People's Republic of China

The war in Vietnam seriously heightened the tension between the USA and the Asia-Pacific region, including America's own allies. The PRC condemned American involvement in Vietnam as 'imperialism' and cited Taiwan as another key example of its expansionism in the region. Mao also claimed that the UN was dominated by the imperialist policies of the West.

STUDENT STUDY SECTION

ToK Time

Think about the following questions:
- As a ToK student, what criteria do you use to distinguish between knowledge, opinion and propaganda?
- Would this be more difficult for a child to do?
- What ways of knowing seem to develop as we become more mature? Do these give us a better grasp of truth?

Document analysis

Read the lyrics to this Chinese children's song:

> There is an evil spirit:
> His name is Johnson.
> His mouth is all sweetness,
> But he has a wolf's heart.
> He bombs Vietnam cities
> And hates the people.
> Chinese and Vietnamese are all one family:
> We will certainly not agree to this!
> I wear a red scarf and join the demonstrations with Daddy.
> With small throat but large voice I shout:
> 'U.S. pirates get out, get out, get out.'

Quoted in L. Mitchinson, *China* (Bodley Head, 1966)

Question

How useful is this source as evidence of Chinese public opinion about the Americans during the Vietnam War?

The PRC and decolonization

The PRC's interest in supporting revolutionary/decolonization movements in the developing world was not simply a pursuit of limited ideological goals in those specific countries. It aimed to ultimately replace the USSR as the world leader of international revolution, and to end Western imperialism by supporting anti-colonial movements.

At the **Bandung Conference** in 1955, PRC Premier Zhou asserted that the USA was the key danger to world peace. The conference had been held in response to the USA's involvement in setting up SEATO, which was an anti-Communist alliance. At this conference, 29 Asian and African states asserted their neutrality.

In 1966, Dean Rusk outlined the USA's policy towards China to the U.S. Congress:

- The USA does not seek to overthrow the PRC.
- The USA objects to PRC involvement in the affairs of other countries, that is, encouraging revolutionary forces worldwide by providing training.
- Although the PRC is more violent in word than action, it still should not be underestimated.

However, despite the rhetoric and the PRC's propaganda in support of 'revolutionary' movements, such as the 'Shining Path' in Peru, China did not have the resources to make a definitive difference in the developing world. Even when China had developed its own nuclear weapons, it did not have the delivery systems to use them in wars of decolonization. Therefore, the threat to the developing world posed by the PRC, as perceived by the USA and outlined by Dean Rush in 1966, was probably exaggerated.

The USA and the PRC's Cultural Revolution

As mentioned in Chapter Eleven, the Great Leap Forward and the Cultural Revolution led to a collapse in the PRC's ability to conduct any real foreign policy. The American view of the turmoil going on inside China was similar to the Soviet perception – it was a clear demonstration of the out-of-control fanaticism of the Maoist leadership, which seemed to lack both stability and coherency. The PRC was seen as a danger to the region, and a perpetual threat to the delicate balance envisaged by the American State Department that prevented the 'dominoes' from tipping over.

During the Cultural Revolution, the Chinese increased the ferocity of their attacks on the United States and its allies (calling them 'capitalist running dogs'). The PRC seriously feared an American attack aimed at bringing about 'regime change'. This, together with the threat of attack by the Soviets, made the PRC leadership incredibly nervous during the first years of the Cultural Revolution.

STUDENT STUDY SECTION

Cartoon analysis

Question

What is the message of the cartoonist here?

'The New Religion' by Edmund Vaultman, 1966, published in the West.

Sino-American détente in the 1970s

Four key areas were the focus for Sino-American relations in the 1970s:

- Taiwan
- Vietnam
- The United Nations
- The Soviet Union.

Détente between the two powers started in 1969 when the United States began to ease trade restrictions. In addition, the patrols by the U.S. Seventh Fleet in the Taiwan Straits were halted. However, the major turning point in Sino-American relations came when the United States changed its policy towards the PRC and the United Nations.

There followed what has become known as 'ping-pong' diplomacy, where an American table-tennis team was invited to compete in China and secret talks took place between Henry Kissinger and Zhou En-lai. Ultimately there was the historic visit in 1972 of President Richard Nixon to Beijing to meet the Communist leadership, including a very sick Mao Zedong, during which a joint communiqué was issued establishing a new relationship between the two superpowers.

Why did the USA want détente with the PRC?

There were a number of reasons why the United States found that it was now the correct time to move towards détente with the Chinese:

- The situation in Vietnam had led the United States to believe containment was not possible there, and it wanted the PRC's assistance in its exit strategy.
- The USA wanted to put pressure on the Soviet–American attempts at détente.
- Nixon wanted to 'make history'.
- There was public support in the USA for more constructive strategies following the Vietnam War.
- The PRC had developed ICBM capability, so it was now the American view that it was more dangerous *not* to have contact.
- The USA hoped to be able to reduce commitments in Asia, while retaining bases in the Pacific.

These reasons reflect the changing perspectives in the United States on the nature of global Communism. The U.S. administration was beginning to understand that various Communist movements around the world were not as '**monolithic**' as it had long suspected, with President Nixon stating, 'Our foreign policy began to differentiate among Communist capitals'. Nixon suggested that the United States would now 'deal with countries on the basis of their actions, not abstract ideological formulas'. The membership of the UN was also changing, and the USA would not be able to control the vote as regards PRC membership for much longer. Both sides now seemed ready to give up attempts to attain hegemony in Asia. This was the key point of the February 1972 joint Sino-American statement, the Shanghai Communiqué.

STUDENT STUDY SECTION

Document analysis

Document A

Nixon … was gradually modifying his longstanding opposition to having the People's Republic in the United Nations. This was largely because of his moves towards the People's Republic, but also because it had become clear that the United States was about to lose the vote at the UN.

From Margaret Macmillan, *Seize the Hour: When Nixon Met Mao* (John Murray, 2006) p.211

Document B

China exemplified the great changes that had occurred in the Communist world. For years, our guiding principle was containment of what we considered a monolithic challenge. In the 1960s the forces of nationalism dissolved Communist unity into divergent centers of power and doctrine, and our foreign policy began to differentiate among the Communist capitals ... We would deal with countries on the basis of their actions not abstract ideological formulas ... [The U.S. and China] seemed to have no fundamental interests that need collide in the eager sweep of history.

From President Nixon's Foreign Policy Report to Congress, 1973

Document C

Once the Soviet Union could no longer count on permanent hostility between the world's most powerful and most populous nations ... the scope for Soviet intransigence would narrow and perhaps even evaporate. Soviet leaders would have to hedge their bets because a threatening posture might intensify Sino-American co-operation. In the conditions of the late 1960s, improved Sino-American relations became a key to the Nixon Administration's Soviet strategy.

From Henry S. Kissinger, *Diplomacy* (Simon and Schuster, 1995) p.719

Document D

Nixon's active pursuit of détente could not help but make China worry about a possible U.S.–USSR alliance against China. Nixon's opening to China, meanwhile made Russia's leaders fearful of a U.S.–China alliance directed against them.

From S.E. Ambrose, *Rise to Globalism* (Allen Lane, 1971) p.239

Questions

1   Link each of the above documents to one (or more) of the motives listed for why the USA wanted better relations with the PRC.

2   With reference to their origin and purpose, what are the values and limitations of using Documents B and C to research American motivations at this time?

3   Using these documents, and the information so far in this chapter and in the previous chapters of the book, what do you consider to be the most important reason for the USA's pursuit of better relations with Communist China? Explain your answer thoroughly.

● **Examiner's hint:**
For Question 4 you need to integrate both the documents and your own knowledge in your answer. It is important that you include both! Identify key points made in the documents and then develop these with extra information from Chapters Eleven and Twelve.

Why did China want détente with the USA?

There were various reasons why China thought it was the right time for détente with the United States.

- In the 1960s and 1970s the PRC saw the USSR as its main rival, so it wanted to reduce tensions with the USA.
- China could gain concessions on key foreign policy issues, for example, UN membership, Taiwan, U.S. withdrawal from Vietnam and Indochina as a whole.
- The PRC was worried about a resurgent Japan, and wanted its power limited.
- The PRC maintained that the détente would be 'temporary', and that it would remain vigilant against U.S. imperialism and aggression. Mao had argued in an article in 1940, 'On Policy', that it was legitimate to play off enemies and to do whatever was necessary to defeat the main enemy at a given time.
- Moderation of their stance against the West could improve the PRC's standing in the Third World.

STUDENT STUDY SECTION

Document analysis

Document A

Word went out to party officials to prepare for Nixon's visit by studying Mao's negotiations with the Guomindang after the Second World War. 'Why shouldn't we negotiate with President Nixon?' Zhou asked a visiting British journalist. 'For instance, in the past we talked with Chiang Kai-shek.'

Margaret Macmillan, *Seize the Hour: When Nixon Met Mao* (John Murray, 2006) p.203

Document B

In September with the fear of Soviet attack building … Zhou En-lai [was sent] a … report which underlined … earlier conclusions. 'The last thing the U.S. imperialists are willing to see is a victory by the Soviet revisionists in a Sino-Soviet war, as this would [allow the Soviets] to build up a big empire more powerful than the American empire in resources and manpower.' Although in the long term China was struggling against both powers, its strategy should be to use one against the other.

Margaret Macmillan, *Seize the Hour: When Nixon Met Mao* (John Murray, 2006) p.143

Document C

While they blamed the United States for Japan's resurgence, they also recognized that the United States could act as a brake on its rearmament and expansion.

From Margaret Macmillan, *Seize the Hour: When Nixon Met Mao* (John Murray, 2006) p.233

Document D

It was only in June 1970, after his anti-American manifesto of 20 May had flopped, and when it was inescapably clear that Maoism was getting nowhere in the world, that Mao decided to invite Nixon to China. The motive was not to have a reconciliation with America, but to relaunch himself on the international stage.

From Jung Chang and Jon Halliday, *Mao: The Unknown Story* (Random House, 2005) p.601

Questions

1 Documents A, B and C are all extracts from Margaret Macmillan's book *Seize the Hour*. Which key motives for the PRC's interest in better relations with the USA are suggested by Macmillan?

2 What extra reason for improved relations is given in Document D?

3 Using these documents, this chapter, and the broader contextual understanding you have gained from Chapter Eleven in this book, what do you think is the key reason why Mao and the PRC sought better relations with the USA at this time? (See Examiner's Hint on page 141)

What did China gain from détente with the United States?

The People's Republic of China attained some of its objectives and several benefits from pursuing détente with the Americans:

United Nations membership: It was unrealistic of the PRC to hope to become a member of the United Nations in the 1950s as the General Assembly was dominated by Western countries. To become a member it would need a majority vote in the General Assembly. Every year a vote was taken on PRC membership, and each time it was defeated. In 1961 the United States had sufficient support for the 'important questions' resolution to pass, which meant the question of PRC membership would now need a two-thirds majority.

In 1965, the U.S. ambassador to the UN, Adlai Stevenson, outlined why United States did not believe the PRC should be a member state:

- The CCP was not the legitimate government of China – it had come to power through force, not by democracy. It also used force to maintain its power.
- It had a record of aggression, and was thus not a 'peace-loving' nation.
- Its sponsorship of revolutionary groups in the developing world would hamper UN work in these areas.
- Taiwan had an honourable record, and should not be expelled.

However, as UN membership grew, it was the non-aligned states and developing countries that began to dominate the General Assembly (see Chapter Fifteen). Indeed, in 1970 the General Assembly finally voted in favour of the Chinese UN seat transferring to Beijing. However, it was not the neccessary two-thirds majority. In 1970, the United States initiated the 'two Chinas' policy. This suggested that Beijing take the Security Council seat for China, while Taiwan still maintain representation in the General Assembly. This solution was rejected by both Chinas.

Finally, in the summer of 1971, President Nixon announced his imminent visit to the PRC and also stated that the United States would no longer oppose Beijing's admission to the UN. The USA failed to prevent the expulsion of Taiwan. In reality, the Americans were simply accepting the inevitable.

Result of UN membership for PRC: The PRC now had the power of the veto in the UN Security Council. It could be used to block resolutions, an example of this being a PRC veto which prevented the admission of Bangladesh to the UN in 1971. This was done in retaliation for the 'victory' of the USSR and its Indian allies over the PRC-backed Pakistan in the Indo-Pakistan War. With its wider access to diplomatic contacts through the UN, the PRC also gained better links with countries in the developing world. It was able to increase its prestige and influence, to present views on the world stage, and publicly support its allies and denounce its enemies (including the USSR).

President Richard Nixon and his Secretary of State, Henry Kissinger, meeting with PRC Chairman Mao Zedong and Premier Zhou En-lai.

Taiwan: It had always been the Chinese Communist view that Taiwan belonged to China, and that it was not a negotiable issue. Indeed, Macmillan suggests that Taiwan was as important to the PRC as their problems with the USSR. When Zhou met Kissinger in July 1971 he said of Taiwan: 'That place is no great use for you, but a great wound for us.'

In 1972 Nixon declared, 'The ultimate relationship between Taiwan and the mainland is not a matter for the U.S. to decide'. This was a key foreign policy objective for the PRC and was a main reason for their pursuit of détente. However, progress towards reunification was very slow – the United States did not want to hurry its transference of official recognition to the PRC, nor was it comfortable with the idea of 'giving up' Taiwan.

The issue dragged on until U.S. President Jimmy Carter finally established full diplomatic relations with China in 1979. At the same time, arms sales to Taiwan were halted. As historian Hsu comments, 'The majority of Americans … found it hard to oppose the simple mathematics of … relations with 900 million people on mainland China compared with the 17 million on Taiwan'.

However, Jimmy Carter was defeated by the fiercely anti-Communist Republican candidate, Ronald Reagan, in the 1980 presidential election, and a renewed 'Cold War' ensued. Reagan again committed the United States to protecting Taiwan. He resumed arms sales and Sino-American relations deteriorated. Even though the PRC had failed to reunite Taiwan with the mainland, it had to remain relatively diplomatic over the issue. China did not want to provoke the USA at a time when relations with the USSR remained tense.

Japan: The improved relations with the United States had, as the Chinese hoped, an impact on their relations with Japan. On 12 August 1978, China and Japan signed a friendship treaty. The relationship developed over the next few years, particularly in economic ties. Within five years of their friendship treaty, China had become second only to the United States as a trading partner with Japan. This had an additional benefit for the PRC as it was a further pressure on the Soviet Union. The Soviets were concerned at this new friendship between historic enemies, and the situation led to more fears in the USSR of being 'encircled'.

STUDENT STUDY SECTION

Document analysis

Document A

Cartoon by Chappette, published in the West in 1979.

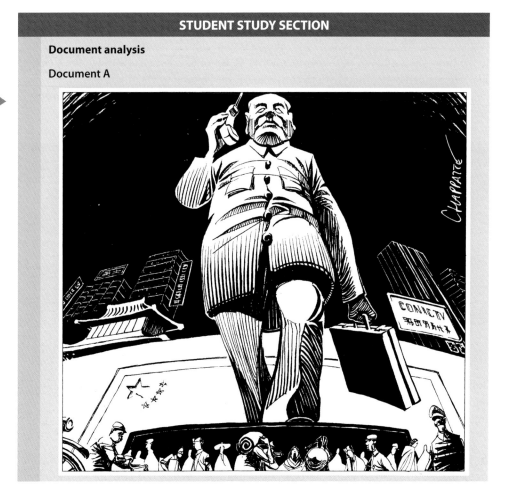

What did the U.S. gain from détente with the PRC?

The Americans also gained certain benefits from détente with the PRC.

Vietnam: There was something of a **paradox** in the American attempt to use the PRC to help them get out of Vietnam. Although better relations had been useful in adding weight to the American side in negotiations, it tended to be indirect. In other words, it was more the leverage that the Sino-American détente gave them with the Soviets that assisted in negotiations with the North Vietnamese. The drawback was that the Americans were never convinced – after the War in Korea – that China would be true to their word and stay out of Vietnam. Some historians, such as Kissinger, have suggested this led the USA to half-measures in Vietnam for fear of provoking Chinese intervention. Nevertheless, as Fitzgerald points out:

... a truce ... was finally signed in January 1973. The Americans firmly believed that Soviet pressure had played an important part in softening Hanoi's negotiating position.

From James Fitzgerald, The Cold War and Beyond *(Nelson, 1995) p.127*

This pressure had been achieved, at least in part, by the new U.S. policy towards China.

Wider contacts: In addition, the new U.S. policy towards China did result in pressure on the USSR to maintain détente with USA. However, the Americans were ultimately unwilling to 'play the China card' in relations with the USSR. They feared creating even more instability, especially if the Soviets began to feel encircled. It had some impact on relieving the U.S. commitment to mainland Asia. The less aggressive stance pursued by the Americans towards the Asian superpower was popular both in Asia and Europe. To a certain extent, it also made up for the U.S. government's loss of face over its changed policy as regards the PRC's seat at the UN.

Question

According to Hsu, what are the key benefits for the Americans of better relations with China?

Review question

To what extent was the Sino-Soviet détente equally beneficial to the USA and the PRC?

The PRC and the Cold War

China emerges as a significant factor in the development of the Cold War. The importance of Communist China's role in the Cold War changed over time. The PRC's influence grew in line with their nuclear power status, their increasingly hostile relationship with the USSR and, ultimately, their growing rapprochement with the USA. This shift in the balance of power resulted in the Cold War becoming more of a 'tri-polar' (USA, USSR, PRC) conflict rather than 'bi-polar' (USA, USSR).

Tiananmen Square, the PRC and the United States, 1989

Following the death of Mao Zedong in 1976, the removal of the fiercely anti-American Gang of Four, and the modernization initiatives of Deng Xiaoping, relations between the PRC and the United States became more co-operative on one level. During the Reagan administration there had been some degree of 'cooling off' in terms of the diplomatic developments between the two powers, but this had not been a return to the 1960s period of hostility. As Macmillan writes, 'While Sino-American relations did not go back to what they had been before Nixon's visit, they did not move ahead either.'

In 1989, the Tiananmen Square pro-democracy protests in Beijing were violently crushed by the government in China (see Chapter Eleven). This flagrant abuse of human rights led to protests on the streets in many Western countries, including the United States. Despite the public demands for a tough response to the actions of the PRC, ultimately Tiananmen Square made little difference to China's international position, including its relations with the United States. There was worldwide condemnation, but no diplomatic isolation or **economic sanctions**. The United States did not want to damage its trade links with the PRC.

STUDENT STUDY SECTION

Document analysis

Document A

Deng accuses U.S. of deep role in democracy protest

Mr Deng Xiaoping, the Chinese paramount leader, yesterday accused the United States of being deeply involved in the country's 'counter-revolutionary rebellion', dealing the most damning blow so far to reconciliation. Mr Deng told Mr Richard Nixon, the former U.S. President, that while China had not done anything to damage America in the past decade 'frankly speaking, the U.S. was involved too deeply in the turmoil and counter-revolutionary rebellion which occurred in Peking not long ago'.

The Times newspaper, 1 November 1989.

The United States, the PRC and the end of the Cold War

In the early 1990s, the new Russian government withdrew its forces from the Pacific. At the same time, the United States did not renew the lease on its naval base in the Philippines. With the ending of the Cold War proper, Communist China was left dominant in the western Pacific. The PRC really was the leader of Communist nations now, but this was at a time when Communism was in crisis. The former satellite states in Eastern Europe had all seen their Communist regimes collapse, some quietly and some with bloodshed.

Instead of seizing its opportunity to export its particular brand of Communism, the new leadership in China focused on its development as a world power. This meant establishing its economic power rather than concentrating on its ideological concerns. In 1992 the United States gave the PRC '**most favoured nation status**'. Trade links have boomed. The United States and China are now important economic partners, with mutually vital interests and investments.

ToK Time
What are the advantages and disadvantages for historians writing about the history of a country or region which has a different culture to their own?

Question

What future problems for Sino-American relations are identified in Documents A and B?

Exam practice

Attempt to draw up a 'thermometer' of Sino-American relations using the events covered in this chapter. There are some starting points shown here:

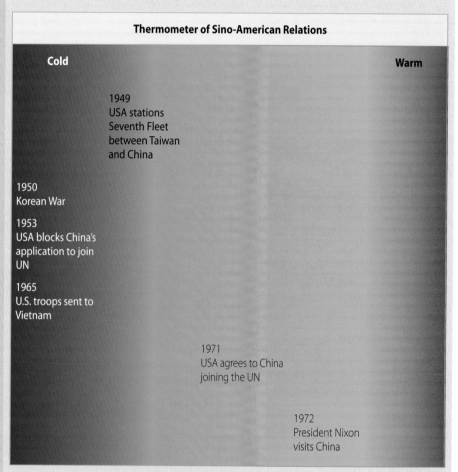

Thermometer of Sino-American Relations

Cold — Warm

1949
USA stations
Seventh Fleet
between Taiwan
and China

1950
Korean War

1953
USA blocks China's
application to join
UN

1965
U.S. troops sent to
Vietnam

1971
USA agrees to China
joining the UN

1972
President Nixon
visits China

Approaching essay questions on Sino-American relations

1   *Why was there a Sino-American détente in the 1970s?* Consider the long-term and short-term causes. Or consider a thematic approach.

2   *Why was there a Sino-American détente in the 1970s, and to what extent was it successful?* Use your plan from the first question to answer the first part of this question. You will now need to analyse the successes and failures for China and then for the USA in the second part of the essay. You should assess the success and failure of détente based on the 'aims' outlined in this chapter, and to what extent they were achieved for each country.

Approaching essay questions on China and the Cold War

3   *Analyse the role of China in the Cold War.* Using the information in this chapter and Chapter Eleven attempt to draw up a thematic approach. This will help you avoid a chronological or narrative response. Consider the changing nature of relations between the PRC and both the USSR and the USA. The rise of Communist China to superpower status, and the importance of 'tri-polar' rather than 'bi-polar' relations in the Cold War, should be included.

One thematic approach that could be used for Question 3 is the following:

Main body of essay

Part 1: Argue that Communist China's key role was in increasing tension in the Cold War, that the PRC made the Cold War more dangerous and war more likely. Include examples of events that support this view.

Part 2: The counter-argument could be that the role of the Communist Chinese in the Cold War was actually a **catalyst** for better relations between the USA and the USSR, that is, the transition of a bi-polar situation to a tri-polar was a key reason for détente between the USSR and the USA.

Include examples of events to support this view.

Conclusion

This could consider how the role of Communist China changed over time during the Cold War.

13 WHY DID DÉTENTE END IN A SECOND COLD WAR?

While reading this chapter, consider the following essay questions:
- Why did détente take place?
- Did détente actually lead to any fundamental changes in the attitudes that the USA and the USSR had towards each other?
- What were the achievements of détente?
- Why did détente collapse?
- To what extent can détente be seen as a failure?

The period known as 'détente' started around 1968 and finally ended in 1980 with the victory of Ronald Reagan in the U.S. presidential election. The term détente means 'a relaxation of tension' and, during the 1970s, it was the word used to describe the attempts of the USA and the USSR to establish a more stable and co-operative relationship. It is also used to describe the improvement in relations between the USA and China, and between Western Europe and the Soviet Union. After 1980, however, détente between the USA and USSR was replaced with a period that became known as the 'second Cold War'.

Détente timeline

1968	Richard Nixon elected U.S. president
1969	Nuclear Non-Proliferation Treaty signed by over 100 countries
1970	SALT talks open in Vienna
1971	Treaty to denuclearize the seabed signed by 74 countries
	Nixon accepts invitation to visit China
	UN admits China to membership (Taiwan expelled)
1972	Nixon visits China
	Nixon visits USSR for summit with Leonid Brezhnev
	SALT I signed
	East Germany and West Germany sign Basic Treaty
1973	Washington Summit between Nixon and Brezhnev
	Yom Kippur War
1974	Moscow Summit between Nixon and Brezhnev
	Nixon resigns over Watergate; Gerald Ford becomes president
	Vladivostok Summit between Ford and Brezhnev
1975	Helsinki Final Act signed by 35 countries
1976	Jimmy Carter elected as U.S. president
1978	Carter warns USSR against involvement in domestic affairs of other countries
1979	USA and China open diplomatic relations
	Shah flees Iran
	Carter and Brezhnev sign SALT II agreement in Vienna
	U.S. Embassy in Tehran seized and diplomats taken hostage
	USA announces plans to deploy cruise missiles
	Soviet forces invade Afghanistan
1980	U.S. Senate suspends SALT II debate
	Ronald Reagan elected U.S. President
1981	U.S. hostages released by Iran
1982	Death of Brezhnev; Yuri Andropov becomes Soviet leader
1983	Reagan explains SDI
	USSR shoots down Korean Airlines flight 007 over its airspace
	First cruise missiles arrive in Europe
1984	Death of Andropov; Konstantin Chernenko becomes Soviet leader
	Reagan re-elected U.S. president

What were the reasons for the Soviet–American rapprochement?

One of the factors pushing the superpowers towards an improvement of relations was the growing awareness of the dangers of nuclear war. As you have seen, the early 1960s saw serious confrontations over Berlin and Cuba and, by the late 1960s, both the United States and the Soviet Union were ready to take steps to reduce the risk of nuclear confrontation. This was also made possible by the fact that by 1969 the USSR had reached nuclear parity with the United States, meaning it now had a similar nuclear capability to the USA and so, for the first time, could negotiate from a position of equality.

Both superpowers also had their own individual reasons for wanting a relaxation of tensions.

The USSR's reasons for détente

One of the key reasons the USSR needed better relations with the United States was that its economy was stagnating. In order to deal with its economic problems, and also to improve the standard of living for Soviet citizens, it needed to be able to transfer economic resources from the production of armaments to production of consumer goods, and also to import technology from the West.

A second key factor was the USSR's deteriorating relationship with China. As was discussed in Chapter Twelve, the Sino-Soviet split had almost ended in war in 1969 and it was now crucial for the USSR to keep China isolated from the West by itself seeking an improved relationship with the West.

The USA's reasons for détente

Détente was initiated by Richard Nixon, who was elected president in 1968, and his National Security Adviser, Henry Kissinger. Nixon needed to find a way of ending the Vietnam War and he also wanted the United States to follow a more realistic foreign policy which would take account of the changing international situation. This was in pursuit of *realpolitik*:

Henry Kissinger called for a 'philosophical deepening' of American foreign policy. By this he meant adjusting to the changed international order. The Kennedy and Johnson administrations, Kissinger argued, had focused too much on victory in one rather isolated area – Vietnam – at the expense of the global balance of power. The world was shifting from a bipolar balance of power between Washington and Moscow to a multipolar balance shared among five great economic and strategic centres – the United States, the Soviet Union, Western Europe, Japan and China.

John Mason in The Cold War *(Routledge, 1996) p.51*

Therefore, Nixon hoped to use détente to get the USSR and also China to put pressure on North Vietnam to end the war and, at the same time, to retain and 'deepen' the USA's global role – through negotiation rather than confrontation. Arms control would also free up resources that could be used to deal with the faltering American economy.

Henry Kissinger
Henry Kissinger was Richard Nixon's National Security Advisor and was considered to be an expert on international relations. Under first Nixon, and later President Ford, for whom he was Secretary of State, he travelled all over the world establishing contacts with leaders of different countries. He was a skilled negotiator and played a key role in negotiations to end the Vietnam War, in Arab-Israeli peace negotiations (1973–1978) and in setting up key meetings for Nixon with the USSR and China as part of the détente process.

Cartoon analysis

'Captain Brezhnev Runs Aground', a cartoon by Jeff MacNelly from the *Chicago Tribune* newspaper.

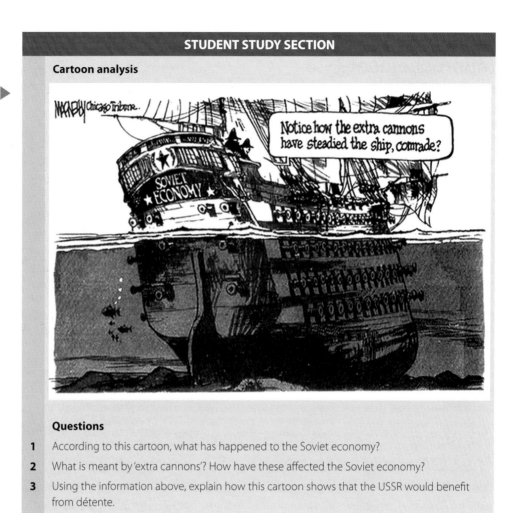

Questions

1 According to this cartoon, what has happened to the Soviet economy?

2 What is meant by 'extra cannons'? How have these affected the Soviet economy?

3 Using the information above, explain how this cartoon shows that the USSR would benefit from détente.

What were the reasons for PRC–USA rapprochement?

Chapters Eleven and Twelve have discussed in detail Sino-American and Sino-Soviet relations. China's relations with the Soviet Union were at a very low point in the late 1960s. China was worried about international isolation and so saw improved relations with the United States as a way to prevent this and, at the same time, get back at the Soviet Union. For the USA, an improved relationship with China was part of the new *realpolitik* approach to foreign policy.

The principal reason for seeking a rapprochement with China was to restore fluidity to the overall international situation. If there are five players and you can't deal with one of them, this produces rigidity. Secondly, we wanted to demonstrate to the American public that Vietnam was an aberration, that we had ideas for the construction of peace on a global scale.

Henry Kissinger, interviewed on the CNN television series, **The Cold War**

In addition, the Americans knew that working with the Chinese would give them extra 'leverage', or negotiating power, in their dealings with the Soviets.

What were the reasons for improved East–West relations in Europe?

There was also pressure for détente from Europe. Events in 1968 had shown political instability in both East and West Europe with the Soviet invasion of Czechoslovakia, and student riots and strikes in France, which had seriously undermined President Charles de Gaulle. The new chancellor of West Germany, **Willy Brandt**, took the lead in trying to improve relations between the two Germanys. He believed that not only West Germany, but also the whole continent, would benefit from a reduction of tensions and greater links between East and West. His policy of encouraging the opening of channels between East and West became known as *Ostpolitik*.

From the Soviet side there was also impetus for improved relations in Europe. A formal peace treaty accepting the new borders of Europe after World War Two had never been signed, and the Soviets wanted to win Western acceptance of the division of Germany and formalize the existing territorial situation in Eastern Europe.

What were the successes of détente?
Arms agreements between the USA and the USSR: SALT I

After the Cuban Missile Crisis, the USA and the USSR signed several arms control agreements (see page 101) The most significant arms control agreement, however, was SALT I (the Strategic Arms Limitation Treaty), signed in 1972. This treaty covered agreement in three areas:

The ABM Treaty: ABMs (Anti-Ballistic Missiles) were allowed at only two sites, each site containing no more than 100 missiles. As discussed in Chapter Ten, this limitation was key for ensuring the continued emphasis on MAD and thus the deterrence of nuclear war.

The Interim Treaty: This placed limits on the numbers of ICBMs (Inter-Continental Ballistic Missiles) and SLBMs (Submarine-Launched Ballistic Missiles).

The Basic Principles Agreement: This laid down rules for the conduct of nuclear war and development of weapons, and committed the two sides to work together to prevent conflict and promote peaceful co-existence. It was followed in 1973 by the Agreement on the Prevention of Nuclear War, which said that if a nuclear conflict looked imminent, both sides would '… immediately enter into urgent consultations with each other and make every effort to avert this risk'.

John Mason writes that SALT I, 'began a process of institutionalized arms control, confirmed the Soviet Union's parity with the United States, and reduced tension between the two nuclear powers' (Mason, *The Cold War*, p.53). It was followed by a spirit of co-operation as Nixon made visits to Moscow in 1972 and 1974, and Brezhnev visited Washington in 1973.

However, there were also severe criticisms of SALT I for not going far enough in limiting nuclear weapons, particularly because it did not mention MIRVs (Multiple Independently Targeted Re-entry Vehicles). Stephen Ambrose writes that this omission made the treaty 'about as meaningful as freezing the cavalry of European countries in 1938, but not the tanks'. (*Rise to Globalism*, Penguin, 1993).

SALT II

Many areas for discussion still remained and negotiations for SALT II began in 1974, with the treaty finally being signed in 1979. This treaty had agreements on:

- a limit on the number of strategic nuclear delivery vehicles (ICBMs, SLBMs and heavy bombers) for each side.
- a ban on the testing or deployment of new types of ICBMs, heavy mobile ICBMs and rapid reload systems.

This was the most extensive and complicated arms agreement ever negotiated. However, by the time it was signed, both Democrats and Republicans were criticizing the arms control process as one that accomplished little and which gave advantages to the Soviets. It was never ratified by the U.S. Senate.

Agreements between the two Germanys and the Soviet Union

Willy Brandt in 1970 kneeling at the memorial to the victims of the Warsaw Ghetto. Egon Gahr, who was an adviser to Willy Brandt, said in an interview that 'Brandt was a stroke of luck for German history. For the Americans he symbolized reliability – he had proved himself the defender of Berlin against the menace of the East. And for the East, he was a resistance fighter against the Nazis.' (Gahr in an interview on the CNN television series, *The Cold War*)

A number of treaties were made between the Soviet Union, East Germany and West Germany in the early 1970s:

The Moscow Treaty: This was signed in August 1970 between the Soviet Union, Poland and the Federal Republic of Germany. It recognized the border between East Germany and West Germany and also formally accepted the post-World War Two border in the East with Poland.

The Final Quadripartite Protocol (1972): This was a major victory for Willy Brandt as it agreed to the maintenance of the 'status quo' in Berlin, confirming that the West had a legal basis for its access routes to the city. Therefore, West Berlin had a much greater degree of security.

The Basic Treaty (1972): This was signed by East Germany and West Germany. It accepted the existence of two Germanys. West Germany now recognized East Germany and agreed to increase trade links between the two countries.

These agreements did much to reduce tension in Europe, though they were criticized by some in the United States for giving legal recognition to Soviet control over Eastern Europe and formalizing the Cold War divisions in Europe.

Agreements between the United States and China

There were also several significant areas of improvement in relations between the USA and China:

- The USA dropped its objections to China taking its seat on the Security Council. Therefore, mainland China (the PRC) replaced Taiwan.
- Trade and travel restrictions between the two countries were lifted.
- Sporting events between the two countries took place, the most famous being the visit of the U.S. table-tennis team to Beijing (so-called ping-pong diplomacy).
- Nixon visited China – the first American president to do so.

Détente between the United States and China was spurred on by the deterioration of relations between China and the USSR, and it also gave the USA more leverage and bargaining power in its arms agreements with the USSR. This became know as 'triangular diplomacy'. The USA, however, did not abandon Taiwan and continued to stand firm in its support of Taiwan's independence from mainland China.

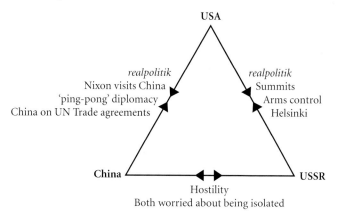

This diagram shows triangular diplomacy between the USA, the USSR and China.

The 'high point of détente': the Helsinki Agreement

Kissinger, Brezhnev, Ford and Gromyko outside the U.S. Embassy in Helsinki, 1973.

At the Moscow summit of 1972, President Nixon agreed to participate in a European Security Conference. This was held in Helsinki in 1973. It was attended by 33 countries and produced a final agreement (the Final Act) on 1 August 1975. This took the form of three so-called 'baskets':

- **Basket 1**: This was the security basket. It followed Willy Brandt's *Ostpolitik* negotiations with the Soviet Union and recognized that Europe's frontiers were 'inviolable', that is, they could not be altered by force. Thus both East Germany and West Germany were now recognized by both sides of the Cold War divide.

- **Basket 2**: This was the co-operation basket. It called for closer ties and collaboration in economic, scientific and cultural fields.

- **Basket 3**: This was the human rights basket. All of the signatories agreed to respect human rights and individual freedoms, such as freedom of thought, conscience or religion, and freedom of travel.

Given the Soviet attitude towards human rights, Basket 3 was clearly the most controversial of the agreement. The West hoped that it would undermine Soviet control in the satellite states, and organizations were set up to monitor Soviet action against the principles set out in the Helsinki Agreement. However, for Brezhnev, the important aspects of the Helsinki Agreement were Baskets 1 and 2, and he was thus prepared to sign the agreement despite Basket 3.

Another result of détente was co-operation in space. On 17 July 1975, three U.S. astronauts and two Soviet cosmonauts met up when their spacecrafts docked 140 miles above the earth. Co-operation in what was seen as a key area of Cold War conflict – the space race – seemed symbolic of the improved international atmosphere.

STUDENT STUDY SECTION

Document analysis

Views on the Helsinki Agreement

Document A

No one should try, on the basis of foreign policy considerations of one kind or another, to dictate to other peoples how they should manage their internal affairs. It is only the people of each given State, and no one else, who have the sovereign rights to decide their own internal affairs … A different approach is flimsy and perilous ground for the cause of international co-operation.

Leonid Brezhnev, speech at the Helsinki Conference, 31 July 1975

Document B

The members of the Politburo read the full text. They had no objections when they read the first and second articles. When they got to the third 'humanitarian' article, their hair stood on end. Suslov said it was a complete betrayal of Communist ideology. Gromyko then came up with the following argument: The main thing about the Helsinki treaty is the recognition of the borders. That's what we shed our blood for in the Great Patriotic War. All 35 signatory states are now saying these are the borders of Europe. As for human rights, Gromyko said, 'Well, who's the master of this house? We are the masters of this house and each time it will be up to us to decide how to act. Who can force us?'

Anatoly Dobrynin, former Soviet Ambassador to United Nations, interviewed on the CNN television series, *The Cold War*

Document C

The Soviet Union and the Warsaw Pact nations did not recognize that the human rights provision was a time bomb. We the United States believed that if we could get the Soviet Union and the Warsaw Pact nations to respect human rights that was worth whatever else was agreed to in the Helsinki Accords.

Former President Gerald Ford, interviewed on the CNN television series, *The Cold War*

Document D

Critics of the Helsinki Conference found it difficult to reconcile many provisions of the Final Act with the Soviet invasion of Czechoslovakia in 1968, the Brezhnev Doctrine justifying that invasion and the dismal record on human rights in the Eastern bloc countries. The West seemed to gain nothing more than vague promises of good behaviour from the Soviet Union. When the Eastern bloc governments made no real improvements in their handling of human rights issues, disillusionment with détente set in rapidly in the West.

John Mason in *The Cold War* (Routledge, 1996)

Document questions

1   Read Documents A and B. What was the attitude of the Soviets towards
    a Basket 1 of the Helsinki Agreement?
    b Basket 3 of the Helsinki Agreement?
2   In what way does Document B support Document A?
3   According to Gerald Ford (Document C) what was the attitude of the United States towards
    Basket 3? Why do you think that he refers to Basket 3 as 'a time bomb'? (Document D gives a
    clue about this.)

Review question

What do you consider to be the most important achievements of détente?

Why did détente between the USA and the USSR come under pressure?

Détente came under pressure for a number of reasons. Firstly, many in the United States felt that the arms agreements were benefiting the Soviets – that the USSR was building up a strategic superiority based on its ICBMs.

Secondly, actions in the Middle East and Africa seemed to indicate that the Soviet Union was continuing to expand its influence.

- When the Yom Kippur War started in October 1973, the USA suspected that the USSR had known in advance about Egypt's surprise attack on Israel. Following the agreement mentioned earlier, which the USA and the USSR had signed promising to inform each other of any conflict that might threaten world peace, the attack on Israel and its aftermath 'definitely damaged the trust between the leadership of both countries' (Anatoly Dobrynin).

- The Soviet Union was also involved in the civil war in Angola, supporting the Popular Movement for the Liberation of Angola (MPLA) with military aid. Soviet aid, along with aid given by Cuba, was key to the success of the MPLA.

- The Soviets and Cubans were also involved in supporting Ethiopia against Somalia in 1977. The scale of Soviet intervention was worrying to the Americans and it seemed that the Soviets were involved in some grand scheme of expansion in several key areas of the world. In fact, it was more a case of the Soviets randomly assisting Marxist rebels throughout the world. As Dobrynin notes, this policy was a kind of 'ideological bondage', which did not in fact benefit the Soviet Union in the long term.

Thirdly, as already mentioned, there was disillusionment over the Soviet Union's attitude towards the human rights 'basket' of the agreement made at Helsinki. Under Jimmy Carter, who was elected U.S. president in 1976, the United States increasingly tried to link economic deals to improved human rights when trading with the USSR, for example, to tie improved trading conditions to the Soviet Union allowing Soviet Jews to emigrate. This 'linkage' was deeply resented by the Soviet Union.

All of these factors meant that by the end of the 1970s 'the complexities and contradictions of détente had become explosive' (James Fitzgerald, *The Cold War and Beyond*, Nelson, 1992 p.136).

Why did détente collapse?

Détente was already struggling to survive by the late 1970s, but it collapsed completely when the Soviets invaded Afghanistan in 1979. The reasons for this invasion are discussed in more detail in Chapter Sixteen, but for the Americans this invasion seemed final proof of 'real' Soviet intentions, that is, their determination to spread their influence beyond their borders and thus, as Carter put it, to be a serious threat to world peace. Carter responded to Soviet actions by refusing to approve SALT II, stopping all electronic exports to the Soviet Union and forbidding U.S. athletes from participating in the 1980 Moscow Olympic games. He also pledged to increase defence spending in real terms for each of the next five years, and announced the Carter Doctrine which committed the United States to intervention if the Soviets threatened Western interests in the Persian Gulf.

This map shows Iran and neighbouring countries. ▶

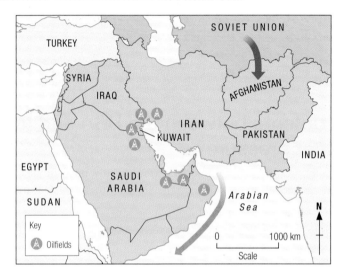

Did détente fail? The historiography of détente

Writers in the mid 1970s, and of course the autobiographies of Richard Nixon and Henry Kissinger, stress the positive achievements of détente in terms of reducing tension and the threat of nuclear war. This view is supported by Post-revisionist historians, such as Bowker and Williams in *Superpower Détente, a Reappraisal* (Sage, 1988). They point out that détente was a necessary strategy to deal with the international situation and to find methods of managing competition 'in a way which prevented them from degenerating into hostilities'.

John Lewis Gaddis also points out that to call détente a failure is to misunderstand what détente was about in the first place. It was not ever intended to end the arms race, to internally reform the Soviet Union in the area of human rights or to prevent Soviet–American rivalry in the developing world. It was intended to turn 'a dangerous situation into a predictable *system*' and indeed American–Soviet relations in the late 1960s and the 1970s were arguably less dangerous than were the first two decades of the Cold War.

The Carter administration and the Iran crisis

Jimmy Carter was a Democrat who was elected President in 1976 – the first president from the southern states since the American Civil War. He had some notable achievements during his presidency, such as the Camp David Agreements on the Middle East which brought peace between Egypt and Israel. However, he faced difficult issues in foreign policy and was often inconsistent due to the fact that his two key advisers, Zbigniew Brzezinski (National Security Adviser) and Cyrus Vance (Secretary of State) had very different views on these issues – Brzezinski being much more hardline in his approach to the Soviets than Vance.

The most damaging event for President Carter was the takeover of Iran by radical Muslim fundamentalists led by Ayatollah Ruhollah Khomeini. This forced the U.S.-backed Shah to flee his country. The Shah had been a valuable anti-Communist ally in the Middle East and his fall was a major defeat for U.S. foreign policy. When President Carter allowed the Shah to enter the United States for medical treatment, Iran retaliated by seizing the U.S. Embassy in the Iranian capital, Tehran, and taking 52 diplomats as hostages. The intention was to hold the hostages until the Shah was returned to Iran for trial. When the United States tried to rescue the hostages in a covert military operation, the mission ended in failure. The hostages were later released at the beginning of the Reagan presidency.

The rightwing of American political history, however, interprets détente as a weak policy that allowed the Soviet Union to continue to strengthen itself and gain access to Western technology at the expense of American interests. One of the main supporters of this view is Richard Pipes, who views détente as nothing more than a 'trick' on the part of the Soviets. The collapse of the Soviet Union in the late 1980s is seen as a result of hardline policies towards the Soviet Union. Détente had failed because it had helped to keep the Soviet Union going.

ToK Time
Review your ToK notes on 'paradigms'. Could it be argued that a key problem for détente in the longer term was that there had been no real 'paradigm shift' in the way the USSR or the USA perceived each other? To what extent are 'paradigms' cultural, or guided by religion or politics?

The Second Cold War

Ronald Reagan had been elected to power on a wave of anti-Communist feeling and a belief that the USA had to reassert its power in the world. Reagan also believed that détente had been a failure:

So far détente's been a one-way street which the Soviet Union has used to pursue its own aims. I know of no leader of the Soviet Union, since the Revolution and including the present leadership, that has not more than once repeated in the various Communist congresses they hold their determination that their goal must be the promotion of world revolution and a one-world Socialist or Communist state.

Ronald Reagan, quoted in the International Herald Tribune, *31 January 1981*

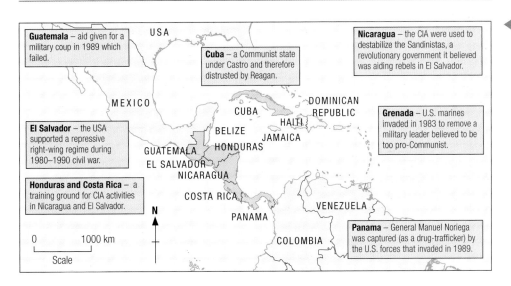

This map shows U.S. involvement in Central America in the 1980s.

Reagan put his tough anti-Soviet policy into action in a number of ways:

- Defence spending was increased by 13 per cent in 1982 and over 8 per cent in each of the following two years.

- New nuclear weapons were developed, including the stealth bomber and Trident submarines.
- A new Strategic Defense Initiative was announced in 1983 ('Star Wars').
- The Reagan Doctrine was announced. This gave assistance to anti-Communist insurgents as well as anti-Communist governments – for example, the Contras, a right-wing guerrilla group fighting against the Communist government of the Sandinistas in Nicaragua. The USA also supported an unpopular right-wing government in El Salvador against a growing popular revolt by the left and, in 1983, U.S. forces invaded the Caribbean island of Grenada and deposed its left-wing government (see map on page 159).
- He used aggressive language towards the Soviets, calling them an 'evil empire' and 'the focus of evil in the modern world.'

Reagan was supported in his hardline approach by Prime Minister Margaret Thatcher of the United Kingdom.

The renewed tension in the Cold War was not helped by the situation in the Soviet Union, where ageing and infirm leaders prevented any kind of initiative or strong leadership. Brezhnev died in 1982 to be succeeded first by Yuri Andropov – who was already an ill man when he took over – and then Konstantin Chernenko in 1984, who himself only lived another year.

The most dangerous point in this 'second cold war' era was the shooting down by the Soviets of a Korean airliner which had flown into Soviet airspace. All of the 269 passengers were killed and there was outrage in the West. The Soviets claimed it was a CIA spy plane and refused to give any clarification as to the situation that had led to shooting down a civilian Boeing 747. Reagan's administration condemned Moscow for what it called a 'callous and brutal attitude to human life'.

On 28 September 1983, Yuri Andropov denounced the actions pursued by the United States as 'a militarist course which poses a grave threat to peace', and concluded that 'one begins to doubt whether Washington has any brakes at all to prevent it from crossing the line before which any sober-minded person must stop' (Yuri Andropov, 'Statement' in the Soviet newspaper, *Pravda*, 28 September 1983).

However, this bleak situation in the Soviet–American relationship was to change radically with the appointment of Mikhail Gorbachev as Premier of the Soviet Union in 1985.

Essay work

Planning essays is an essential way to revise topics as you approach examinations. In pairs or groups, plan out the following essays. Your plan should include:

- an introduction written out in full
- the opening sentence for each paragraph
- bullet points giving an idea of the information to go in each paragraph
- a conclusion written out in full.

Essay questions

1 'Détente defined, not friendship, but a strategy for relationships among enemies.'
   What brought about détente and what changes, if any, did it cause in East–West relations?

2 To what extent did the Cold War become less confrontational between 1970 and 1980?

3 'Despite the claims of those who promoted détente, its achievements were limited'. How far do you agree with this opinion?

4 How and why did détente collapse in the late 1970s and early 1980s?

Document analysis

The following documents all relate to the SALT talks.

Document A

SALT was silent on the issue of multiple independently targeted re-entry vehicles (MIRVs) so the Russian advantage in missile numbers was matched by the US advantage in deliverable warheads. The agreement did not cover medium-range and intermediate-range missiles, nor bases in Europe. However, SALT was an important first step. It would eventually usher in a new era of détente between the superpowers. In 1972 the SALT I Treaty effectively froze the military balance between the Soviet Union and the U.S. They now realized that each side must be able to destroy each other, but only by guaranteeing its own suicide.

An extract from Jeremy Isaacs and Taylor Downing, *Cold War: An Illustrated History, 1945 – 1991* (Little, Brown and Co. 1998).

Document B

The effort to achieve strategic arms limitation marked the first, and the most daring, attempt to follow a collaborative approach in meeting military security arrangements. Early successes held great promises, but also showed the limits or readiness of both superpowers to take this path … The early successes of SALT I contributed to détente and were worthwhile … There was remarkable initial success on parity and on stability of the strategic arms relationship but there was insufficient political will (and perhaps political authority) to ban, or sharply limit, MIRVs.

An extract from a book by former American diplomat and member of the U.S. SALT I delegation, Raymond L. Garthoff, *Détente and Confrontation: American Soviet Relations from Nixon to Reagan* (Brooking Institution, 1994).

Document C

The domestic political difficulties of the Nixon administration contributed to the failure to conclude a new SALT treaty … The main obstacle to progress on arms control, however, was the evident unwillingness of both superpowers to abandon the arms race with each other. Behind the public advocacy of détente and disarmament, lay the reality that the freeze on missile numbers in SALT I had never been intended to prevent either side from continuing to develop and modernize its existing weapons.

An extract from a book by a lecturer in American diplomatic history at the University of Exeter in the UK, Joseph Smith, *The Cold War 1945 – 1991* (OUP, 1998).

● **Examiner's hint:**
Here are some questions you should consider while planning your essays:

- Does the essay specify dates? How does this affect your choice of information to be included?
- Does the essay title give clues as to the structure you should follow?
- Is there a quote which you need to refer to/explain/ come back to in your conclusion?
- Does the question require you to make a judgement?
- Where can you include historiography?

Each group should present its essay plan to the rest of the class. How much overlap of content is there between the different essay plans?

Document questions

1   Remember to look back to Chapter Five at the guidelines to answering questions on documents and the Examiner's hint on page 141.

2   In what ways do the views expressed about SALT I in Document A support the conclusions expressed in Document B?

3   What are the value and limitations of Documents B and C for historians studying the SALT agreements?

4   How successful was arms control during the 1970s? Use these three documents and also the information in the rest of this chapter to answer this question. Refer to the documents directly in your answer.

14 WHAT WAS THE IMPACT OF THE COLD WAR ON THE UNITED NATIONS?

While reading this chapter, consider the following essay questions:

1 How far did the Cold War have an impact on the effectiveness of the United Nations?
2 How did the rivalry between the USA and the USSR affect the working of the United Nations?
3 What was the role of the United Nations in the Cold War?

Timeline of United Nations and the Cold War

1941	**Aug**	Atlantic Charter agreed by Roosevelt and Churchill
1943	**Nov**	Tehran Conference
1944	**Aug**	Dumbarton Oaks Conference
1945	**Feb**	Yalta Conference
	April	San Francisco Conference
1946	**Feb**	UN's first Secretary General, Trygve Lie, takes office
1948	**April**	Berlin Crisis
1950	**June**	North Korea invades South Korea
	July	UN resolution authorizes Korean force under U.S. 'Unified Command'
	Aug	Soviets return to Security Council
	Nov	'Uniting for Peace' resolution passed by General Assembly
1953	**April**	Dag Hammarskjöld, second UN Secretary General takes office
	July	Armistice signed in Korea
1956	**July**	Nasser nationalizes Suez Canal
	Oct	Soviets crush Hungarian Uprising
		U.S. draft resolution calls for withdrawal of Israel from Suez
	Nov	UN establishes United Nations Emergency Force sent to Suez
1958	**June**	UN Observation Group sent to Lebanon
1960	**June**	Congo gains independence
	July	Congolese Prime Minister Lumumba asks for UN assistance
		UN establishes operation force for Congo (ONUC)
	Sept	Lumumba under UN protection
		Khrushchev claims ONUC 'pro-Western' force
1961	**Jan**	Lumumba murdered
	Feb	Security Council authorizes ONUC to use force if necessary
	Aug–Oct	UN unsuccessful operations against secession group in Congo
	Sept	Death of Hammarskjöld; U Thant of Burma succeeds him
1962	**Oct**	Cuban Missile Crisis
1963	**Jan**	Congolese 'secession' finally ended under UN pressure

The flag of the United Nations Organization.

◀ This timeline reflects the events covered in this chapter and is not a comprehensive catalogue of the UN's involvement in international crises in the second half of the 20th century. Some significant themes are not covered here, such as much of the UN's involvement in the Middle East during the Cold War.

1964	June	Withdrawal of ONUC from Congo
1967	May	UNEF withdrawn from Suez
1971	Oct	People's Republic of China replaces Taiwan as 'China' in UN
1975	April	Civil war breaks out in the Lebanon
1978	March	Israel invades Lebanon
1979	Dec	Soviet invasion of Afghanistan
1982	June	Israel re-invades Lebanon
1988	April	UN mission to Afghanistan and Pakistan established
1989	Nov	Berlin Wall comes down
1990	March	UN completes mission in Afghanistan and Pakistan
1992	Jan	Boutros Boutros-Ghali of Egypt becomes Secretary General
	March	UN protection force established for the former Yugoslavia
	April	United Nations Operation in Somalia established
1995	March	UN withdraws from Somalia
	Nov	Dayton Agreement signed on Bosnia

The UN and the Cold War: the background

The United Nations had been planned in the Atlantic Charter of 1941. The subsequent Allied meetings at Tehran (1943) and at Yalta and Potsdam (1945) continued to develop the plans for this new international organization. The Allies wanted to build a safer world, and to prevent a world war ever happening again. The key aims of the new United Nations Organization were to:

- maintain international peace and security
- develop friendly relations among nations
- achieve international co-operation in solving problems
- act as the centre for collective action (Article 1 of the United Nations Charter).

So, the first purpose of the United Nations was essentially the same as that of its ill-fated predecessor, the League of Nations – keeping peace. However, the Allies attempted to redress what they saw as the main reasons for the League's failure to maintain peace, that is, the lack of commitment to peacekeeping from member states, particularly in providing military back-up. This problem had been exacerbated by the need to attain a unanimous decision to act on any resolution.

The basic idea of 'collective security', where member states work together to stop aggressor states and potential conflict, was to be the key working principle of the United Nations. The main advocates for the new organization were Roosevelt and Churchill. Indeed, the Charter itself was generally an Anglo-American document.

STUDENT STUDY SECTION

Research task

Compare and contrast the Covenant of the League of Nations (Articles 10 and 16) with the Charter of the United Nations (Articles 39–51, Chapter VII).

Does the United Nations Charter appear to give the organization more strength than the Covenant of the League of Nations? (You can find the Charter at www.un.org)

The structure of the United Nations Organization

The Allies wanted to promote the idea of 'the equal right of men and women and nations large and small' and to establish the conditions under which 'justice and respect for the obligations arising from treaties and other sources of international law can be maintained.' There are six main areas in the United Nations structure:

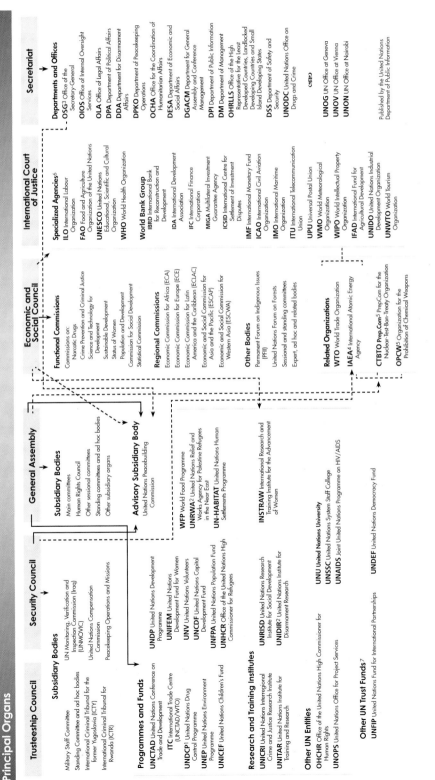

The United Nations System

Principal Organs

Trusteeship Council

Subsidiary Bodies

Military Staff Committee
Standing Committee and ad hoc bodies
International Criminal Tribunal for the former Yugoslavia (ICTY)
International Criminal Tribunal for Rwanda (ICTR)

Security Council

Subsidiary Bodies

UN Monitoring, Verification and Inspection Commission (Iraq) (UNMOVIC)
United Nations Compensation Commission
Peacekeeping Operations and Missions

Programmes and Funds

UNCTAD United Nations Conference on Trade and Development
 ITC International Trade Centre (UNCTAD/WTO)
UNDCP[1] United Nations Drug Control Programme
UNEP United Nations Environment Programme
UNICEF United Nations Children's Fund

UNDP United Nations Development Programme
 UNIFEM United Nations Development Fund for Women
 UNV United Nations Volunteers
UNCDF United Nations Capital Development Fund
UNFPA United Nations Population Fund
UNHCR Office of the United Nations High Commissioner for Refugees

WFP World Food Programme
UNRWA[2] United Nations Relief and Works Agency for Palestine Refugees in the Near East
UN-HABITAT United Nations Human Settlements Programme

Research and Training Institutes

UNICRI United Nations Interregional Crime and Justice Research Institute
UNITAR United Nations Institute for Training and Research

UNRISD United Nations Research Institute for Social Development
UNIDIR[2] United Nations Institute for Disarmament Research

INSTRAW International Research and Training Institute for the Advancement of Women

Other UN Entities

OHCHR Office of the United Nations High Commissioner for Human Rights
UNOPS United Nations Office for Project Services

UNU United Nations University
UNSSC United Nations System Staff College
UNAIDS Joint United Nations Programme on HIV/AIDS

Other UN Trust Funds[7]

UNFIP United Nations Fund for International Partnerships

UNDEF United Nations Democracy Fund

General Assembly

Subsidiary Bodies

Main committees
Human Rights Council
Other sessional committees
Standing committees and ad hoc bodies
Other subsidiary organs

Advisory Subsidiary Body

United Nations Peacebuilding Commission

Economic and Social Council

Functional Commissions

Commissions on:
Narcotic Drugs
Crime Prevention and Criminal Justice
Science and Technology for Development
Sustainable Development
Status of Women
Population and Development
Commission for Social Development
Statistical Commission

Regional Commissions

Economic Commission for Africa (ECA)
Economic Commission for Europe (ECE)
Economic Commission for Latin America and the Caribbean (ECLAC)
Economic and Social Commission for Asia and the Pacific (ESCAP)
Economic and Social Commission for Western Asia (ESCWA)

Other Bodies

Permanent Forum on Indigenous Issues (PFII)
United Nations Forum on Forests
Sessional and standing committees
Expert, ad hoc and related bodies

Related Organizations

WTO World Trade Organization
IAEA[4] International Atomic Energy Agency
CTBTO Prep.Com[5] PrepCom for the Nuclear Test-Ban-Treaty Organization
OPCW[5] Organization for the Prohibition of Chemical Weapons

International Court of Justice

Specialized Agencies[6]

ILO International Labour Organization
FAO Food and Agriculture Organization of the United Nations
UNESCO United Nations Educational, Scientific and Cultural Organization
WHO World Health Organization

World Bank Group

IBRD International Bank for Reconstruction and Development
IDA International Development Association
IFC International Finance Corporation
MIGA Multilateral Investment Guarantee Agency
ICSID International Centre for Settlement of Investment Disputes

IMF International Monetary Fund
ICAO International Civil Aviation Organization
IMO International Maritime Organization
ITU International Telecommunication Union
UPU Universal Postal Union
WMO World Meteorological Organization
WIPO World Intellectual Property Organization
IFAD International Fund for Agricultural Development
UNIDO United Nations Industrial Development Organization
UNWTO World Tourism Organization

Secretariat

Departments and Offices

OSG[3] Office of the Secretary-General
OIOS Office of Internal Oversight Services
OLA Office of Legal Affairs
DPA Department of Political Affairs
DDA Department for Disarmament Affairs
DPKO Department of Peacekeeping Operations
OCHA Office for the Coordination of Humanitarian Affairs
DESA Department of Economic and Social Affairs
DGACM Department for General Assembly and Conference Management
DPI Department of Public Information
DM Department of Management
OHRLLS Office of the High Representative for the Least Developed Countries, Landlocked Developing Countries and Small Island Developing States
DSS Department of Safety and Security
UNODC United Nations Office on Drugs and Crime

UNOG UN Office at Geneva
UNOV UN Office at Vienna
UNON UN Office at Nairobi

Published by the United Nations Department of Public Information

> Diagram showing the structure of the United Nations.

NOTES: Solid lines from a Principal Organ indicate a direct reporting relationship; dashes indicate a non-subsidiary relationship.

1 The UN Drug Control Programme is part of the UN Office on Drugs and Crime
2 UNRWA and UNIDIR report only to the GA
3 The United Nations Ethics Office and the United Nations Ombudsman's Office report directly to the Secretary-General
4 IAEA reports to the Security Council and the General Assembly (GA)
5 The CTBTO Prep.Com and OPCW report to the GA
6 Specialized agencies are autonomous organizations working with the UN and each other through the coordinating machinery of the ECOSOC at the intergovernmental level, and through the Chief Executives Board for coordination (CEB) at the inter-secretariat level
7 UNFIP is an autonomous trust fund operating under the leadership of the United Nations Deputy Secretary-General. UNDEF's advisory board recommends funding proposals for approval by the Secretary-General.

The General Assembly was to be a forum for discussion and decision-making for all member states. Each state, no matter how small, was given a vote. However, the Security Council of the United Nations was the most powerful body of the organization. The General Assembly could be *invited* by the Security Council to make recommendations when they were considering a dispute – but this was not required.

The Security Council was to be a sort of executive body, and would preside over the most important and critical issues – including the use of military intervention to resolve a dispute. Force would only be considered when absolutely necessary. There were initially to be four permanent members of the Security Council, the USA, the UK, the USSR and China, later rising to five with the inclusion of France. It was hoped that all other states would be guided by their decisions.

The Soviets were willing to accept apparent Security Council domination by pro-Western states (with Chiang's Taiwan representing China as the West refused to recognize the legitimacy of Mao Zedong's PRC), as each permanent member had the power of the 'veto'. Veto power gave each Security Council permanent member the power to block a decision agreed on by the other four.

The main principles of the United Nations

According to its Charter, the UN has the following main functions:
- to be a forum for discussion and decision
- to meet as a syndicate for action
- to employ non-forcible measures to improve the world
- to spread moral values and higher standards in international relations.

However, the ideological differences between the USA and the USSR predictably led to differences in the superpowers' interpretation of the UN's key ideas.

Firstly, both superpowers were concerned over issues of sovereignty. Neither the USA nor the USSR wanted its sovereign rights subordinated to the UN. Their powers of veto in the Security Council meant that they could usually block anything they considered against their country's best interests. But at the same time as the situation was bi-polar, it meant that the veto could also prevent them doing what they wanted to do. Therefore, the United Nations could only act when its most powerful members agreed to it.

Three key principles of the UN Charter

The *Collective Security Principle* underpinned most of the key principles of the UN Charter. Members were to take 'effective collective measures' to prevent and remove threats to peace and to suppress aggressive acts. Any call to action must come from the Security Council. However, with the Security Council dominated by the USA and the USSR, both with their powers of veto, it was clear that the Cold War blocs and not an independent United Nations would dominate what was interpreted as a threat to peace or an aggressive act.

The Charter did not allow for intervention in 'domestic matters' and this could be viewed as an important omission, as it allowed for the development of spheres of influence in the Cold War. The respective superpowers asserted that any 'suppression' of groups seen as anti-American or anti-Soviet in their sphere of influence was legitimate. There was also no clear directive for action in self-defence if one member state attacked another.

The *Regional Principle* allowed for the development of regional arrangements or agencies for dealing with threats to peace in a region, as long as they worked in line with UN principles. With Security Council authorization, these could be used to enforce UN resolutions. However, regional groupings were often developed within the superpower blocs.

The *Association Principle* set down that all 'peace-loving states' could be members of the United Nations. This principle, however, led the USA and the USSR into dispute, as they did not agree on which states qualified as genuinely 'peace-loving'. There was opposition to countries perceived as being in the Capitalist or socialist blocs. For example, between 1946 and 1961 the Soviet Union used its veto 96 times to block the memberships of Ceylon, Ireland, Italy, Jordan and Spain. The USA and its Western allies did likewise over the memberships of Albania, Bulgaria, Hungary and Romania. In addition the USA stopped the membership of Vietnam until 1976 and backed the representation of China by Taiwan at the UN until 1971. Thus, from the very outset, the Cold War had a direct impact on the very membership of the UN.

With the developmentof the Cold War in Europe, the early optimism soon ended, particularly in the West, for the potential of the United Nations. This new international organization was going to be hindered in its work by the bi-polar tension between the United States and the Soviet Union. The balance of power was held by the superpowers in the UN, and its role in the Cold War was to reflect this.

American expectations

Indeed, the superpowers had very different expectations of the United Nations. American hopes for the new institution, according to historian D.J. Whittaker, 'now strike us as very optimistic, even evangelistic'. The former isolationists had no practical experience as leaders in peacetime. The United States primarily believed that the international collective represented by the UN would support U.S. values. The UN was to promote only moderate and constructive change. Revolutionary and violent change was to be suppressed. The foundation for peace would be built on fostering U.S.-style economic objectives in a global free market.

President Harry S Truman declared to the opening conference of the UN in San Francisco: 'The powerful nations have a duty to assume responsibility for leadership toward a world of peace … By their own example the strong nations of the world should lead the way to international justice.'

Soviet expectations

The Soviet Union's expectations of the United Nations were very different. The Soviet delegates set out to use the UN to promote their ideological beliefs, both politically and economically opposed to the U.S. model. They saw the United Nations' role as purely to prevent another great war. The Soviets aimed to encourage revolutionary change but, perhaps paradoxically, they also wished to retain the balance of power. Economic and social change could not be based on a global free market, but on freeing people from exploitation. The Soviets were suspicious of the UN's Charter and of the International Court of Justice, as some key clauses appeared to support capitalist principles. Ultimately, the USSR viewed the UN's role as far more marginal than expressed in the initial hopes of the United States.

STUDENT STUDY SECTION

Review activity

In pairs, draw up a bullet point list of the key differences between the USA and the USSR in their interpretations of the UN Charter and the role of the United Nations.

The UN and nuclear weapons

At the onset of the UN, it was presumed that it would be responsible for atomic weapons control, but the superpowers ignored this function of the United Nations and sought to control atomic weapons through bi-lateral agreements.

The UN and the emergence of the Cold War

The post-war 1940s saw the development of the Cold War between the USSR and the USA. It soon became evident that the Cold War would have a defining impact on the role and operation of the United Nations. As Senator William Fulbright commented about the first years of the UN, it was 'a history of retreat from false hopes and of adjustment to the reality of a divided world.'

Inevitably, the potential of the United Nations as a viable world force for peace-making and peacekeeping was made very difficult, if not impossible, by the fact at its core were the two superpowers working against one another. It was unlikely that there would be much co-operation between the Americans and the Soviets, and this would have a dramatic impact on the ability of the UN to pursue its Charter meaningfully.

The United Nations took a back seat in the developments in Europe during 1945–1949. There was no 'collective' response to the Soviet occupation of Eastern Europe. The UN did not interfere when Truman declared his 'Doctrine' for Greece and Turkey. There was no UN alternative to the economic aid offered by the Americans to rebuild Western Europe, and bolster their political influence there. The USSR's intervention in Czechoslovakia in 1948 received mere condemnation from the UN. When the first real crisis of the Cold War developed in Germany, and the superpowers were on the brink of war over Berlin in the blockade of 1948–1949, the UN was powerless to intervene. As D. J. Whittaker suggests, by the end of the 1940s it was clear that 'Europe's collective security relied on the superpowers pulling back from the brink, without any prospect of UN intervention'.

Therefore, as the Cold War developed in the late 1940s, there was a very real danger that the UN would be at best marginalized or, at worst, become irrelevant as all major disputes increasingly became the focus of superpower hostility. The United Nations found that the only way of avoiding irrelevance was in pursuing the 'mediation principle'; in other words 'peacekeeping' would give the United Nations a role in the Cold War.

STUDENT STUDY SECTION

Document analysis

Document A

'Bicycle Built for Two', a cartoon by John Collins, 1947.

Document B

For the Americans, that term [justice] meant political democracy, market capitalism, and – in principle if not always in practice – respect for the rights of individuals. For the British and French, still running colonial empires, it meant something short of that; for the Chinese Nationalists, facing the prospect that the Chinese Communists might eject them from power, it meant even less. And for Stalin's Soviet Union, 'justice' meant the unquestioning acceptance of authoritarian politics, command economies, and the right of the proletariat to advance, by whatever means the dictatorship that guided it chose to employ, towards a worldwide 'classless' society ... It was hardly surprising, then that the United Nations functioned more as a debating society than as an organization capable of defining principles and holding states accountable to them.

Extract from John Lewis Gaddis, *The Cold War* (Penguin, 2005), p.159

Questions

1 What is the message of the cartoonist in Document A?

2 Explain the differences between each of the five permanent members of the Security Council and their understanding of 'justice' as explained in Document B.

3 What does Gaddis mean when he says that the UN functioned more as a 'debating society'?

The UN and the global Cold War: the 1950s

By 1950, the Cold War was poised to take on global dimensions. As hostility increased between the superpowers the apparent viability of the UN decreased further, international relations were increasingly determined by individual countries aligning with one or other of the superpowers. As historian Norrie Macqueen suggests, the 'idea of [an] independent "disinterested" global body seemed … unworkable'.

In April 1950, U.S. NSC-68 (see Chapter Five) stated that the USSR was a 'slave society' and claimed that the spread of Communism must be resisted by force. The rise of McCarthyism led to accusations in the United States that Americans working for the UN were in fact working for the Soviets – spying against the USA. Nevertheless, the United States had the majority of support in the UN at this time, and many saw the UN's role as a tool of American foreign policy. Indeed, this attitude to the UN was made clear by an aide of Truman in 1948, who wrote, 'The United Nations is a God-given vehicle through which the United States can build up a community of powers … to resist Soviet aggression and maintain our historic interests'.

The Soviets also saw the UN as being turned into a tool of the Western capitalists, a key example of which was the American refusal in 1949 to recognize Mao's new People's Republic as the legitimate Chinese government. The USSR was boycotting the United Nations as a result of this when the Korean War broke out in 1950.

1950s Case Study 1: Korea 1950-53

The Security Council had the responsibility to decide on which crises were real threats to peace or 'acts of aggression', and then decide on what action to take. As discussed in Chapter Five, the UN sent a military force to Korea in response to the invasion of the South by the North in 1950.

The Soviet Union had vetoed the South Koreans joining the UN, and the USA would not recognize the legitimacy of the North Korean government. On 25 June 1950, the Security Council learned of the full-scale invasion of the South and discussions began on what the UN response should be. The faith that the United States had in the UN at this stage can be seen in how it took this crisis straight to the UN and was ready to fight under its flag.

However, the USSR was not present due to its **boycott**, and this meant that the Security Council was made up solely of pro-Western powers. The USSR, therefore, was not there to use its veto. This made a mockery of the UN's principle of collective security.

Following a Security Council resolution on 25 June 1950 calling for the withdrawal of Northern troops from the South, on 27 June a resolution was passed recommending UN members to assist the South. Meanwhile, the United States had begun its own unilateral efforts – it had sent in air strikes and a bombardment by the 7th fleet. On 30 June, using Article 51 'collective self-defence' as its justification, U.S. troops based in Japan were sent to Korea.

With no Soviet veto, an Anglo-French resolution was passed by the Security Council on 7 July, calling for a 'Unified Command' to fight in Korea. Under the command of U.S. General Douglas MacArthur, the UN force was primarily an American army. The USA had, in reality, seized the initiative and sought UN resolutions after the event. MacArthur was under the control of the U.S. government first, and merely had to inform the Security Council of decisions and outcomes. This was not a truly multilateral force, with other troops mainly from NATO countries.

However, the situation in the UN changed dramatically at the beginning of August when the USSR returned to the Security Council, at a point when it was the Soviets' turn to hold the presidency of the Council.

The American objective was now to take the North, and ultimately to reunify Korea under a Western-style government. However, there was no real mandate from the UN to cross into the North. With the USSR back in the Security Council, a resolution backing this plan would be vetoed. The Americans then came up with a plan that would change the balance of power in the UN in their favour.

The United States planned to get around the power of the veto in the Security Council by transferring power to the General Assembly, where they had majority support. On 3 November 1950, the General Assembly passed the 'Uniting for Peace' resolution. This resolution stated that decisions over security could be transferred to the General Assembly when action by the Security Council was blocked by veto.

As Norrie Macqueen writes,

In effect the United States arranged to move the constitutional goal posts to serve its military and political objectives. If the Charter gave the Soviet Union the power to block enforcement with its veto, the Charter could be changed.

Norrie Macqueen in **The United Nations Since 1945: Peacekeeping and the Cold War** *(Longman, 1999) p.17*

The Soviets were incensed. The key reason they had agreed to join the UN was so that they would have the power of veto in the Security Council. The 'Uniting for Peace' resolution made this worthless. In addition to this, another Security Council resolution calling on China to withdraw from Korea was blocked by the USSR, but then passed by a General Assembly vote.

However, as the military situation became more difficult with the People's Liberation Army from China in force by 1951, the Americans changed their objectives. They no longer pushed for unification, and Truman sacked MacArthur. With the limitation of U.S. aims, the UN could take back more of a mediator role and seek a compromise. An armistice was agreed in July 1953.

The UN action in Korea was generally seen in the West as a success for UN enforcement. However, it was seen in the Soviet Union as merely an anti-Communist force, with the West perceived as having manipulated the UN. Indeed, Khrushchev later warned the Security Council that his country would 'never entrust the security of the Soviet Union to a foreigner.'

By this stage, not all Americans remained convinced of the UN's capabilities either. The general view in Washington, which was shared by George Kennan and also held by the U.S. Joint Chiefs of Staff, was 'Faith in the ability of the United Nations as presently constituted to protect, now or hereafter, the security of the United States would mean only that the faithful have lost sight of the vital security interest of the United States.'

For the United Nations the Korean War simply provided the empirical proof of what its members and officials had come to accept: that collective security and Cold War were incompatible.

From Norrie Macqueen, **The United Nations Since 1945: Peacekeeping and the Cold War** *(Longman, 1999) p.18*

STUDENT STUDY SECTION

Cartoon analysis

'Tank trap' by John Collins, 1950.

Questions

1   What is the message of the cartoonist?

2   Does this cartoon support the idea that the UN was a 'tool of American foreign policy'?

1950s Case Study 2: the Suez Canal Crisis, 1956

Although Korea was viewed by many as a failure for the UN in its role as an independent organization during the Cold War, its role in the Suez Crisis is seen more favourably.

In 1953, the UN had a new Secretary General, a Swede named Dag Hammarskjöld. He was seen by many countries as more 'independent' than his predecessor, who had been viewed as pro-Western. Hammarskjöld had a new vision for the role of the UN in the context of the Cold War. He wanted the UN to act *before* a military collective security response was needed. His idea was for peacekeeping forces to be focused on preventing the development of conflict.

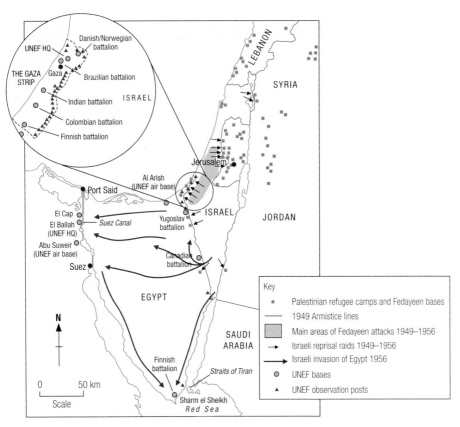

This shows Egypt and Israel at the time of the Suez Canal Crisis.

The origins of the Suez Crisis lay in the actions of the Egyptian President, Gamal Abdel Nasser. Although he had initially received American backing for his ambitious Aswan Dam project, he had then provoked U.S. hostility by receiving arms from Czechoslovakia. With funding now withheld, Nasser retaliated by nationalizing the Suez Canal. The canal had been built by the French, but was part-owned by the British. It was a vital waterway for British and French shipping. Neither the British nor the French could tolerate Egyptian control of Suez, and so the British initiated a plan with the Israelis to take back control.

The plan was for Israel to launch an attack on the Canal Zone, and for the British and French to then send in a force to 'protect' the area from the ensuing conflict. The USA was not informed of this plan. On 29 October 1956, Israel launched its attack.

The United States was furious when it heard about the attack, and called a Security Council meeting on 30 October to discuss the crisis. A U.S. draft resolution called for the withdrawal of Israeli forces and, as a pointed criticism of Britain and France, also called on other UN members not to intervene. For the first time, Britain applied its veto.

Some historians have claimed that this was the worst internal crisis faced by the Western bloc during the Cold War.

The crisis was then passed to the General Assembly and on 4 November the Assembly passed a resolution creating the first UN peacekeeping force, the United Nations Emergency Force (UNEF). This force would maintain its independence by including forces only from countries outside the Security Council. The UNEF force had a limited mandate, and had to follow tight restrictions on its authority:

- It would be in occupation only temporarily, to establish stability and the cessation of conflict.
- It would have no role in the political or military conditions of the region.
- It would have no power within Egypt, only being located along ceasefire lines.
- Costs were to be borne by individual contributors.

The USSR remained concerned at the transfer of power to the General Assembly and was worried about the development of UNEF. However, the Soviets tolerated the mission, as it was a further embarrassment to the West, since the UK and France had been the cause of the crisis.

UNEF forces began to arrive in Egypt on 15 November 1956. Before the end of December, British and French troops had been withdrawn. In terms of its aims, this first peacekeeping force was successful. However, for the UN in the Cold War context, this success was muted. The Americans and Soviets had not been working against each other during the crisis, so this was really the key factor as to why UNEF had been effective.

1950s Case Study 3: the Hungarian Uprising, 1956

The brutal crushing of the Hungarian Uprising (see Chapter Sixteen) was a failure for the United Nations. The rising happened, unfortunately for the Hungarians, at the same time as the Suez Crisis. This meant that the UN was quite literally looking the 'other way', that is, focusing on the Middle East rather than Europe at the time.

The Hungarian government had appealed to the UN for assistance, but the USSR vetoed the Security Council resolution which requested Soviet withdrawal from Hungary. The General Assembly then passed the same resolution, and a committee was set up to investigate the crisis. However, the Soviets simply refused to co-operate with the committee. This rendered the UN powerless. Unlike the pressure successfully exerted on Britain and France in Egypt, the Soviets responded by ignoring the UN.

The Hungarian Uprising demonstrated that the superpowers were beyond the control of the UN. The UN could only exert authority over lesser powers, and when it had the backing of the USA and the USSR.

STUDENT STUDY SECTION

Review activity

Statement by the new Hungarian government to the Security Council, 12 November 1956:

Soviet troops are here for the purpose of restoring law and order, and at the request of the Hungarian government. We cannot permit UN observers to enter Hungary, since the situation is purely an internal affair of the Hungarian state.

Question

What problems were there for the UN in dealing with the issue of 'internal affairs' in the Cold War context?

Impact of the Cold War on the UN's first decade

The Cold War had had a rather negative impact on the early years of the United Nations. The American-led mission in Korea had ultimately broadened the conflict into a war with China. It had also gone beyond the UN's principal mandate. The success of the independent UN 'peacekeeping' in Suez was limited, as it was only possible because both superpowers had backed the campaign.

The UN had failed to act during the Soviet invasion of Hungary. It also failed to act against American interference in the internal affairs of sovereign states in the 1950s. Using covert operations, the USA was involved in the overthrow of the Iranian government in 1953 and in Guatemala in 1954.

Research question

Research how the USA was involved in Iran in 1953 and in Guatemala in 1954, and the responses of the UN.

The UN and the Cold War: the 1960s
Case Study: The Congo

In the 1960s, African states began to emerge from colonial domination. Many African nationalist movements became embroiled in the ideological battle between the East and the West. These former colonies often needed support in setting up their new independent administrations and infrastructures, and were economically vulnerable after the withdrawal of their European colonizers.

The Congo had been under the colonial rule of Belgium. The Belgians left on 30 June 1960, not wanting to engage in a potentially drawn out conflict with growing Congolese nationalist groups. Belguim had announced its imminent withdrawal only six months beforehand, and the Congo was not adequately prepared for independence. For example, there were no Congolese-trained doctors, lawyers or military officers.

The Crisis Only two weeks after independence, the new regime was already in trouble. On 12 July, the new Prime Minister, Patrice Lumumba, and the President, Joseph Kasavubu, asked the UN for help with a 'domestic crisis'. The new country's national army (the *Armée Nationale Congolese* – ANC) had mutinied. There remained in the Congo a large Belgian population, and so the Belgian government sent in troops to protect its nationals from the rampaging ANC.

To add to the general internal chaos, the local leader of the mineral-rich southern province of Katanga, Moise Tshombe, declared that his territory was independent. The Lumumba government believed that Tshombe had made this declaration under the influence of the British and the French, who it believed wanted control over the potential riches of this region.

There were several key problems for the United Nations in dealing with the crisis in the Congo. These included how to:
- achieve the withdrawal of Belgian forces
- restore public order
- defend a UN force, as the Congolese national government was not in control
- avoid interference in local politics. This would be very difficult as the UN would be acting on behalf of the Lumumba government against the group who had seceded.
- prevent the crisis drawing in the superpowers.

The UN response Working with a similar idea to the peacekeeping force that was deployed during the Suez Crisis, Hammerskjöld appealed to the Security Council for a force to be sent to oversee the withdrawal of Belgian troops. The resolution was put forward in the Security Council by Tunisia and passed. Britain and France did not use their vetoes to block the resolution, but did abstain from the vote. A UN force called *Operation des Nations Unies au Congo* or ONUC was set up. This would be the most difficult mission for the UN since its creation.

Prime Minister Lumumba had at first turned to the superpowers for help. However, both the USA and the USSR had referred him back to the UN. This suggests that, initially, neither superpower had seen the Congo as a vital interest to them. They also perhaps foresaw the potential for a drawn out conflict in the country.

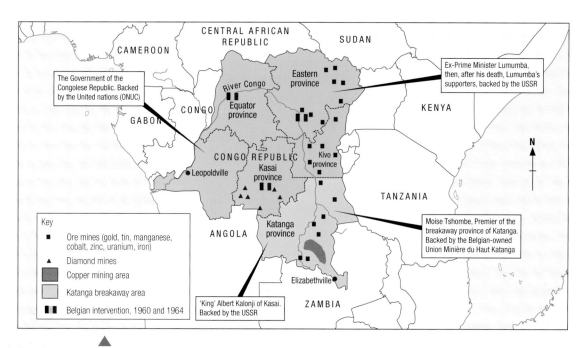

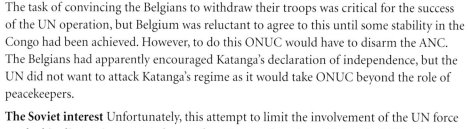

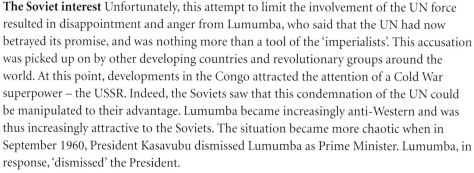

This shows the Congo at the time of the independence crisis.

Joseph Kasavubu.

The task of convincing the Belgians to withdraw their troops was critical for the success of the UN operation, but Belgium was reluctant to agree to this until some stability in the Congo had been achieved. However, to do this ONUC would have to disarm the ANC. The Belgians had apparently encouraged Katanga's declaration of independence, but the UN did not want to attack Katanga's regime as it would take ONUC beyond the role of peacekeepers.

The Soviet interest Unfortunately, this attempt to limit the involvement of the UN force resulted in disappointment and anger from Lumumba, who said that the UN had now betrayed its promise, and was nothing more than a tool of the 'imperialists'. This accusation was picked up on by other developing countries and revolutionary groups around the world. At this point, developments in the Congo attracted the attention of a Cold War superpower – the USSR. Indeed, the Soviets saw that this condemnation of the UN could be manipulated to their advantage. Lumumba became increasingly anti-Western and was thus increasingly attractive to the Soviets. The situation became more chaotic when in September 1960, President Kasavubu dismissed Lumumba as Prime Minister. Lumumba, in response, 'dismissed' the President.

The UN's ONUC force was now directly caught up in the internal politics of the Congo. As the crisis intensified, the Secretary General's Congo representative, Andrew Cordier, decided to redress the chaos by closing all the air fields and shutting down the state capital's radio station. Instead of bolstering the control of the government, these actions strengthened Lumumba's enemies. He now could not move or deploy loyal troops, nor could he use the only means of mass communication in the Congo to persuade the Congolese people that they should support him. Cordier's actions were thus perceived as being 'anti-Lumumba'. It was seen as further evidence of the pro-Western nature of the UN.

For the Soviets, UN peacekeeping forces were merely tools of American foreign policy. The Suez mission had been tolerated, as the crisis was a huge embarrassment for the allies of the United States. The Congo crisis was becoming more and more ideological, and there was a correspondingly increased interest from the Soviets in how the crisis was being dealt with by ONUC forces. Even though Cordier was replaced by an Indian national, the USSR condemned ONUC as a pro-Western force both culturally and politically. In September, in the Security Council, the Soviets denounced the failure of the UN to 'confront imperialism' in the Congo. The USSR declared that the UN was working against the 'radical aspirations' of the 'third world' and stated that this was counter to the best interests of the new African and Asian nations in the UN. The Soviets went further, and declared that the Secretary General himself was responsible for the 'Western conspiracy' in the Congo.

Believing that the balance of power in the UN was swinging in its favour, on 23 September 1960 the Soviet leader, Khrushchev, addressed the Security Council on ONUC's failings. He challenged the role of the Secretary General, claiming that he had too much power, and that this power was wielded in favour of the Western imperialists. The position should be abolished: 'There are neutral nations, but no neutral men'.

Khrushchev said that the office should be replaced by a 'troika', that is, a body of three representatives from 'the three distinct groups of states': Western, Communist and Afro-Asian. Khrushchev claimed that this would mean neither side in the Cold War could exploit the power of this office, although the Soviets themselves were hoping to exploit the Afro-Asian group who would be more inclined to be pro-Soviet than friendly to the former colonial powers of the Western bloc.

When it came to it, there was little support for the 'troika' idea. The historian Norrie Macqueen points out that 'The troika system, would … have formalized the bi-polar structure of the Cold War international system into a permanent feature of the UN's architecture.' The USSR allowed its 'troika' plans to be dropped. It was determined to follow the direction of the Afro-Asian regions, as the Sino-Soviet split had undermined its influence in the developing world.

Secretary General Dag Hammarskjöld survived Khrushchev's attack as he was still viewed in many countries as pro-UN rather than specifically supporting American foreign policy ambitions.

The crisis intensifies The crisis in the Congo demonstrated that UN involvement could cause a situation to deteriorate further, and worse still, draw in the superpowers, broadening the conflict. By late September 1960, superpower involvement in the Congo seemed imminent.

In mid-September, the ANC commander, Mobutu Sese Seko, announced an army coup. He then expelled Soviet and other Eastern bloc diplomats from the capital, Leopoldville. The Soviets believed that the West was behind this. Hammarskjöld was now seriously worried that Lumumba would appeal for the direct involvement of the USSR. However, something unexpected happened: Mobutu and Kasavubu drew together and this new alliance led Lumumba to ask for protection, not from the Soviets, but from the UN.

Patrice Lumumba.

In November 1960, although originally wanting reconciliation between Lumumba and Ksavubu, with Western encouragement the General Assembly accepted a delegation from Kasavubu and Mobutu and in so doing indirectly accepted their regime.

In response to yet another 'betrayal' by the UN, Lumumba left the protection of the UN in Leopoldville. He intended to reach his supporters, and organize an attack on the new regime. However, Lumumba was quickly captured by Mobutu's ANC troops. A few weeks later he was handed over to Tshombe's secession government in Katanga, where he was then brutally murdered.

The results of his murder for the UN's ONUC mission were considerable. It seemed clear that its protection of Lumumba was very poor. In addition, ONUC's failure to stop him being handed over to Tshombe seemed more than just ineffective. Indeed, it was perceived as very 'convienient' for the Americans and the West that Lumumba had been removed. Although the evidence is still not clear, it has been claimed that there was CIA involvement in the decision to hand him over to the Katangan regime.

In response to the murder, countries such as Indonesia and Morocco removed their contingents from ONUC, and other countries threatened to do the same. The USSR again demanded the dismissal of the Secretary General.

The UN authorizes force On 21 February 1961 the Security Council authorized ONUC to use force if necessary to prevent full-scale civil war in the Congo. This went beyond Hammarskjöld's principle of peacekeeping. By this point, the United States had a new President – John F. Kennedy. Kennedy was perceived to have a more 'sensitive' attitude towards the African and Asian nations, and it was hoped that he would be a calming influence on the American approach to the crisis in the Congo.

With Lumumba dead, Katanga now became the focus of the crisis. Although ONUC troops were present in the region, Tshombe's administration had been relatively stable and prosperous, and ONUC forces had not interfered. However, Katanga's success was due to the support of Europeans and white African states. The reality was that the majority of UN member states were hostile to the regime in Katanga. In addition, ONUC's role in Katanga was not clear. Did 'preventing civil war' mean that ONUC could or should crush the secession?

Although pressure from the superpowers had decreased in the Congo by mid-1961, with both sides supporting the objective of a unified Congo, Hammarskjöld was under pressure. His peacekeeping force still did not have a peace to enforce. Katanga simply ignored all UN efforts to negotiate reunification. The regime was able to do this as it was backed by European advisers and an army led by European mercenaries.

In August 1961, the next crisis developed as Conor Cruise O'Brien, the Secretary General's representative, ordered ONUC forces to arrest and expel all foreign forces in Katanga in an attempt to undermine the European backing for Tshombe. This ended in complete failure for ONUC forces, and gave Tshombe more confidence to ignore UN calls for a compromise.

Mobutu Sese Seko.

O'Brien launched a bigger attack a few weeks later, and initially announced that ONUC forces had been successful in crushing the Katanga secession. However, the Security Council was furious, as it had not been consulted. As Western bloc countries and Hammarskjöld did not support the mission, ONUC forces pulled back. The UN wanted to assert its control over events in the Congo, particularly now that the superpowers were less likely to be drawn in.

The conclusion of the crisis On 17 September 1961, Hammarskjöld flew to meet Tshombe in Northern Rhodesia in an attempt to find a resolution. The plane crashed en route and Hammarsjköld was killed. He was replaced by the first non-European Secretary General, U Thant of Burma.

The division in the UN over the Congo was no longer really along Cold War lines, but rather along the lines of 'imperialist countries' versus 'Afro-Asian countries'. Indeed, the United States itself was moving against the European position.

In addition, the 'non-aligned' bloc (see Chapter Fifteen) was gaining in influence in the UN. They attacked the UN failure against the Katanga regime. In November, the Security Council passed another resolution authorizing ONUC to use more force to crush the Katanga regime. By the end of 1962, the UN was in control of Katanga, and the Congo was reunified. ONUC forces were withdrawn in June 1964.

But there was a further 'twist' in the story, as Tshombe was elected as the new Prime Minister of Congo. Mobutu replaced Kasavubu as Head of State in 1965. Mobutu wielded the real power in the Congo. He remained in power for more than three decades. His regime, created by the UN, was one of the most corrupt in the world.

Document analysis

Document A

'Big Game Hunter' by John Collins, 1961.

Document B

The Security Council … Urges that the United Nations take immediately all appropriate measures to prevent the occurrence of civil war in the Congo, including arrangements for cease-fires, the halting of all military operations, the prevention of clashes and the use of force, if necessary, in the last resort;

Urges that measures be taken for the immediate withdrawal and evacuation from the Congo of all Belgian and other foreign military and paramilitary personnel and political advisers not under the United nations Command, and mercenaries;

Calls upon all states to take immediate and energetic measures to prevent the departure of such personnel for the Congo from their territories, and for the denial of transit and other facilities to them;

Decides that an immediate and impartial investigation be held in order to ascertain the circumstances of the death of Mr Lumumba and his colleagues and that the perpetrators of these crimes be punished …

UN Document S/RES/143, 14 July 1960, which was passed with Britain, China and France abstaining

Questions

1. What is the message of the cartoonist in Document A?

2. Which of the recommendations made in Document B may have led Britain and France to 'abstain' from the vote?

Review activity

Discuss as a class or in small groups the following question: What does the case study of the Congo suggest about the limitations and dangers for UN intervention in crises during the Cold War?

Impact of the Cold War on the UN in the 1960s

Throughout the 1960s, the United Nations continued to engage in 'peacekeeping' missions around the world, even though the Congo had been nothing less than a series of failures for the UN. The UN's work was generally in areas the superpowers did not find strategically important. It was clear that the UN could only function with authority when the interests of the USA and the USSR were not threatened.

When the USA attempted to force regime change in Cuba in 1961 with the invasion of the Bay of Pigs (see Chapter Nine), the UN did not get involved. As had been the case with the Soviet aggression in Eastern Europe, the UN avoided becoming engaged in the superpowers' spheres of influence. However, because the Cold War had gone 'global', this philosophy extended to any country or region where the superpowers had identified interests.

STUDENT STUDY SECTION

Document analysis

[during the Cuban Missile Crisis] '... *the great power tussles of the Cold War were waged in a very new kind of arena, in which rhetoric and political rationalizations of the great powers could be tested and judged by an increasingly informed and concerned audience. First there was the presence of the ever-expanding United Nations, a court of world opinion which both U.S. and Soviet Union took seriously enough to invest heavy diplomatic and financial resources. Second, there was television.*

From Martin Walker, *The Cold War* (Vintage, 1994) p.161

Questions

1   Martin Walker suggests that the UN's importance in the 1960s during the Cold War was as a 'court of world opinion'. Explain what he means.

2   What is Walker implying about the relevance of the UN when he compares it to 'television'?

The UN and détente: 1968–1979

The emergence of the period of détente meant a relaxation of tension between the superpowers. Some of the ways in which détente was brought about, fear of Mutually Assured Destruction, for example, meant that both the USA and the USSR were more ready to look for agreement between each other when conflicts arose, rather than inciting an escalation of tension. Therefore, during détente, the USA and USSR were more ready to work with the UN and its idea of 'peacekeeping'.

In addition, by the late 1960s not only had relations between the superpowers changed, but the UN had also changed. The balance of power shifted from Western domination to a majority of newly independent and/or 'non-aligned' states. By the end of the 1960s, the Americans no longer could be confident of having things their own way in the General Assembly. The Soviets had always been suspicious of Western influence in the UN, and were now more comfortable with the new balance of power.

It could be because of these changes that during this period UN forces had a number of limited successes. They were involved in achieving a ceasefire in Kashmir when fighting broke out in 1965 between India and Pakistan, and again in Cyprus when violence erupted between the Greek and Turkish Cypriots in 1974.

However, as had been the case in the Hungarian Uprising a decade before, the UN proved impotent in the face of superpower aggression. Soviet forces invaded Czechoslovakia in 1968. The USSR had sent forces in to crush what it perceived to be a move away from Soviet control by the Czech leadership (see Chapter Sixteen). Once again the Security Council had

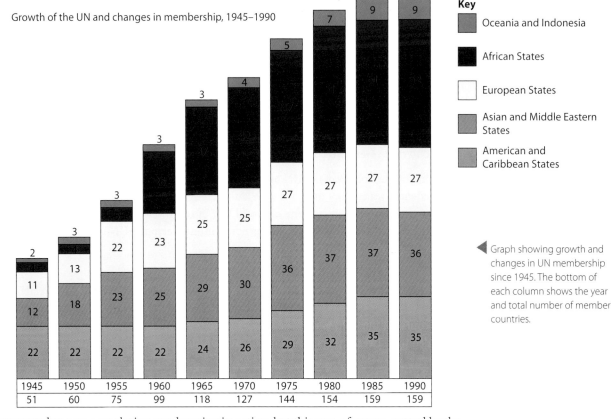

Growth of the UN and changes in membership, 1945–1990

Key

- Oceania and Indonesia
- African States
- European States
- Asian and Middle Eastern States
- American and Caribbean States

1945	1950	1955	1960	1965	1970	1975	1980	1985	1990
51	60	75	99	118	127	144	154	159	159

◀ Graph showing growth and changes in UN membership since 1945. The bottom of each column shows the year and total number of member countries.

attempted to pass a resolution condemning its action, but this was, of course, vetoed by the USSR. The Soviets claimed to the UN that the Czechs had requested their assistance – the Czechs denied this. The UN was powerless to stop the Soviet Union.

The UN was again powerless when the United States attempted to force regime change in Chile. In October 1970, the democratically elected Marxist government of Salvador Allende took office. The CIA had been involved in covert attempts to undermine Allende in the election campaign, but he had still been elected. President Nixon then authorized the CIA to 'unseat him'. For the next three years the CIA attempted to destabilize the Allende government. Finally, in September 1973, a military coup successfully took control in Chile. Salvador Allende was dead, possibly by suicide. The Chilean government was under the leadership of an anti-Communist General, Augusto Pinochet. The UN had not responded.

The UN and the second Cold War

In the 1980s, when the USA and the USSR resumed the rhetoric and hostility of the pre-détente period of the Cold War, the UN's dependence on the superpowers was again revealed. Unable to reach agreement on responses to crises in the Security Council, peacekeeping missions ended.

In the 1950s and 1960s peacekeeping had provided the UN with a means of sealing off superpower involvement in local conflicts peripheral to their main interests. In the 1970s, when cold war gave way to détente, it had offered the superpowers themselves a tool for the management of relationships with troublesome clients. Now, in the 1980s, with bi-polar competition sharpened once again and the Second Cold War underway, no third phase of UN peacekeeping emerged to meet the new situation.

Norrie Macqueen in The United Nations Since 1945: Peacekeeping and the Cold War *(Longman, 1999)*

ToK Time

This is from a speech made by Mikhail Gorbachev to the United Nations on 7 December 1988:

We are entering an era in which progress will be based on the common interests of the whole of humankind. The realization of this fact demands that the common values of humanity must be the determining priority in international politics ... This new stage requires the freeing of international relations from ideology.

Read the extract from Gorbachev's speech.

- What, if any, are the 'common interests of the whole of humankind'?

- Can 'common interests' be defined internationally? How dependent are these on political beliefs? Religious beliefs? Cultural paradigms?

- Can nation states ever be free from 'ideology' and 'self-interest' in their pursuit of foreign policies?

It could be argued that the UN's key function of responding to potential conflict situations was only possible when the Cold War was not played out in the Security Council.

The UN and the end of the Cold War

After considering the influence of the Cold War on the effectiveness and relevance of the United Nations, it would seem obvious that with the end of the Cold War there would be a new optimism about the potential for the UN in the 'new world order'. The UN would no longer be held to ransom by the opposing forces of the East and West, crippling its ability to respond to crisis. Genuine 'collective security' was a real possibility.

At the end of the Cold War, the UN began to launch new peacekeeping missions on an unprecedented scale. More missions were launched in the decade following 1988 than in the three decades following the end of World War Two. However, the end of the Cold War's dominance did not mean the end of superpower influence on the UN.

Case Study 1: Somalia

During the Cold War, the USSR and the USA were both involved directly and indirectly in African states, particularly in the 1960s and 1970s. However, these events had little impact on the course of the Cold War. The Soviet Ambassador to the United States in the 1990s concluded that 'Twenty years later no one (except historians) could remember them.'

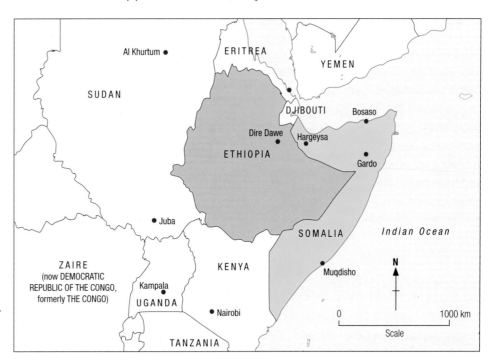

This map shows the borders between Somalia and Ethiopia in the early 1990s.

Somalia had initially drawn the interest of the superpowers during the Second Cold War period because of its strategic position (see map). When war broke out between this former Soviet ally and the new Marxist regime in neighbouring Ethiopia in 1977, the USA was drawn in. The Americans had supported the regime in Somalia as the Soviets had backed the 'revolutionary' regime in Ethiopia. However, when the Cold War ended, the USA and the former USSR lost interest.

This was bad news for the government of Somalia and the government of Ethiopia, as they were both very unpopular, and were dependent on their superpower supporters to retain control. In Somalia, Siyad Barre's regime fell in early 1991. However, the UN only became involved in early 1992 when it became clear that a million and half people were starving. After the initial UN mission failed to protect aid workers, the United States offered to send 30,000 troops to crush the armed factions. In December 1992, the Security Council voted for the establishment of a Unified Task Force under U.S. command.

After brutal fighting, much of which was filmed by television crews on the ground, the situation had not improved. Essentially there was no central authority to protect. In addition, in the developing world there remained much hostility and suspicion of the USA, so in May 1993 the UN resumed control of the mission in Somalia. Fighting continued, and the United States, under pressure from public opinion after the deaths of over 100 'peacekeepers', decided to withdraw from Somalia in March 1995.

The UN intervention in Somalia was discredited as the USA had taken a dominant role. The limitations of the UN in the new post-Cold War era were exposed. It seemed that without the balance of power afforded to it by the USSR, the UN would become ever more a tool of U.S. policy. It also meant that the USA might be able to ignore the UN with impunity.

Case Study 2: Bosnia

When the initial crisis broke out in the former Yugoslavia in 1991, the UN accepted that a European response might be the best solution. NATO forces were sent to Bosnia to protect the area from Serbian forces. However, the UN was ultimately drawn in as NATO troops were not able to resolve the conflict between local Muslims, Croats and Serbs. In March 1993, a dual UN–NATO force became involved. But there was tension between the two organizations from the start. After the UN had abandoned Srebrenica to Bosnian Serbs and a massacre had taken place, NATO forces seized the initiative. NATO ultimately won a sustained air offensive against the Serbs and secured the end of the conflict through the Dayton Accord of November 1995.

The Bosnian crisis again highlighted the problems facing the UN in a one-superpower world. With the end of the Cold War, the resistance of member states to genuine multilateralism and 'collective security' became clear. States did not want to follow policies that were not in line with their own foreign policy aims. There also remained old suspicions and tensions left over from the Cold War. Any consensus that could be achieved was limited.

Ultimately, it had been NATO and not the United Nations that had secured peace in Bosnia. The UN had proved unable to make the military commitment necessary to enforce its resolutions.

Thus, the initial optimism about the new authority and capabilities of the post-Cold War UN faded. In Somalia the problem of the dominance of the only remaining superpower was highlighted, and in Bosnia the belief in the UN as an effective force against conflict was undermined.

STUDENT STUDY SECTION

Document analysis

Document A

The really serious problem, which had been brewing since the end of the Cold War and the emergence of the USA as sole superpower, was about the future relationship between the UN and the USA. Tension began to mount as soon as the Bush administration took office in 2001: within its first year the new government rejected the 1972 Anti-Ballistic Missile treaty, the 1997 Kyoto Protocol … Tensions reached a climax in March 2003, when the U.S. government aided and abetted by UK, decided to attack Iraq … The challenge for the UN in the coming years is how best to harness and make use of the power and influence of the USA instead of being impeded or stampeded by it.

From Norman Lowe, *Mastering Modern World History* (Palgrave, 2005) p.189

Document B

A President can't subordinate his decision making to a multilateral body. He can't sacrifice one ounce of our sovereignty to any organization.

Statement by Vice-President George H.W. Bush, August 1988

Questions

1   What key issues does Norman Lowe highlight in Document A as future problems for the post-Cold War United Nations?

2   What is Vice-President George Bush's view of the UN in Document B?

The legacy of the Cold War for the United Nations

For almost forty years the Security Council was a ring for a heavyweight contest between the titans, the United States and the USSR, egged on by their partisan supporters.

From David J. Whittaker, United Nations in the Contemporary World (Routledge, 1997)

The deploying of 'peacekeepers' gave the UN a role during the Cold War. It 'rescued it from military irrelevance'. This Cold War view of the UN has outlived the Cold War, and is still seen today as a primary function of the UN.

In June 1992, the UN Secretary General, Boutros Boutros-Ghali, produced a report on peacekeeping, 'An agenda for peace'. The report attempted to analyse the purpose of peacekeeping in the post-Cold War era, or as Boutros-Ghali put it, after the collapse of 'the immense ideological barrier that for decades gave rise to distrust and hostility'. It was assumed that the key effect of the Cold War on the work of the UN was to push states into alliance with one superpower or the other. This polarization meant the idea of collective action could not work.

Unfortunately, 'the Agenda for Peace' actually exposed the continued limitations of 'collective security'. This was because the post-Cold War world was dominated by self-interested states, disinclined to involve themselves in any collective action that was not directly in line with their own foreign policy objectives.

The UN and the Cold War: conclusion

In the 1950s, the view of the Soviet Union towards the UN was that the organization was virtually another Western alliance system. The 'Uniting for Peace' resolution perpetuated this perception, as the balance of power in the General Assembly was in the United States' favour. The decolonization movements of the 1960s, and the emergence of newly independent states in Africa and Asia, shifted the balance of power in the UN and gave the Soviet Union renewed interest in the potential of the organization.

However, ultimately, the impact of the Cold War on the role of the United Nations was more significant than the impact the UN had on the development and course of the Cold War. There were times when states were able to stand up to the dominance of the superpowers, for example the non-alignment movement, but even this did not really empower the UN as an independent organization.

The UN's success was dependent on the support of the superpowers, or in certain cases, their indifference. Often the UN had little choice but to remain 'passive' in the face of Soviet or U.S. aggression. In addition, when the UN did get involved in 'peacekeeping' operations it often had a negative impact on relations between the USA and the USSR. Peacekeeping missions often aggravated the tensions between the Soviets and the Americans.

There was a generally accepted view that the Cold War had held the UN hostage and frustrated its ability to function effectively. However, this perception may have been an exaggeration, as during the post-Cold War era the UN has had similar problems of controlling the domination of the USA, and has shown itself limited in achieving collective security through military action. Perhaps the Cold War was a 'smoke-screen' and the fundamental weakness of the United Nations is, and always was, the unwillingness of states to hand over some degree of sovereignty to an international organization.

STUDENT STUDY SECTION

The UN and the Lebanon 1975–1999

The UN's involvement in the Lebanon reflected the shifting pattern of the Cold War. This included the move towards a relaxation of tension during détente, and then the renewed hostility of the Second Cold War period and finally the impact of the end of the Cold War. The case study of the Lebanon is thus a good example of how the UN's peacekeeping credibility was directly related to relations between the superpowers.

A civil war raged in the Lebanon from 1975. The situation was increasingly complex, and made more so by a dispute between the Palestinians and the Lebanese Christians over a border in the south of the country. Israel had been supporting the Christians, and in 1978 invaded the south in an attempt to stop attacks on its territory, which it claimed were being launched from guerrilla bases in this area.

In June 1978, under pressure from the UN, the Israelis agreed to withdraw and hand over policing of the frontier to the UN. However, with détente under pressure, the Soviet Union would not be drawn into working with the Security Council on a resolution. As the plans for a peacekeeping force were drawn up in March 1978, the USSR abstained from voting in the enabling resolutions. This gave the mission less credibility from the start.

The UN interim force in Lebanon (UNIFIL), numbering around 7000 troops, oversaw the Israeli withdrawal and had some success in stabilizing the border. However, this was sporadic, and it was unable to stop violations of the frontier, attacks, assassinations and hostage-taking. Israel invaded again in June 1982, following an increase in attacks across the border. When the Israelis withdrew again in 1985, UNIFIL was left attempting to secure an even larger 'security zone', which made it more difficult. When Mikhail Gorbachev came to power in the USSR, Soviet abstention from support for UNIFIL ended, and this gave more credibility to the force. Now all the permanent members of the Security Council were behind it.

UNIFIL had a more credible mandate. However, the end of Cold War divisions, together with more unity of purpose in the UN, did not end the conflict in the Lebanon. Hezbollah launched renewed attacks from South Lebanon against Israel, and in April 1996 Israel responded by occupying most of the region, a position that continued until 1999. UNIFIL again in 1999 oversaw an Israeli withdrawal.

Question

In what ways does the Lebanon case study highlight the limitations of the Cold-War-dominated UN and its continued lack of authority in the post-Cold War era?

Research activity

Having read this chapter on the United Nations and the Cold War, it would be beneficial to add to the case studies included here. Divide the class into groups and have each group research one of the following case studies. It should be noted that the UN and the Middle East is a far larger research task and could be split between groups.

1   UN involvement in the Middle East conflict:
    From the withdrawal of Britain in 1948

2   UN involvement in India and Pakistan conflict:
    From the 1949 observer mission

3   UN involvement in Cyprus:
    From attempted coup in 1974

4   UN involvement in Angola:
    From withdrawal of Portugal in 1975

5   UN involvement in Iraq:
    From the Iraqi invasion of Kuwait in 1990

6   UN involvement in Rwanda:
    From establishment of the UN Mission for Rwanda in 1993

Each group should then feed their research findings back to the class.
How do these findings highlight the problems the UN had with operating during the Cold War?

This map shows the location of some of the conflict case studies. ▶

India – Pakistan, 1947-9, 1965, 1971

Korean War, 1950-3

UK

SPAIN

USA

CHINA

S. KOREA
N. KOREA

EGYPT

INDIA

Vietnam – China, 1979

PAKISTAN

Iran – Iraq 1980-8 'Gulf War',

The Vietnam War, 1965-73, Massive US involvement

Syria

Lebanon

Cyprus

IRAN

Rwanda, 1993–

Isreal   Jordan

IRAQ

Angola, 1975–

ARGENTINA

Arab – Israeli Wars, 1948-9, 1956, 1967, 1973, 1982-5

UK – Argentina, 1982

Essay question

- How far did the Cold War have an impact on the effectiveness of the United Nations?

Essay frame

Introduction: Outline impact of superpower divide on the structure, aims and membership of the UN.

Main body: You could adopt a thematic or a chronological approach here.

Paragraph 1: 1950s

Paragraph 2: 1960s

Paragraph 3: Détente period

Paragraph 4: Second Cold War

Paragraph 5: Continued limitations in the post-Cold War era

Conclusion: Key effects of the Cold War on the UN contrasted with its continued problems

Now attempt to create an essay frame for the following question:

- 'The major obstacle to successful international peacekeeping between 1945 and 1965 was the impact of Cold War politics on the United Nations. 'To what extent do you agree with this assertion?

In pairs, plan these two following essays from the introduction to the conclusion, and then discuss your plans with another pair of students. (See page 161 for hints on what to include on your plans.)

1   Explain how the rivalry between the USA and the USSR affected the working of the United Nations.

2   Analyse the role of the United Nations in the Cold War.

15 WHAT WAS THE IMPACT OF THE NON-ALIGNED STATES ON THE COLD WAR?

 Consider these essay questions as you read the chapter:
- Why did the Non-Aligned Movement develop?
- How successful was the Non-Aligned Movement in resisting superpower domination during the Cold War?

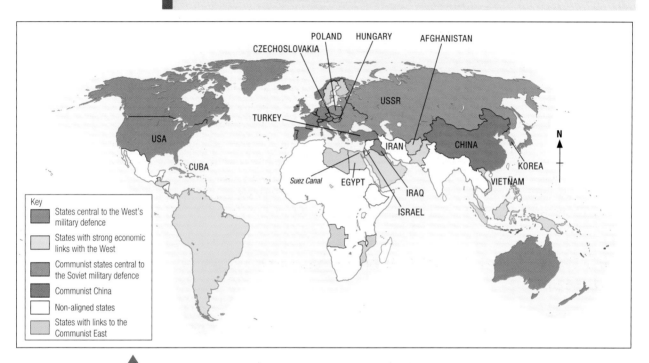

This map shows the distribution of the non-aligned countries throughout the world.

The Cold War, decolonization and the Third World

During the Cold War, the non-aligned countries were those states that rejected alliances and ties with either superpower.

This group was viewed as the 'Third World', as it had decided to take a 'third path' that was not in line with the American system or the Soviet system. These states attempted to avoid becoming part of Cold War politics, which they saw as potentially destructive for their countries. Some historians now believe that the Cold War needs to be considered not only from the perspectives of Washington and Moscow, but also from the viewpoints of the states that came to be called the Third World. Indeed, historian Odd Arne Westad argues that the 'most important aspects of the Cold War were connected to the political and social development of the Third World'.

 The Third World
The Third World was a term that grew out of the development of the Western capitalist world bloc and the Communist world bloc in order to describe those countries which belonged to neither of the two powerful groups. It later became synonymous with economics, and the idea that the Third World was uniform in its lack of economic development. The term 'Third World' became linked to the economic idea of 'the developing world' and in some cases the terms became confused. This is not the correct way to describe the non-aligned states, as it quickly becomes obvious that there are economic differences between, for example, India and Senegal. The Non-Aligned Movement itself was an idea pioneered in Eastern Europe by Yugoslavia.

However, the policy of avoiding superpower alignment was not the only factor that linked many of the non-aligned states. At the end of World War Two, the Cold War developed simultaneously with the growth of **decolonization** movements in Africa and Asia. The European colonial powers were exhausted at the end of World War Two, and former colonial territories seized their opportunity to rid themselves of their imperial rulers. As can be seen on the map on the previous page, many of the non-aligned states were former colonial possessions, and a key factor in their unity was a desire to resist 'imperialists' and give support to anti-imperialist movements around the world.

Although this anti-imperialist stance at times is viewed as anti-European, many of the non-aligned states were also increasingly perceived as anti-American during the Cold War. Indeed, even though the USA had condemned European imperialism and had supported its demise, the United States itself was accused of 'neo-colonialism'. The colonial empires of Spain and Portugal in the Americas had ended, but the independence of the former European colonial possessions was limited by the 'informal' U.S. imperialism that followed. In addition, the United States went on to create 'spheres of influence' around the globe as the Cold War intensified. This was seen by some non-aligned states as an extension of its neo-colonialism.

Nevertheless, certain important leading members of the Non-Aligned Movement (NAM) were anti-Soviet in outlook, believing that the USSR was as guilty of 'imperialism' as the USA. NAM wanted to exert pressure on both superpowers regarding their growing nuclear arsenals. The non-aligned states feared that the Cold War could lead to a nuclear exchange.

What were the aims of the Non-Aligned Movement?

The Indian Prime Minister, Jawaharlal Nehru first used the term 'non-aligned' in a speech setting down the principles for Sino-Indian relations in 1954. At a meeting in 1961, using the points from this speech as a foundation, the criteria for a 'non-aligned' state was established. To be considered non-aligned, countries must not join in alliances or defence pacts with the main world powers. Not only would this allow them to retain a degree of autonomy from superpower domination by not committing to either side in the Cold War, it would also enable them to go one step further and attempt to manipulate the bi-polar divide to their own advantage. They would do this by ensuring that they left 'openings' to ally with either the USA or the USSR, and thus would continue to be courted by both. On the other hand, if pressure from one superpower got to be too much, they could threaten to ally with the other.

As more and more former colonial states achieved independence, the 'non-alignment bloc' grew. By the mid-1960s the developing world came to represent more than half the membership of the United Nations (see graph on page 181). Many of the states were non-aligned, and so NAM gained in importance and influence once the developing world became the majority in the General Assembly, shifting the balance of power away from the USA. At times, many of these states had backing from the Communist bloc countries.

If they could manage to act as a bloc with their increased numbers in the General Assembly, NAM could potentially hold the balance of power. Many smaller states in the United Nations believed that the non-aligned states brought in 'fresh debate' to the General Assembly. Two groups made up the movement:

- the Non-Aligned Movement of 115 states, formed in Belgrade, Yugoslavia in 1961
- the Group of 77 established after the UN Conference on Trade and Development in Geneva in 1964.

The non-aligned bloc would at times work together in the UN General Assembly, or in committees, but they did not have an overriding unity, and would not act as a bloc on all issues. The Group of 77 worked to gain support for developing countries by putting pressure on industrial nations. This was necessary as many of the non-aligned states were in desperate need of economic aid and modernization. The non-aligned states attempted to exert some influence during the Korean War (1950–1953), the crisis in the Congo (1960), the Suez Crisis (1956), the Soviet invasion of Afghanistan (1979), the Falklands War (1982), and the Iran–Iraq War (1980–1984).

The Cold War and the origins of the Non-Aligned Movement

Marshal Tito's post-war Yugoslavia was dedicated to Communism, but did not want to sacrifice its hard fought for sovereignty to Moscow (see Chapter Sixteen). When this led to a split with Stalin in 1948, the Americans offered aid to Tito. Tito saw this as an opportunity to safeguard his country from Soviet invasion, reasoning that Stalin would not invade if it might provoke a war with the United States. The U.S. Navy 6th Fleet was operating just off the Yugoslav coast at this time, which probably heightened the Soviet fear of U.S. involvement.

There is some evidence that this did impact on the USSR, which refrained from invasion and focused on assassination plots instead. Nevertheless, in line with non-aligned thinking, Tito avoided getting too close to the United States, as he did not want it pressurizing him to introduce Capitalism back into Yugoslavia. When Stalin died in 1953, Tito invited Nikita Khrushchev to the Yugoslav capital, Belgrade. At this meeting, Tito was treated as an equal by Khrushchev, who hoped that there was an opening for a rapprochement.

Further evidence of the success of Tito's position on non-alignment came in 1956 when Khrushchev and George Malenkov (see page 75) embarked on a hazardous and exhausting trip to see Tito. They sought his 'approval' for the crushing of the Hungarian uprising. They had taken the trouble to come to him, and not vice versa, thus showing the impact that non-alignment could have.

It was successes like this that provided the non-alignment inspiration for Jawaharlal Nehru of India and Zhou En-lai of China, both leaders who wanted to resist the bi-polar superpower domination.

Marshal Tito of Yugoslavia.

The growth of the Non-Aligned Movement

India and China were countries that had thrown off the control of their colonial powers, and neither wanted to replace these restraints with one or other of the superpowers.

The USA had backed Pakistan after the partition of India and supported its U.S.-friendly leadership. For India and Nehru, NAM was a way of striking back at the Americans without having to ally with the Soviet Union. It would also offer India some degree of influence as a potential non-aligned world leader, demonstrating that there were alternatives to 'taking sides' in the Cold War.

Following the Sino-Soviet split, there were several reasons for the People's Republic of China to join NAM:
- It wanted to avoid hegemony over China by the USA or the Soviet Union.
- It was keen to present itself as leader of the newly liberated former colonial states.
- It believed that this movement could work in line with its presentation of Marxist ideology.

Jawaharlal Nehru of India.

The first conference of non-aligned states took place at Bandung in Indonesia in April 1955. It was initiated by Tito, and then supported by Nehru and Zhou En-lai, all of whom realized that they shared common aims in the Cold War environment. The main purpose of the Bandung Conference was to increase the membership in the independent bloc by fostering 'neutrality' in the Cold War. Tito also emphasized his concern that the arms race between the Soviets and the Americans could lead to an all-out nuclear war. At Bandung, the principle of 'peaceful resolution' of disputes was established as a key principle for member states.

Nasser, non-alignment and the Cold War

General Nasser of Egypt was one of the leaders who attended the conference. He was impressed with the views and arguments presented. Nasser decided that he would pursue a neutral position in the Cold War. He also understood a key idea of non-alignment – that of exploiting attempts by both the USSR and the USA to coerce successfully non-aligned countries into becoming part of the superpower spheres of influence.

By following this non-aligned philosophy of 'courting' the superpowers, Nasser triggered a crisis in the Middle East. He initially courted the Americans and managed to persuade them to fund the construction of the Aswan Dam project. Then he decided to move towards the USSR by buying arms from Czechoslovakia.

In the ensuing crisis over the Suez Canal (see Chapter Fourteen), Nasser balanced the superpowers against one another and emerged the winner. He kept the canal, humiliated the colonial powers, checked his involvement with the USA and the USSR and emerged as the leader of Arab nationalism. This was a clear Cold War victory for a non-aligned state.

The Non-Aligned Movement demonstrated that the superpowers could not always push the smaller states around, nor could they always get what they wanted. The very fact that the nature of the Cold War led the Soviets and the USA to believe that they 'needed' to bring neutral states over to their sides in itself gave these countries a weapon to wield against the superpowers. As Gaddis comments, 'Tails were beginning to wag the dogs.'

Cartoon analysis

'The Voice from the Floor', by John Collins, 1956.

Questions

1 What is the message of the cartoonist?

2 What did Gaddis mean by his statement: 'Tails were beginning to wag the dogs'?

3 Attempt to sketch your own cartoon under the heading: 'The tail is beginning to wag the dog'.

Research task

Research the involvement of Kwame Nkrumah of Ghana and Sukarno of Indonesia in the early development of NAM.

The Cold War and the Non-Aligned Movement in the 1960s and 1970s

As a group or 'bloc' the Non-Aligned Movement had more influence in the General Assembly of the UN by the 1960s. The key political content of the movement at this time was:

- to encourage solidarity of member states
- to warn superpowers against spreading the Cold War in the Third World
- to apply pressure against using war as means of settling disputes
- to counter imperialism
- to stand committed to restructuring the world economic order.

NAM held a summit meeting in Belgrade in 1961. This meeting coincided with the crisis in Berlin. In response, the non-aligned heads of state present at the meeting sent the same letter to both Kennedy and Khrushchev, warning them against the threat of war and urging for a 'peaceful solution'. Although the impact of these letters is difficult to quantify, the fact that the NAM states saw themselves as a group powerful enough to 'lecture' the superpowers shows the belief they possessed at this stage in the movement.

In addition, many of the non-aligned states represented countries that had shifted the balance of power away from the United States in the General Assembly of the UN. This meant that in the 1960s the Non-Aligned Movement had to be taken seriously by both superpowers.

Although NAM continued to grow, it was as early in the movement's development as 1962 that the idea of a 'bloc' began to collapse. In 1962, the Sino-Indian border war broke out. War between two of the movement's most powerful members – India and China – undermined its credibility. Indeed, India moved closer to the Soviets during the dispute with China. This was a big blow to the idea of 'solidarity' and of course the key Bandung principle of 'peaceful resolution'.

By the end of the 1960s all the original non-aligned leaders were gone. Nehru died in 1964 and Nasser died in 1970. The non-aligned regimes in Indonesia and in certain African states were overthrown.

Castro and NAM

When Fidel Castro came to power in Cuba in 1959, many Latin American countries saw his 'revolution' as a victory over American imperialism. Castro's foreign policy aims quickly became focused on giving Cuban support to groups 'struggling against imperialism around the globe'.

In 1970, a non-aligned conference was organized in the Zambian capital, Lusaka. However, by this time, much of the early belief and enthusiasm for NAM had evaporated. Many of the post-colonial regimes in Africa failed in the 1970s, and these countries moved away from non-alignment and towards the USSR. Cuba's leading role in NAM was questioned by some states, as its relationship with the Soviets clearly meant it had a degree of 'alignment' with a superpower.

The Americans did not want to support NAM as its members often assumed an anti-colonial stance in the UN and this could lead the United States into conflicts with its European allies. The USA wanted to focus on preventing the spread of Communism, and thus wanted the NAM states to be clearly aligned with their side in the Cold War. The USA could not accept that many Third World countries wanted to back Communist or socialist regimes. For example, Henry Kissinger viewed Salvadore Allende's victory in Chile in the 1970s as being caused by an 'irresponsible electorate' rather than the result of a genuinely informed choice by the Chileans.

Many states chose to align with the Soviets as they needed economic development, and the USSR promised aid and support. The Soviet Union also offered support for the political movements that were attempting to realize modernization. For example, whereas the United States wanted to resist the revolutionary forces in Vietnam, Khrushchev offered arms and money. Therefore, many NAM leaders, even when they were more nationalist than Communist, turned to the Soviets for assistance.

The 1979 NAM Summit meeting in Havana

Initiated by the Chairman of NAM at the time, Fidel Castro, the Havana Summit considered the possibility of a 'natural alliance' with the Soviet Union. The Jamaican Prime Minister Michael Manley made a pro-Soviet speech, and praised Castro for strengthening the forces against Western imperialism.

STUDENT STUDY SECTION

Document analysis

*For this reason we agreed in Havana to reaffirm that the quintessence of the non-alignment policy, in accordance with its original principles and fundamental nature, is the struggle against imperialism, colonialism, neocolonialism, apartheid, racism, including **Zionism**.*

Fidel Castro in a speech to the United Nations on 12 October 1979 in his position as chairman of NAM.

Question

What does Castro see as the key aims of the Non-Aligned Movement by the end of the 1970s?

The Cold War and the Non-Aligned Movement in the 1980s and 1990s

In 1979 the members of NAM turned against each other over the Soviet invasion of Afghanistan. Those non-aligned states that were allied or friendly to the USSR were in support of the invasion; however, other states, including many Muslim countries, were strongly opposed to it.

The Non-Aligned Movement was supposed to be non-aligned with either Russia or America. But then when countries like Cuba and Vietnam joined it which were clearly aligned to the Soviet Union, and countries like Singapore would plead, as it were, the Western cause, it began to look less like a non-aligned movement than something else.

Dr Geoffrey Stern of the London School of Economics

By the end of the 1980s, the Third World, as Odd Arne Westad commented, had ceased to exist as 'a meaningful political or economic concept.' Dramatic economic and political changes had begun in the 1970s, which had moved many African, Asian and Latin American countries in very different directions. For example, some South-East Asian countries had embarked on rapid economic development, whereas most of Latin America was, in contrast, stagnating economically. In Africa, the Balkans and certain parts of South Asia, ethnic and religious differences became more important than ideological ones. Political Islam was on the rise and often usurped secular politics.

The Non-Aligned Movement continued to hold international conferences and summits. But, exacerbated by the end of the Cold War, the focus shifted away from political issues and on to the promotion of solutions for global economic problems. Membership of NAM continued to grow until by 2000, there were 113 members and 17 observer states.

Some historians have suggested that NAM has struggled to find relevance since the end of the Cold War. This might suggest that despite the other factors that led to its development, such as decolonization and economic under-development, the Non-Aligned Movement was essentially a product of the Cold War. Jonathan Fryer, an expert on international affairs, puts it this way: 'it was a movement that basically set itself up as something which it is not, rather than something which it is ... In other words, it was meant not to be associated with Washington and not to be associated with Moscow. It is very much a child of the Cold War'.

STUDENT STUDY SECTION

Research activities

Questions

1   Research the rise, development and actions of one political Islamist group from the 1970s.

2   Divide the class into small groups or pairs. Each group should research the issues and decisions made at one of the following NAM summits:
    - First Conference: Belgrade, September 1–6, 1961
    - Second Conference: Cairo, October 5–10, 1964
    - Third Conference: Lusaka, September 8–10, 1970
    - Fourth Conference: Algiers, September 5–9, 1973
    - Fifth Conference: Colombo, August 16–19, 1976
    - Sixth Conference: Havana, September 3–9, 1979
    - Seventh Conference: New Delhi, March 7–12, 1983
    - Eighth Conference: Harare, September 1–6, 1986
    - Ninth Conference: Belgrade, September 4–7, 1989
    - Tenth Conference: Jakarta, September 1–7, 1992
    - Eleventh Conference: Cartagena de Indias, October 18–20, 1995.

3   In the conferences following the end of the Cold War, how far would you agree that NAM agendas and discussions could be viewed as 'anti-American'?

Review activity

For this chapter, you must create your own timeline on the Non-Aligned Movement. You will need to do this before you attempt the essay questions below. You should not only include the information from this chapter, but also include the research material you and your class find when working through the student activities.

Essay questions

1 Why did the Non-Aligned Movement develop, and how successful was it in resisting superpower domination during the Cold War?

Essay content hints

Include the different factors that led to the development of NAM in the opening of this chapter. Consider not only the case studies of NAM resistance of the superpowers in this chapter, but also look at the map of non-aligned states and consider examples of other NAM states covered in other chapters.

Remember that several NAM states ended up in some sort of alliance with one or other of the superpowers.

2 How far do you agree with the statement that the movement for non-alignment was a development of the Cold War?

Essay content hints

Consider the origins of the movement as you have done for Essay Question 1. These should include not only the Cold War, but also decolonization and economic motives. Then analyse the development of the movement, and consider the extent to which the Cold War motivated NAM membership and the actions of NAM states.

ToK Time

Read the source extract below:

The peoples of the Americas and Asia … played pivotal roles in the history of the Cold War, which, as we now know, was not just fought by the superpowers and Europe. It was also fought with this Third World, by the Third World, in collaboration with other Third World countries. Only if we understand the history of these countries can we begin to understand the world we live in today – where … the Chinese Communist Party still governs the world's most populous nation.

Tanya Harmer, from the article 'The Cold War in Asia and the Americas 1949–75' in *20th Century History Review*, April 2006

Why is it important to understand the history of other nations if we are to understand the world we live in today?

16 CHALLENGES TO SOVIET CONTROL 1945–1980

When reading the chapter, consider the following essay questions:
- What was the nature of Soviet control over the satellite states?
- How successful were challenges to Soviet control?
- Why did the USSR intervene in Afghanistan and what was the impact of this invasion on the development of the Cold War?

This map shows the satellite states of the Soviet Union. ▶

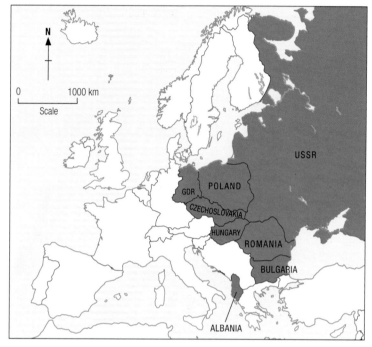

Between 1944 and 1948, the Soviet Union under Josef Stalin established control over the countries on its borders. By 1949, Hungary, Czechoslovakia, East Germany, Romania and Poland were on the eastern side of the 'iron curtain'. For each of these countries, the system established by Stalin meant tight Soviet control:

- The establishment of one-party rule, including installation of national leaders dependent on the USSR.
- Nationalization of private enterprise.
- The establishment of Soviet-style Five Year Plans. Heavy industry was encouraged and agriculture collectivized.
- Integration of the economy of Eastern Europe with the Soviet Union to offset the weakness of industry and agriculture in the USSR. Each country had to produce what the USSR needed: for example, Poland produced coal and steel ships. The satellite states were not to co-operate economically with each other, however. This situation was one of exploitation of the satellite states for the economic advantage of the USSR, and it had disastrous effects on any attempts at economic modernization in the satellites.

This economic and political system was backed up by:
- social and ideological controls (Cominform, secret police)
- censorship of all media
- suppression of religious freedom
- military presence of Soviet troops
- political purges.

However, from 1945 onwards there were attempts by the satellite states to resist this extreme level of Soviet control.

1948	**June**	Yugoslavia expelled from Cominform
		Purges begin in other satellite states to get rid of 'Titoists'
1953	**June**	Riots in Czechoslovakia
	June	Strikes break out in East Germany and Soviet troops restore order
1956	**Feb**	Khrushchev gives de-Stalinization speech
	June	Polish workers' revolt suppressed by Soviet troops
	October	Soviet suppression of Hungarian uprising
1968	**April**	Dubcek reveals plans for modernization of Czechoslovakia
		The Prague Spring
	August	Warsaw Pact forces invade Czechoslovakia
	Sept	Brezhnev announces Brezhnev Doctrine
		Albania leaves Warsaw Pact
1979	**Dec**	Soviet forces invade Afghanistan
1980	**Aug**	Strikes in Poland. Gdansk agreements recognize Solidarity
1981	**Dec**	Martial law imposed in Poland

The challenge of Yugoslavia

◀ This map shows Yugoslavia in 1945.

The Yugoslavs had organized a successful resistance campaign against the Germans during World War Two and had liberated their country in 1945. Marshal Tito was one of the resistance leaders. He had been head of the Yugoslav Communist Party since 1937 and was elected leader of the new republic in 1945. Tito was popular because he had resisted the Germans. Therefore, in Yugoslavia the establishment of Communism was not due to Soviet influence. Moreover, Tito was not interested in being tied too tightly to Moscow, and wanted to be free to trade with the West as well as with the Soviets. In addition, the Yugoslavs were unhappy with Stalin's lack of support for Tito's claim to Trieste, for the Greek Communists or for a Balkan Federation.

Tensions came to a head in 1948. Stalin expelled Yugoslavia from Cominform, which then declared that the Yugoslav party was 'in the hands of murderers and spies' and cut off economic aid. However, these actions failed to topple Tito who was able to continue without Soviet support. His regime remained Communist, but Tito followed his own road to Communism, which also involved full contact and trade with the West and acceptance of aid from the International Monetary Fund (IMF). (See page 190 for Tito's involvement in NAM.)

Why was Tito able to survive?

Because of his resistance against the Nazis in World War Two, Tito was a popular leader; the government had not been installed by the Soviet Red Army (the Red Army left in 1944) and did not depend on Soviet support to remain in power. In addition, from 1950 Tito received both military and economic aid from the USA, which enabled him to maintain his independence from the Soviet bloc.

What was Stalin's reaction to Tito?

Having failed to get rid of Tito, Stalin took his revenge on suspected 'Titoists' by carrying out East European purge trials. By using fabricated charges, leaders, such as the Hungarian foreign minister Laszlo Rajk, were demoted, tried and either imprisoned or executed during the late 1940s.

Although this got rid of open Tito sympathizers, secret sympathizers remained. The exploitative and repressive nature of the regimes in the satellite states meant that Soviet rule was resented by ordinary people and never achieved any popular support. Thus on several occasions, from 1945 onwards, there were to be more challenges to Soviet control: East Germany in 1953, Poland and Hungary in 1956, Czechoslovakia in 1968 and Poland in the 1980s.

Challenge in East Germany, 1953

It was the combination of relaxation of controls with continuing repression which helped to trigger the East German riots of 1953. East Germany was facing a crisis at this time due to the mass exodus of East Germans to the West through Berlin. Beria, the Deputy Soviet Prime Minister, suggested that the USSR should get rid of the unstable and expensive GDR by selling it to the West. This idea was not taken up, as his colleagues still believed that it was possible to work towards a unified Socialist Germany. However, the East German leader, Walter Ulbricht, was forced by the Soviet government to take a more conciliatory approach in his policy of forced collectivization of farms and socialization. Unfortunately, this softer approach came too late and no attempt was made to reduce the high production targets, which had been set for the workers by Ulbricht. This created a dangerous situation and, on 16–17 June, workers in Berlin and elsewhere in East Germany rose up in revolt.

STUDENT STUDY SECTION

Document analysis

We, the working-people from the district of Bitterfeld demand:

1. The immediate resignation of the so-called German Democratic government which has come to power through manipulation of the elections
2. The creation of a provisional government consisting of the progressive working-people
3. Admission of all the big West German democratic parties
4. Free and secret direct elections within four weeks at the latest
5. Release of all political prisoners (the plain political ones, the so-called fiscal criminals, and those persecuted because of their religious confession)
6. Immediate abolition of all borders and withdrawal of the People's Police
7. Immediate normalization of the social standard of living
8. Immediate dissolution of the so-called National Army
9. No reprisals against even a single striking worker

Demands of the East Berlin Strike Committee, 1953 (telegram sent to the government of the GDR)

Question

From these demands, what can you learn about the actions and policies of the East German Government?

This was the first time that anything like this had happened in the Soviet sphere of influence and the uprising was quickly suppressed by Red Army troops; however, the revolt was very embarrassing for the Soviet Union. Beria was arrested and executed for being a Western agent. The idea of having a friendly neutral Germany was abandoned. Repression continued and Ulbricht and Khrushchev now concentrated on building up the GDR as a separate state.

Challenges to Soviet control under Khrushchev

Khrushchev and de-Stalinization

In 1956, at the Twentieth Congress of the Communist Party, Khrushchev proclaimed his policy of de-Stalinization. Although for a time this did strengthen his position at home, it seriously weakened his authority over Communism elsewhere. It is ironic that Khrushchev got rid of Stalin's weapons of terror and yet he had to use more force than Stalin had ever done in order to keep control in Hungary.

Khrushchev and Tito

As part of his attack on Stalin, Khrushchev claimed that Stalin had made a major error concerning Tito and Yugoslavia. He argued that had Stalin understood Tito and the national cause he represented, Yugoslavia would never have broken away from the East European bloc. He thus restored relations with Yugoslavia, visiting Tito in 1955 and 1956. However, Tito continued to maintain his non-aligned status in his relationship with the USSR.

Khrushchev and Poland

In revising the USSR's relations with Yugoslavia, Khrushchev did not intend to revise the USSR's relations with its other satellite states. However, many of the satellite states saw Khrushchev's approach to Yugoslavia as a sign that he also would accept them finding their own way with regard to Communism.

In Poland at the end of June 1956, workers in the industrial city of Pozan revolted. During the next few months, the Polish Communist Wladyslaw Gomulka, who had been outlawed in Stalin's day, was brought back to political prominence as First Secretary (without Khrushchev's approval) and he implemented a rapid de-Stalinization programme. On 19 October 1956, Khrushchev flew to Warsaw and Soviet military forces moved into intimidating positions. However, Gomulka refused to be intimidated by Khrushchev, even threatening to arm the Polish workers to resist the Soviets. Importantly, however, Gomulka also told Khrushchev that he had no intention of taking Poland out of the Warsaw Pact. This calmed Khrushchev's fears. He agreed to allow Gomulka to remain in power; this was, significant as it was the first time that the Soviet Union had compromised with another Communist state on its choice of leader. In fact, Gomulka turned out to be a trusted ally of Khrushchev and the freedoms acquired by the Poles in 1956 were gradually taken away.

Khrushchev and Hungary

Khrushchev, however, did not compromise over Hungary, and it was here that it became clear that Khrushchev was as determined as Stalin to maintain Soviet control over the satellite states.

What was the American reaction?
The United States felt that it had to do something to help the East Germans. It therefore called for a four-power foreign ministers' conference to discuss the future of Germany, but also continued provocative broadcasts from its radio stations in West Berlin to try to prolong the unrest in East Germany.

Khrushchev's de-Stalinization speech
(see also Chapter Seven)
In 1956, Khrushchev gave a speech to the Twentieth Congress of the Communist Party, in which he denounced Stalin. He criticized the excesses of Stalin's regime and denounced Stalin's crimes and the growth of the 'cult of personality'. This was shocking to the Communist world.

Communists were not used to having mistakes admitted at the top, and certainly not on this scale. It was, as Secretary of State Dulles commented at the time, 'the most damning indictment of despotism ever made by a despot'.
John Lewis Gaddis, *The Cold War* (Penguin, 2005) p.107

Stalin's statue being taken down during the Hungarian revolution.

The Suez Crisis

This occurred after President Nasser of Egypt took the decision to nationalize the Suez Canal. The British, French and Israelis invaded Egypt to take back control of the canal, but faced condemnation from both the USA and the USSR as a result. Britain and France were forced to withdraw and Nasser retained control over the canal. (See Chapter Fourteen for more details.)

News of the Polish success had spread to Hungary, where people lived under the repressive regime of Matyas Rakoski. Crowds took to the streets and demanded that Rakoski be replaced with the more moderate Imre Nagy. Khrushchev agreed to this, but riots continued. Khrushchev ordered the Red Army to restore order, but, surprisingly, it failed to do this, and Nagy was able to negotiate the withdrawal of Soviet forces on 28 October 1956. Shortly afterwards he announced that Hungary would leave the Warsaw Pact and become a neutral state. He was also planning to share power in Hungary with non-Communist groups.

This was something that Khrushchev could not tolerate and, aware that the attention of the West was focused on the Suez crisis, Soviet forces launched a general offensive against the Hungarians. There was bitter fighting in the streets of Budapest. Twenty thousand Hungarians and 3000 Soviet troops were killed, but the Soviets were successful in bringing Hungary back under their control. A new Hungarian government under Janos Kadar was created and Imre Nagy was later executed by the Soviets.

What actions did the USA take?

The Hungarian revolt had been encouraged by CIA broadcasts on Radio Free Europe which led Hungarians to believe that they would get U.S. support. However, the Americans made it clear to the Soviet leaders that the United States would take no action to save Nagy. It is true that U.S. attention was being diverted by the Suez Crisis, but there is no evidence that President Eisenhower ever considered interfering in Hungary. This was because he believed (probably mistakenly) that Khrushchev might have been prepared to risk nuclear war rather than lose this satellite state.

Why did the Soviets act differently in Hungary and Poland?

In Poland, the Communist Party had retained control, while in Hungary they had lost control. Nagy's decision to declare Hungary a neutral state would have meant the exclusion of Soviet influence and a weakening of the defensive ring of states established on its Western borders since 1944. Khrushchev's actions in Hungary showed that de-Stalinization did not mean a softening of the USSR's fundamental attitudes. When the Communist Party was in danger of losing control over state machinery, or where its control of the Eastern bloc was challenged, it was prepared to use whatever pressure was necessary to pull the satellites back into line.

STUDENT STUDY SECTION

Document analysis

Document A

We have almost no weapons, no heavy guns of any kind. The Hungarian people are not afraid of death. You can't let people attack tanks with their bare hands. What is the United Nations doing? … Civilized people of the world! Our ship is sinking. Light is fading. The shadows grow darker over the soil of Hungary. Help us!

The above are extracts from radio messages sent by Hungarian rebels during the fighting.

Document B

A Socialist state could not remain an indifferent observer of the bloody reign of Fascist reaction in People's Democratic Hungary. When everything settles down in Hungary, and life becomes normal again, the Hungarian working class, peasantry and intelligentsia will undoubtedly understand our actions better and judge them aright. We regard our help to the Hungarian working class in its struggle against the intrigues of counter-revolution as our international duty.

From an editorial in *Pravda* dated 23 November 1956

What were the results for Khrushchev and the Soviet Union?

Khrushchev's position in the USSR was strengthened by the events in Hungary and Suez. It also meant that the Soviets could now feel confident that there would be no American influence in their area of control. However, events also made clear that the Warsaw Pact (unlike NATO) was not based on voluntary participation, and that the USSR could not always rely on the loyalty of its satellite states.

STUDENT STUDY SECTION

Cartoon analysis

This cartoon, entitled 'Trainer Khrushchev's Problem', by Leslie Illingworth was published in *Punch*, (a British magazine) on 31 October 1956.

Questions

1 Using your knowledge of events in Eastern Europe, explain the actions of the different bears in the cartoon.

2 What is the overall message of the cartoonist?

Soviet leader Leonid Brezhnev.

Brezhnev and the challenge from Czechoslovakia, 1968

In the 1960s the dissatisfaction felt by the Czech people at their repressive regime came to a head. Alexander Dubcek became First Secretary of the Communist Party in 1968 and this marked the beginning of what became known as the 'Prague Spring'. Aiming to create 'socialism with a human face', Dubcek introduced measures to modernize and liberalize the economy. There were also to be wider powers for trade unions, expansion of trade with the West and freedom to travel abroad. In June he even abolished censorship and encouraged criticism of the government. Conscious of what had happened to Hungary in 1956, he was careful to assure the USSR that Czechoslovakia would stay in the Warsaw Pact and remain a valuable ally.

What actions did the Soviets take?

Soviet leader Leonid Brezhnev and the other leaders of the Warsaw Pact became increasingly worried at the events in Prague, and the USSR decided to resort to force. In August 1968, Soviet troops, together with other members of the Warsaw Pact, invaded Czechoslovakia and ended the Prague Spring. A new government was installed under Gustáv Husák, which was subservient to Moscow.

What were the results of the invasion of Czechoslovakia?

In order to justify his actions in Czechoslovakia, Brezhnev laid down what became known as 'the Brezhnev Doctrine':

There is no doubt that the peoples of the socialist countries and Communist parties have and must have freedom … theirs must damage neither socialism in their own country nor the fundamental interests of other socialist countries … This means that every Communist party is responsible not only to its own people, but also to all the socialist countries and the entire Communist movement. Whoever forgets this is placing sole emphasis on the autonomy and independence of Communist parties, lapses into one-sidedness, shirking his internationalist obligations …

The Brezhnev Doctrine as quoted in Pravda, 26 September 1968

Thus the actions of one socialist country were recognized as affecting all. Therefore, collective action to deal with any threat to the socialist community was viewed as justified and necessary. It was now clear that any attempt at 'liberalism' by a state in the Eastern bloc would not be tolerated. As a result, reform plans throughout the region were abandoned, with disastrous economic consequences to the future of the Soviet bloc.

The invasion of Czechoslovakia seriously damaged the international reputation of Communism and the Soviet Union. Yugoslavia, Albania and China condemned the Soviet action. In Western Europe, many Communists stopped looking to Moscow for guidance. However, it had no major impact on East–West relations. It slowed down the détente process, but did not throw it off course.

Moscow's goals in Czechoslovakia led most observers on both sides of the Iron Curtain to regard the intervention as a decisive Soviet victory. Relations with the West experienced some setbacks

... *Ultimately, however, the need to involve Moscow in negotiations with North Vietnam overcame American indignation ... The invasion ... created instant tensions with the East European nations that had not taken part in the operation. As for the nations remaining in the Soviet-led alliance, the invasion confirmed that autonomous political reforms would no longer be tolerated ... [also] the invasion seriously damaged Moscow's ability to build a united front against the Chinese.*

Matthew Ouitmet gave this overall assessment of the effects of the invasion of Czechoslovakia in The Rise and Fall of the Brezhnev Doctrine in Soviet Foreign Policy *(University of North Carolina Press, 2003)*

STUDENT STUDY SECTION

Cartoon analysis

"Out, Out, Brief Candle!"

'Out, Out, Brief Candle!' by Herblock, 1968.

Cartoon questions

1   Explain what is happening in the cartoon.

2   What is the cartoonist's message about Brezhnev's actions with regard to Czechoslovakia?

Review question

To what extent did the Soviet actions in Czechoslovakia have more impact on their relations with other Communist countries than with the West? Refer also to Chapter Eleven (pages 126–7) in answering this question.

The challenge from Poland in the 1980s

In the late 1970s, dissatisfaction with the poor economic situation in Poland resulted in industrial unrest, food shortages and strikes. The opposition to the government centred on the port city of Gdansk, and in 1980 the Gdansk shipyard workers went on strike. They were led by an unemployed shipyard worker named Lech Walesa, and were successful in securing economic and political rights, including the right to strike and form free trade unions. This led to the establishment of the independent trade union movement called Solidarity. By 1981, Solidarity claimed a membership of 10 million and was seen as a threat to the USSR. The Red Army sent troops to the Polish border, but did not invade. Stanislaw Kania, the new leader of Poland, convinced Brezhnev that he could restore order himself, and it is also possible that American warnings against the use of force kept back the Soviet troops. However, reliable elements of the Polish army were used to seize control of the government in December 1981. The loyal General Wojciech Jaruzelski was installed as prime minister and he declared marital law, banned Solidarity and arrested thousands of activists. By 1983, the government was in firm control, but the economic problems, along with continued support for Solidarity, remained (see Chapter Seventeen).

The declaration of martial law in Poland along with the invasion of Afghanistan helped to weaken détente, which was already struggling to survive at this point.

STUDENT STUDY SECTION

Review exercise

Copy out the grid below and summarize the challenges to Soviet control:

	Nature of challenge	Soviet reaction	Western reaction	Consequences
Yugoslavia 1948				
East Germany 1953				
Poland 1956				
Hungary 1956				
Czechoslovakia 1968				
Poland 1980				

To what extent were Soviet leaders following Stalin's structural legacy?

The system set up by Stalin in Eastern Europe – his 'legacy' – is outlined at the beginning of this chapter. Although Khrushchev attempted to carry out de-Stalinization and to improve relations with Tito, there was no fundamental change in the relationship between the Soviet Union and the satellite states as established under Stalin. This was even more the case during Brezhnev's leadership:

- Power remained centralized in Moscow; economically the satellite states continued to develop their economies to suit that of the Soviet Union. After the Brezhnev Doctrine was introduced, all economic experiments in the Soviet bloc aimed at modernization and increased competitiveness came to an end.
- The leaders of the satellite states remained men who were loyal to Moscow.
- When any of the states attempted to resist or deviate from this situation, the Red Army was used ruthlessly to restore order and maintain the system; the Brezhnev Doctrine justified this as necessary for preserving socialism throughout the Eastern bloc.

The challenge from Afghanistan

The Brezhnev Doctrine was also used as a reason for invading Afghanistan in 1979. Although not part of the official Soviet sphere of influence, the USSR was anxious to prevent a situation developing in Afghanistan that might threaten Soviet security.

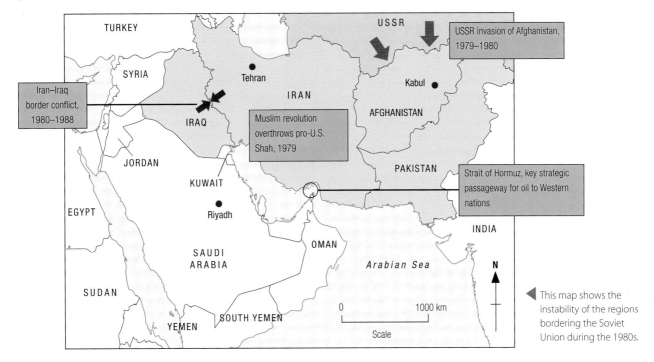

This map shows the instability of the regions bordering the Soviet Union during the 1980s.

Why did the Soviets intervene in Afghanistan?

In April 1978, the People's Democratic Party (PDP) of Afghanistan seized power. This was a pro-Soviet organization and received economic assistance from Moscow. However, the new government's social and economic policies, which included land reform, women's rights and secular education, were resisted by both the fundamentalist Muslim groups and factions within the PDP. One faction was led by Hafizullah Amin, who came to power in a coup in September 1979.

However, there was continued instability in the country because of anti-Muslim policies, and Afghan Muslims began joining the *Mujahedin*, which declared a *jihad*, or holy war, against the supporters of Amin. Amin's regime became increasingly dependent on Soviet aid. However, relations between the Soviets and Amin were strained and Amin also began to initiate contact through the CIA with the U.S. government. This triggered rumours that Amin himself had been recruited by the CIA. To the Soviets there seemed to be no alternative but to intervene militarily and replace Amin with the pro-Soviet Babrak Kamal.

The official Soviet reasons for invading Afghanistan included the following:
* The USSR did not want the 'Afghan Revolution' defeated and Afghanistan turned into a Shah's Iran.
* The USSR believed that the victory of the 'counter-revolution' would result in a 'bloodbath' caused by religious zealots and vengeful feudal lords.
* The USSR believed that a victory for the counter-revolution's forces would allow for massive American military involvement in Afghanistan. This was a country bordering the USSR, and thus a threat to Soviet security.
* The USSR claimed that it would have 'ceased to be a great power' if it turned away from taking 'unpopular, but necessary, decisions'.

The impact of the revolution in Iran on the Soviet Union

In January 1979 the Shah of Iran (who had been backed by the USA) was removed in an Islamist uprising and replaced by the Ayatollah Khomeini – a Muslim fundamentalist. The implications of this for the United States have already been discussed (see Chapter Thirteen, page 159). However, this new regime threatened Soviet security as well. The Central Asian Republics of the USSR – bordering Afghanistan – had significant Muslim populations and the spread of Islamic fundamentalism could destabilize these areas.

In a letter to Brezhnev, Yuri Andropov wrote:

We have been receiving information about Amin's behind-the-scenes activities which may mean his political reorientation to the West. … In closed meetings he attacks Soviet policy and the activities of our specialists. Our ambassador was practically expelled from Kabul. These developments have created, on the one hand, a danger of losing the domestic achievements of the Afghan revolution, and, on the other hand, a threat to our positions in Afghanistan …

In addition, there were unofficial reasons for the invasion:
- The moderate Western response to the invasion of Czechoslovakia may have encouraged the Soviets in their decision to invade Afghanistan.
- Détente was already in difficulties, so the impact that the invasion might have on relations with the USA was not so much of a concern to the Soviet leadership as it might have been several years earlier.

From this point on, the new Kamal regime that replaced Amin was dependent on Soviet military strength to maintain its control against the popular revolutionary troops of the Afghan Islamist forces. However, the problem was, as Westad comments, that Afghan Communism had already 'self-destructed' well before the Soviet invasion:

The basic policy failure of the Soviet Afghan invasion was the belief that foreign power could be used to secure the survival and ultimate success of a regime that demonstrably could not survive on its own.

Odd Arne Westad in The Global Cold War *(CUP, 2007) p.326*

What was the American response to the Soviet invasion of Afghanistan?

The Soviets completely miscalculated the impact that their actions would have on the West. Generally, the invasion was seen in the West not as evidence of maintaining control in an already existing sphere of influence, as had happened in Czechoslovakia, but as evidence of Soviet expansionism. President Carter stated that the invasion might pose the most serious threat to world peace since World War Two and imposed stringent measures against the USSR (see also Chapter Thirteen). As a response, the Carter administration took the following actions:
- The 'Carter Doctrine' was announced – it pledged U.S. intervention in the Persian Gulf if the Soviets threatened its interests there.
- Carter's National Security team decided to resist the Soviet invasion by 'proxy', that is, providing the *Mujahedin* rebels with weapons.

After 1981 President Reagan's more aggressive stance towards the Soviet Union involved a more direct approach in Afghanistan. Reagan increased levels of aid and, in the mid-1980s, began to send U.S. supplies of arms to the *Mujahedin* and their Afghan allies, some via Pakistan:

By 1985, a very complex web of foreign support for the Mujahedin was in place in which the United States worked and co-operated closely with conservative Arab governments and voluntary organizations to jointly fund and operate key initiatives.

From Odd Arne Westad, The Global Cold War *(CUP, 2007) p.355*

As the war of attrition continued to the end of Brezhnev's rule, and through that of Andropov and Chernenko, the impact of direct American aid probably gave the rebels the upper hand:

> … *in Afghanistan, a large covert operation was mounted to arm the Mujahedin rebels through Pakistan. It was, however, only in Reagan's second term, after 1985, that the crucial Stinger anti-aircraft missiles were provided. Easily portable and fired by a single soldier, the Stingers turned the tide of the Afghan War by challenging the Soviet command of the air.*

From Martin Walker, **The Cold War** *(Vintage, 1995) p.287*

The war in Afghanistan cost the lives of more than one million Afghans and 25,000 Red Army soldiers. It also cost the USSR in the region of $8 billion per annum. The reason that the Soviets ultimately pulled out was very much down to the political thinking of the new Soviet leader – Mikhail Gorbachev. He believed that this money was desperately needed for his domestic reforms. Also, the war itself did not fit in with his new philosophy for Soviet foreign policy – the USSR was no longer to foot the bill for supporting the cause of world Communism. Gorbachev announced his intention to pull Soviet troops out of Afghanistan in February 1988. By the following February, the USSR had completed its military withdrawal.

Mujahedin fighters in Afghanistan.

Afghanistan and its impact on détente

The view of the rightwing in the United States is that the invasion of Afghanistan was a key example of how the Soviets were still pursuing the 'Marxist-Leninist' expansionism embodied in their political doctrine. Thus the Soviets were responsible for the breakdown of détente.

The Post-revisionist view is that the Soviet Union was responding defensively to a genuine threat to its security. This threat was also in its 'sphere of influence'. The U.S. response was cynical, and intended to take advantage of the unstable situation caused by Islamic fundamentalism in Afghanistan. It was in fact changes in U.S. foreign policy – as championed by Carter's adviser Zbigniew Brzezinski and then by Reagan's government – that led to the second Cold War and renewed tension, not the Soviet invasion of Afghanistan.

STUDENT STUDY SECTION

Review question

What was the impact of the invasion of Afghanistan on the Cold War up to 1985? To answer this question comprehensively, refer back to Chapter Eleven and Chapter Thirteen.

Research question

To what extent do you agree that Afghanistan was the Soviet Vietnam?

Essay question

To what extent was the Soviet Union successful in maintaining control over its satellite states in the period 1945–1980?

Essay planning hints

Introduction: For your introduction, you need put the question into context, that is, to explain briefly how the Soviet Union tried to control the satellite states and the main challenges to that control that took place up to 1980. Also identify your main line of argument – whether you think that they were or were not successful.

Main body: You want to avoid a chronological run-through and description of the challenges. Keep to the question which is to *assess the success* of the Soviet Union in keeping control. How can you do this?

- You could consider looking firstly at where and in what ways the Soviet Union was successful in keeping control and then where and in what ways it was not successful.
- You may also want to discuss what the cost of its 'successes' were for the satellite states (and future Soviet control), also what factors affected the Soviet Union's success or failure.

Essay skills review activity

The opening words of an essay are key for telling you what exactly you should be aiming to do in your essay, and what the focus of your key arguments should be. Below are essay questions on the Cold War. The opening key words or phrases in each essay question have been italicized. In pairs, briefly discuss what each of the words/phrases is expecting you to do in the essay and how they might have an impact on how you structure the essay:

To what extent was the Soviet Union successful in maintaining control over its satellite states in the period 1945–1980?

How far were the policies of Truman responsible for the cold War?

Assess the importance of the Yalta and Potsdam conferences for the development of the Cold War, 1945 to 1949.

Analyse the impact of the Korean War on the development of the Cold War after 1950.

Account for the growing hostility between China and the Soviet Union up to 1970.

Evaluate the impact of the Cold War on newly independent countries.

Examine the role of ideology in the origins of the Cold War.

Compare and contrast the part played by Vietnam and Afghanistan in the Cold War.

How and why did superpower rivalry dominate international politics after 1945?

In what ways could Stalin be held responsible for the origin and development of the Cold War up to 1953?

17 THE COLLAPSE OF THE SOVIET UNION AND THE END OF THE COLD WAR

There are several questions that need consideration when attempting to explain why the Cold War ended:

- What was the role of Gorbachev? To what extent was Gorbachev forced to end the Cold War?
- What role did the American administration and a renewed arms race play in the fall of the Soviet Union?
- How far did the economic problems within the USSR and its sphere of influence dictate the changes in policy under Gorbachev?
- What was the role of 'people power' and nationalism in the fall of the USSR?

The end of the Cold War baffles us; almost nobody expected it.

Melvyn Leffler

◀ The Berlin Wall is dismantled, 1989.

When Mikhail Gorbachev resigned as president of the USSR on Christmas day 1991, the Soviet Union had ceased to exist. The Cold War was finally over. This monumental turning point in modern world history had occurred, amazingly, with little bloodshed. Perhaps just as astonishing was that no one had predicted this rapid collapse of the 'other' superpower. The United States and British intelligence services were as surprised as the East German border guards when the iconic symbol of the Cold War, the Berlin Wall, was torn down in November 1989. The collapse of the Soviet Empire meant that the Cold War was definitely at an end. However, even before this happened in 1989, relations between the Soviet Union and the United States had changed dramatically.

Timeline of key events leading to the end of the Cold War	
1979	Invasion of Afghanistan
1979	Solidarity movement set up in Poland
1980	Brezhnev dies, succeeded by Andropov
1984	Andropov dies, succeeded by Chernenko
1985	Chernenko dies, succeeded by Gorbachev (March)
	Perestroika reform era begins
1986	*Glasnost* era begins (April)
	Chernobyl nuclear disaster
1987	Washington Summit (December) – Intermediate Nuclear Forces Treaty is signed
1988	Law on State Enterprises (January) – Soviet state no longer responsible for debts on economic enterprises
	Electoral Law – new multi-candidate elections established in USSR and used in the elections for the new Congress of People's Deputies (October)
	Gorbachev's speech to UN – outlines Warsaw Pact troop reductions and a withdrawal of Soviet forces from Afghanistan (December)
1989	Soviet withdrawal from Afghanistan (February)
	Commission on Economic Reform set up to consider ways to reform Soviet economy (July)
	Anti-Soviet movements begin in Warsaw Pact countries. Gorbachev maintains he will not intervene (October)
	Fall of the Berlin Wall (November)
	Malta Summit. Gorbachev and Bush declare the 'end of the Cold War'
1990	Article 6 of USSR constitution is dropped – ends monopoly of the CPSU (Communist Party of the Soviet Union) within the USSR (February)
	Baltic Republics declare independence (Estonia, Latvia and Lithuania), (March – May)
1991	Vilnius Massacre in Lithuania (January)
	Boris Yeltsin elected President of Russia (June)
	Coup against Gorbachev by hard-liners is unsuccessful (August 19-21)
	Yeltsin outlaws CPSU in Russia (August 23)
	Gorbachev resigns as general secretary of CPSU, and dissolves the party (August 24)
	Minsk Agreement – ends the USSR, replaced by Commonwealth of Independent States (CIS)

Mikhail Gorbachev and Ronald Reagan.

What was the impact of Mikhail Gorbachev?

For the Soviet Union, Stalin's 'legacy' meant that politically the Soviet Union remained an authoritarian, one-party state and that economically it was focused on producing military hardware rather than housing, transport, food, consumer goods and health care. 'We can't go on living like this', Mikhail Gorbachev is reported to have said on the eve of his succession as General Secretary to the Politburo. Not only was he the youngest leader to have this position since Stalin, but he was also the first university-educated leader since Stalin.

Gorbachev introduced two key reforming ideas – *perestroika* and *glasnost*. *Perestroika* (restructuring) aimed at restructuring the economy and *glasnost* (openness) was the principle that every area of the regime should be open to public scrutiny. This represented a radical change in politics in the Soviet Union. It involved greater 'democratization', with more people involved in the Communist Party and in political debate.

Through these strategies, Gorbachev intended to make the Soviet system more productive and responsive, and he realized that part of this process also had to involve a reduction in military spending. He knew that, if his reforming ideas were going to work, the Soviets could not rise to the challenge of matching Reagan's SDI system. He decided to abandon the arms race and attempt a negotiated reduction in arms with the USA. It was not just for economic reasons that Gorbachev wanted arms control. 'He called for a new thinking in international affairs, and he said that there could be 'no winners' in a nuclear war. Gorbachev declared the world to be interdependent and likened all its people 'to climbers roped together on the mountainside' (John Mason, *The Cold War*, Routledge, 1996).

The Chernobyl disaster, when an explosion destroyed a reactor at the Chernobyl nuclear power plant in the Ukraine, only heightened Gorbachev's awareness of the dangers of nuclear power. As Anatoly Chernlayev, an aide to Gorbachev, put it, 'Gorbachev knew even before that catastrophe about the danger of nuclear weapons. That explosion showed that, even without war and without nuclear missiles, nuclear power could destroy human kind' (quoted in the CNN television series, *The Cold War*).

Reagan was also interested in disarmament and had previously put forward to the Soviets an arms control proposal known as 'Zero Option', which would eliminate all intermediate-range missiles in Europe. Gorbachev, unlike his predecessors, was prepared to discuss this option. This resulted in the two leaders meeting together in four summits to discuss arms control:

- Geneva Summit, November 1985: No substantial progress was made but the two leaders did agree that 'a nuclear war cannot be won and must not be fought'.
- Reykjavik Summit, October 1986: Talks ended without agreement, mainly because of disagreement over SDI. Gorbachev said that SDI should be 'confined to the laboratory', but Reagan refused to make any concessions. However, the talks also covered the most sweeping arms control proposals in history, and Gorbachev declared that it had 'been an intellectual breakthrough' in relations between the United and States and the Soviet Union.
- Washington Summit, December 1987: An Intermediate-Range Nuclear Force Treaty (INF Treaty) was signed which actually agreed to abolish weapons – land-based missiles of intermediate and shorter range. This was an important first step in reducing the nuclear stockpiles of the two superpowers. Agreement was also reached for the first time on inspection of the destruction of missiles.
- Moscow Summit, May 1988: Again there was disagreement over SDI, but arms reductions negotiations continued. Standing in Red Square, Reagan confessed that he now no longer believed in the 'evil empire'.

Other foreign policy initiatives by Gorbachev were reassuring to the West. By 1988, Gorbachev had announced his plans to withdraw from Afghanistan and he pulled back Soviet aid to its 'allies' in the developing world.

The 'thawing' of the Cold War continued under the new U.S. president, George H.W. Bush. At the Malta Summit between the U.S. and Soviet leaders in 1989, Soviet Foreign Minister Shevardnadze announced that the superpowers had 'buried the Cold War at the bottom of the Mediterranean'.

What was the role of Ronald Reagan?

Clearly, Gorbachev's willingness to tackle the issue of nuclear weapons, along with his new style of politics and doing business with the West, were key to explaining the breakdown of the Cold War. However, many historians also give Reagan credit for this and argue that it was his approach to the Soviet Union in the early 1980s that was crucial for pushing the Soviet Union into arms negotiations. An article critical of the 'Reagan victory school' describes this view below:

As former Pentagon officials like Caspar Weinberger and Richard Perle … and other proponents of the Reagan victory school have argued, a combination of military and ideological pressures gave the Soviets little choice but to abandon expansionism abroad and repression at home. In their view, the Reagan military build-up foreclosed Soviet military options while pushing the Soviet economy to the breaking point. Reagan partisans stress that his dramatic Star Wars initiative put the Soviets on notice that the next phase of the arms race would be waged in areas where the West held a decisive technological edge.

D. Deudney and G.J. Ikenberry, 'Who won the Cold War?', in Foreign Policy, no. 87, Summer 1992, p.124

This 'Reagan victory school' view is therefore critical of the 'détente' approach to relations with the Soviet Union as explained below by Patrick Glynn:

The Jimmy Carter-Cyrus Vance approach of rewarding the Soviet build-up with one-sided arms control treaties, opening Moscow's access to Western capital markets and technologies, and condoning Soviet imperial expansion was perfectly designed to preserve the Brezhnev-style approach, delivering the Soviets from any need to re-evaluate (as they did under Gorbachev) or change their policies. Had the Carter-Vance approach been continued … the Cold War and the life of the Soviet Union would almost certainly have been prolonged.

Patrick Glynn, letter to the Editor, Foreign Policy, no. 90, Spring 1993, pp.171–3

STUDENT STUDY SECTION

Document analysis

Read the two sources above again.

Questions

1 Identify three reasons from the first source to explain why Reagan's policies could be seen as responsible for ending the Cold War.

2 What criticisms does Patrick Glynn have of détente?

Other historians, such as Michael MacGwire, also claim that Reagan played an important role, but believe this role was more connected to his views on anti-nuclearism, which helped to convince Gorbachev at the different summits of the possibilities of halting the nuclear arms race. Reagan's character and willingness to engage with Gorbachev was also important:

I know of no one else of a leadership stature in the United States in those days who would have moved forward as Reagan did, to engage Gorbachev, to engage the Western Alliance, to truly lead the Western Alliance, and to take us through what became, of course, a very constructive introductory period to the end of the Cold War.

Rozanne Ridgeway, U.S. Assistant Secretary of State interviewed on the CNN television series, The Cold War

Ridgeway's view is supported by historian R.J. McMahon:

To his great credit, Reagan proved willing first to moderate, and then to abandon, deeply held personal convictions about the malignant nature of Communism, thereby permitting a genuine rapprochement to occur.

From R.J. McMahon, The Cold War, A Very Short Introduction (OUP, 2003) p.162

Review question

Who do you believe played the more important role in bringing about a new relationship between the United States and the Soviet Union – Gorbachev or Reagan?

Long-term factors in the ending of the Cold War
What was the role of the Soviet economy?

Although the actions of Gorbachev and Reagan are important for explaining how events turned out as they did, it is also important to look at the long-term forces that were at work in pushing the Soviet Union into ending the Cold War. By the time Brezhnev died in 1982, both the political and economic policies of the Soviet Union were in crisis.

Under Brezhnev the Soviets spent even more resources on foreign policy. Although involved in important arms treaties with the USA, it was under Brezhnev that the USSR achieved 'parity' with the USA in the nuclear field and, in some areas, surpassed it. This was achieved at a high price. Brezhnev's era is remembered as a period of stagnation and decline in the USSR. This is due to the serious lack of spending not only on consumer goods, but on the domestic economy as a whole. Brezhnev left his successors an economy that was still based on the 'command economy' structure of Stalin's day. It was falling behind in modern technology and industrial output was declining. A large proportion of the agricultural workers lived below the poverty line and grain was imported from North America. Workers had little incentive to work harder or produce better goods. Labour morale was low, with high absenteeism and chronic alcoholism.

When Gorbachev took over, he inherited an economy in serious trouble. It could thus be argued that Gorbachev was forced to take the actions that he did in both internal reform and negotiations with the West. Given this situation in the Soviet Union, some historians argue, in direct contradiction with the historians of the 'Reagan victory school', that keeping the Cold War going through containment and détente played a role in bringing about the end of the Cold War rather than prolonging it.

Document analysis

The West did not, as is widely believed, win the Cold War through geopolitical containment and military deterrence. Nor was the Cold War won by the Reagan military build up and the Reagan Doctrine … Instead, 'victory' for the West came when a new generation of Soviet leaders realized how badly their system at home and their policies abroad had failed. What containment did was to successfully stalemate Moscow's attempts to advance Soviet hegemony. Over four decades it performed the historic function of holding Soviet power in check until the internal seeds of destruction within the Soviet Union and its empire could mature. At this point, however, it was Gorbachev who bought the Cold War to an end …
Raymond L. Garthoff 'Why Did the Cold War Arise and Why Did it End?' in Michael J. Hogan (ed), *The End of the Cold War: Its Meaning and Implications* (CUP, 1992) p.129

Questions

1   Explain the meaning of the following phrases used in the extract:
    - geopolitical containment
    - military deterrence
    - Soviet hegemony
    - internal seeds of destruction.

2   What is the overall message of this document regarding the reasons why the Cold War ended?

3   Compare and contrast what Raymond Garthoff says about the reasons for the end of the Cold War with those given by Patrick Glynn on page 212.

What was the role of nationalism and people power in ending the Cold War?

What no one understood, at the beginning of 1989, was that the Soviet Union, its empire, its ideology – and therefore the Cold War itself – was a sand pile ready to slide. All it took to happen was a few more grains of sand. The people who dropped them were not in charge of superpowers or movements or religions: they were ordinary people with simple priorities who saw, seized, and sometimes stumbled into opportunities. In doing so they caused a collapse no one could stop.

From John Lewis Gaddis, The Cold War *(Penguin, 2005) p.238*

In the late 1980s, a resurgence in nationalist movements began to develop in most of the satellite states. The reasons for this were a combination of the continued deterioration of living standards, the fact that the USSR was becoming less involved in the internal affairs of these countries and the implications of Gorbachev's reforms. Gorbachev made it clear that he was unwilling to use force to maintain control over the satellite states.

In a speech to the United Nations, on 7 December, 1988, he announced that the Soviet Union would cut by half a million men its commitment of troops to the Warsaw Pact. 'It is obvious,' he argued, 'that force and the threat of force cannot be and should not be an instrument of foreign policy … Freedom of choice is … a universal principle and it should know no exceptions'. This was a clear signal to the peoples and governments of Eastern Europe. Gorbachev had made it clear that the Brezhnev Doctrine would not be applied, and 1989 saw an amazing series of revolutions in the satellite states, resulting in the whole Soviet system, including Stalin's legacy, being swept away.

The events of 1989

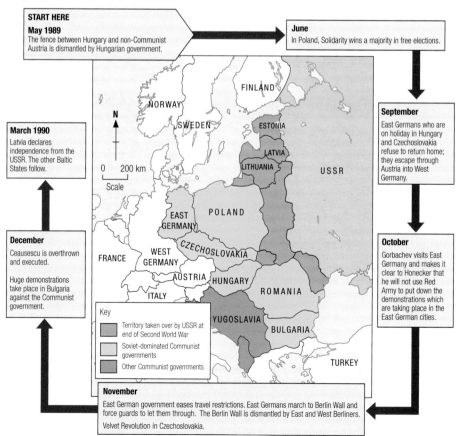

START HERE

May 1989
The fence between Hungary and non-Communist Austria is dismantled by Hungarian government.

June
In Poland, Solidarity wins a majority in free elections.

March 1990
Latvia declares independence from the USSR. The other Baltic States follow.

September
East Germans who are on holiday in Hungary and Czechoslovakia refuse to return home; they escape through Austria into West Germany.

December
Ceausescu is overthrown and executed.

Huge demonstrations take place in Bulgaria against the Communist government.

October
Gorbachev visits East Germany and makes it clear to Honecker that he will not use Red Army to put down the demonstrations which are taking place in the East German cities.

November
East German government eases travel restrictions. East Germans march to Berlin Wall and force guards to let them through. The Berlin Wall is dismantled by East and West Berliners.

Velvet Revolution in Czechoslovakia.

0 200 km
Scale

N

Key

Territory taken over by USSR at end of Second World War

Soviet-dominated Communist governments

Other Communist governments

FINLAND
NORWAY
SWEDEN
ESTONIA
LATVIA
LITHUANIA
USSR
EAST GERMANY
POLAND
CZECHOSLOVAKIA
WEST GERMANY
FRANCE
AUSTRIA
HUNGARY
ITALY
ROMANIA
YUGOSLAVIA
BULGARIA
TURKEY

The process by which the Soviet Union collapsed began in May 1989 when the Hungarian government dismantled the barbed-wire fences on the border with Austria. Thousands of Hungarians and East Germans then crossed over to Austria in order to cross into West Germany.

Events in Poland

In Poland, the union movement called 'Solidarity' had been suppressed in 1981 by General Jaruzelski. He had then declared a state of martial law. Nevertheless, there continued to be popular support for Solidarity due to the combination of economic stagnation that the government failed to solve and support from the Catholic Church. In response to Gorbachev's reforms, Solidarity was legalized in 1988, and some attempt to introduce reforms was made. Solidarity won the first free elections in Poland in 1989. Jaruzelski remained President, but a Solidarity leader became Prime Minster. The Communist Party had been defeated by a huge popular vote, and the government was the first in the Eastern bloc since the 1940s not to be controlled by the Communists. Gorbachev had not intervened to support the old Communist regime and, in the absence of internal or external support, the Polish Communist Party collapsed.

Events in East Germany

Erich Honecker, a hardline Communist, had been the leader of East Germany since 1971. Although considered one of the more 'successful' countries in the Eastern bloc, living standards were well below those enjoyed by their fellow Germans in the West. Honecker used sport as a focus for nationalism, but this did not create a sense of an East German society, and many people still looked forward to the day when Germany would be reunified. Evidence of the insecurity felt by Honecker's regime was the extremely repressive nature of the East German secret police, the Stasi. The Stasi kept files on 5.5 million people. The regime was unpopular, but Honecker was particularly hated. By the mid-1980s there was growing pressure on the government to remove him.

Honecker hoped to consolidate Communist control in East Germany during the celebrations for the 40th anniversary of the GDR. However, people criticized the harsh and repressive East German system and openly demanded reforms. Thousands of East German holidaymakers in Hungary crossed into Austria across the now open border . These 'escapes' were a return to the days before the building of the Berlin Wall – a mass exodus of East Germans (on one day alone 125,000 crossed to the West). More alarming still for the regime were the groups, like the 'New Forum', that decided to stay and resist rather than flee to the West. Honecker wanted to use force to control the swell of anti-Communist party feeling. Gorbachev, however, made it clear that he would not intervene if there were a full-scale revolt. Demonstrations in East German cities continued to grow and a new leader, Egon Krenz, was put in place by the Politburo. In order to try to stem the flow of people from East Germany, the government announced on 9 November 1989 the easing of travel and emigration restrictions. Although not actually intending this to mean an immediate opening of the checkpoints through the Berlin Wall, the lack of clarity in the official statement meant that thousands of East Berliners immediately descended on the checkpoints. The East German guards were taken by surprise and, lacking direction from above, had to go ahead and open the barriers that night. Within 24 hours, the Berlin Wall had ceased to be the symbol of Cold War division and instead its destruction by the people – both East and West Berliners – had become the symbol of the ending of the Cold War. When free elections were held in 1990, parties in favour of unification with West Germany won a majority of seats. East and West Germany were finally reunited on 3 October 1990.

The Berlin Wall comes down ▶ in November 1989.

Events in Hungary

Reform in Hungary came more from within the Hungarian Communist Party itself. Reformers, encouraged by the new policies expounded from Moscow, sacked the hardline leader, Kadar, and then dominated the government. On 23 October 1989 Mátyás Szúrós declared the Third Hungarian Republic and became interim president. Hungary's first free elections were held in 1990.

Events in Czechoslovakia

The changes that took place in Czechoslovakia that led to the downfall of the Communist regime have become known as the 'Velvet Revolution' as there was very little violence. People power can be seen as the clear driving force here. The government was forced to respond to mass demonstrations calling for reform. The campaign was co-ordinated by an organization called the Civic Forum and, in 1989, a leading dissident playwright, Vaclav Havel, was elected president. The Warsaw Pact nations, including the USSR, issued an official statement condemning the 1968 invasion of Czechoslovakia as 'illegal' and promising never to again interfere in each other's internal affairs.

The 'Velvet Revolution' in Czechoslovakia.

Events in Romania

In comparison to the 'Velvet Revolution' in Czechoslovakia, events in Romania were far more violent. Its leader was President Ceausescu and his regime was one of the most repressive in Eastern Europe. However, in December 1989, inspired by news of events in Hungary and by the killing of demonstrators by the Romanian army in Timisoara, there was an uprising against Ceausescu and his wife. When the Ceausescus appeared at a rally in the Romanian capital, Bucharest, one week after the army had killed 71 people in Timisoara, they met with a hostile reception. The army now refused to take action against the demonstrators. Ceausescu and his wife tried to flee, but were arrested by the army and then executed on Christmas Day, 1989.

At the beginning of 1989 the Communists had been in complete – and seemingly permanent – control of Eastern Europe. At the end of the year, they were gone. Democratic coalitions, promising free elections in the immediate future, had taken place in East Berlin, Prague, Budapest, Warsaw and even Bucharest … As a result, the Warsaw Pact had been, in effect, dismantled. The Soviet Union had withdrawn inside its borders. The Cold War in Europe was over.

Stephen Ambrose sums up the events of 1989 in Rise to Globalism *(Penguin, 1991) p.378*

STUDENT STUDY SECTION

Cartoon analysis

Questions

1 Explain what is happening in the cartoon.

2 What is the message of the cartoon regarding events in Eastern Europe?

'The Pace of History Quickens', *The Philadelphia Inquirer*, November 1989.

OOPS! I ACCIDENTALLY HIT FAST FORWARD...

EASTERN EUROPE

HISTORY

11/16/89. THE PHILADELPHIA INQUIRER.

The end of the USSR

Abroad, Gorbachev's policies brought admiration and in 1990 he was awarded the Nobel Peace Prize. At home, however, failure to bring about an improvement in the country's economic situation meant that he became increasingly unpopular. Events in Eastern Europe brought about calls for independence from the republics of the Soviet Union. Thus, during 1991, the Soviet empire disintegrated. In August, the Baltic states of Estonia, Latvia and Lithuania, claimed their independence, as did the republics that had been part of the USSR (see map below).

The former republics of the USSR, which became independent states in 1991.

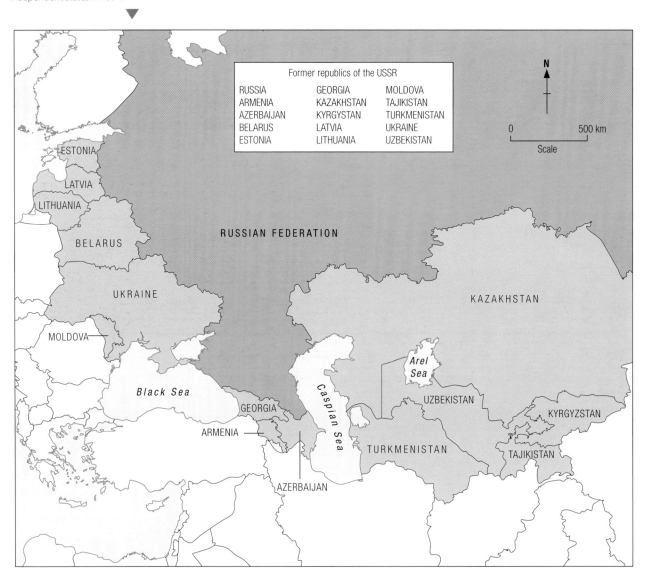

Former republics of the USSR

RUSSIA	GEORGIA	MOLDOVA
ARMENIA	KAZAKHSTAN	TAJIKISTAN
AZERBAIJAN	KYRGYSTAN	TURKMENISTAN
BELARUS	LATVIA	UKRAINE
ESTONIA	LITHUANIA	UZBEKISTAN

This break-up of the Soviet Union intensified hostility towards Gorbachev in the Soviet Union and, in August 1991, there was an attempted coup by Communist hardliners against him. This was defeated by Boris Yeltsin and although Gorbachev was restored, he had now lost authority. On 25 December 1991, Gorbachev resigned as president. The Commonwealth of Independent States was established and the Soviet Union formally ceased to exist.

What was the impact of the fall of the USSR and the end of the Cold War?

The collapse of the Soviet Union had a huge impact on international politics as well as the economic situation of countries that had been dependent on the Soviet Union for aid.

For many in the United States, it seemed that they were the 'winners' and international politics became 'unipolar' with the USA as the only country now capable of having a military alliance around the world. Capitalism seemed to have triumphed. Communism remained the official ideology in only a few states – Cuba, North Korea, Vietnam and China, and even in China and Vietnam, changes in economic controls allowed free-market forces to have an impact.

For Cuba, the drying up of Soviet economic aid, along with the U.S. trade embargo, brought about an economic crisis. Similarly other regimes in Africa formerly supported by the Soviet Union suffered economically. In other states, which had been the focus of superpower conflict and fighting, such as Afghanistan, conflict continued: 'Indeed, many of the Third World countries that had been the focus of excessive superpower interest in the 1970s and 1980s were dubbed "failed states" in the 1990s as civil strife continued unabated and often with relatively little attention from the rest of the world' (Jussi Hanhimäki and Odd Arne Westad, *The Cold War*, OUP, 2004, p.630). The 11 September 2001 attacks on the United States led to a new focus for U.S. foreign policy: the War on Terror … Islamic extremism was identified by the U.S. government as the new global enemy.

STUDENT STUDY SECTION

Research activity
Research the role of Boris Yeltsin, both in the coup against Gorbachev, and later as President of the Russian Federation.

Review activity

1 Draw a spider or flow diagram to show the factors bringing about the end of the Cold War. Distinguish between short and long-term factors on your diagram.

2 A former U.S. Secretary of State said, 'The cold war did not have to end with a whimper; it could have ended with a bang'. What factors do you feel prevented the Cold War ending with a 'bang'?

3 Plan and film a documentary on the collapse of the Soviet Union. Work in groups; you will need to decide on:

   • a title for the documentary

   • who you are going to interview – you will have to take on different roles for the interviews

   • what images you will want to include

   • if you are going to include references to all the countries involved or you if are going to focus on just one or two countries

   • if you are going to portray a particular viewpoint with regard to Gorbachev's actions or if you are going to try to maintain a 'neutral' approach.

Essay question
• To what extent was Gorbachev responsible for bringing about the end of the Cold War?

Essay planning hints

Introduction: Put the question into context. Explain when the end of the Cold War took place. Set out the key factors you will be discussing and your main line of argument.

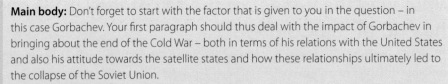

Main body: Don't forget to start with the factor that is given to you in the question – in this case Gorbachev. Your first paragraph should thus deal with the impact of Gorbachev in bringing about the end of the Cold War – both in terms of his relations with the United States and also his attitude towards the satellite states and how these relationships ultimately led to the collapse of the Soviet Union.

You then need to look at other factors:
- the impact of Reagan
- problems within the Soviet Union (you particularly need emphasis on the economic situation here)
- people power.

There are plenty of opportunities for you to bring historiography into this essay; include references to the historians and extracts that are mentioned in this chapter. You should also distinguish between the long- and short-term causes.

Conclusion: You need to decide how far the actions of Gorbachev were the most important factors in the ending of the Cold War. Was he key? Or do you come down on the side of the Reagan victory school? Or maybe the view that the economic situation would have led to the collapse of the Soviet Union anyway?

Research and discussion questions

Below are some research and/or discussion questions on the post-Cold War era:

1 What has been the impact of the collapse of the Soviet Union
a on the European Union?
b on Yugoslavia?
c on NATO?

2 What has been the impact of the end of superpower rivalry on the UN? (Refer back to Chapter Fourteen.)

3 How has the relationship between Russia and the West developed since 1989?

4 Is the situation with regard to nuclear weapons now safer or less stable?

5 Is the 'War on Terror' the new Cold War? Can lessons be taken from the Cold War on how the War on Terror should be fought?

ToK Time

In pairs discuss the following question and feedback to the class: After the fall of the USSR and the end of the Cold War, Soviet archives were opened up to historians for the first time. These archives provided new evidence for researchers to better understand the situation in the USSR and the motives, perspectives and decisions made by its regime during the Cold War.

- How far does this mean that historians in the 1990s were more able to find the 'truth' about the Soviet Union during the Cold War than their predecessors?

Students should attempt to offer examples to support their answers, and add notes from this discussion to their ToK journals.

18 COLD WAR REVIEW AND CONSOLIDATION

This chapter looks at the Cold War as a whole and suggests different study and revision ideas that will help pull together key themes and tackle questions that demand an overall perspective on the Cold War.

What was the role of different U.S. and USSR presidents in the origin and development of the Cold War?

Look at the chart on U.S. Presidential Policies and the Cold War (Appendix III on pages 240–242).

Make sure you understand all the terms and events mentioned. You may also notice that some policies can be interpreted as either a 'success' or a 'failure' depending on the viewpoint you take.

Now copy out and fill in the grid below on the Soviet leaders in the same way, working your way back through this book to find information to help you.

	Stalin Refer to Chapters Two–Five	Khrushchev Refer to Chapters Seven–Nine	Brezhnev Refer to Chapters Thirteen and Sixteen	Gorbachev Refer to Chapter Seventeen
Key policy ideas/beliefs				
How put into practice				
Successes				
Failures				
Legacy				

Using the two grids for guidance, attempt the following essay questions:
1 How sucessful was John F. Kennedy in handling Cold War problems?
2 Assess the impact of the different leaders of the USA and the USSR on the development of the Cold War up to 1964.
3 'Stalin in the period after 1945 and Khrushchev pursued similar objectives in foreign policy; only their methods were different'. Examine the truth of this statement.

What were the key features of the Cold War?

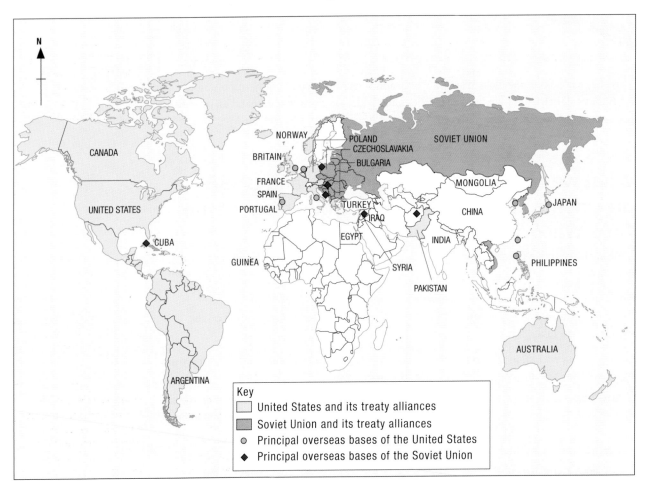

Map showing the different alliances and spheres of influence of the superpowers.

Key
United States and its treaty alliances
Soviet Union and its treaty alliances
○ Principal overseas bases of the United States
◆ Principal overseas bases of the Soviet Union

SEATO	WARSAW PACT	NATO
(1954–1977, with residual 1954 Manila Pact ties remaining with the Philippines and Thailand) Austria Britain France New Zealand Pakistan Philippines Thailand United States	Bulgaria Czechoslovakia East Germany Hungary Poland Romania Soviet Union	Belgium Britain Canada Denmark West Germany Greece Iceland Italy Luxembourg Netherlands Portugal Spain Turkey United States

The Cold War was fought through a variety of methods that included ideological conflict, economic policies, propaganda, the arms race and gaining spheres of influence in different parts of the world.

You need to be able to examine the impact of these different issues or themes regarding the origins and development of the Cold War. There is a grid on the next page to help you – copy it and add extra details.

	Ideology	Economic systems	Security/Arms race	Gaining spheres of influence/Empire building
1945–1949 Origins of Cold War	Ideology becomes increasingly important during this period. Kennan Telegram and Truman Doctrine both focus on Soviets' ideological aims. Cominform set up to spread Communism. Language on both sides becomes increasingly ideological and aims reinforced by propaganda on both sides from about 1947. U.S. propaganda stresses the evils of Communism and the threat it posed to 'Americanism'. Communist propaganda stresses the exploitative, 'fascist' approach of the West in their treatment of workers.	Important in origins as both sides set up own economic systems in their spheres of influence. Marshall Plan designed to strengthen Western governments so that they can resist Communism. Also allows United States to get more markets – seen as American imperialism. Helps intensify Cold War – strong response from Soviets. Satellite states tied together with COMECON.	During this period, the Soviets are working to gain A-bomb so arms race is not such a key factor in origins.	For the Soviets this is key during this period – building up Soviet satellite states. West responds with economic and military sphere of influence in Europe with Marshall Plan and NATO.
1949–1985	Containment plus domino effect becomes key for U.S. foreign policy, reinforced by McCarthyism and growing fear of Communism in United States. Need to 'protect free peoples' now outside Europe as well. Ideology a key reason for U.S. involvement in Vietnam. Downplayed at certain times e.g. during détente when Nixon stresses a more *realpolitik* approach but differences in ideology remain fundamental until 1985. Plays a key role in Second Cold War and language of Reagan.	Economic aid becomes a key tool in securing influence in Third World countries for both USA and USSR. Soviet economic aid given to countries such as Egypt, Angola and Ethiopia in Africa, and Cuba in Central America. USA gives economic aid to right-wing, anti-Communist governments in Taiwan, Thailand, Vietnam and Chile.	From 1949, arms race plays a key role in tension and continuation of hostility. Main aim of both sides is to stay ahead in terms of technology and number of weapons. Even during arms control of détente period, both sides continue to build up weapons. Both sides accept MAD theory and so nuclear weapons keep Cold War going as neither side prepared to risk war – helps détente to develop. Gives huge influence to military-industrial complex in USA.	After China becomes Communist and North Korea attacks South Korea, USA believes in monolithic idea of Communism and sees Soviet sphere of influence spreading. Domino effect takes hold so USA seeks to both stop USSR's influence spreading and to build up own spheres of influence through alliances and military and economic aid. Both sides now attempt to build up spheres of influence in Middle East, Africa and Central America. Brezhnev justifies continued Soviet control in Eastern bloc through Brezhnev Doctrine.
1985–1989	Ideology becomes less important as Reagan and Gorbachev find genuinely common ground and the USSR moves away form the Stalinist legacy in both political and economic spheres.	Economic systems play a key role in end of Cold War; Soviet economic system on verge of collapse.	Plays key role in end of Cold War; spending on nuclear weapons helps to bankrupt the Soviet Union.	Reagan attempts to extend U.S. sphere of influence in Central America through Reagan Doctrine. Soviet sphere of influence collapses with revolutions of 1989.

Themes grid question

In what ways did each of the factors in the grid help start and affect the development of the Cold War?

Again, make sure that you understand and can define key words used above which will appear in essay questions:

- Ideology
- Domino effect
- Containment
- *Realpolitik*
- The different economic systems of capitalism and Communism
- Sphere of influence.

STUDENT STUDY SECTION

Essay questions

Using the grid on page 224 as a starting point for your plans, attempt the following essay questions:

1 Explain the part played by economic issues in the origins and development of the Cold War.

2 To what extent was the Cold War a conflict between two irreconcilable ideologies?

3 'Ideological differences played a key role in the origin and development of the Cold War.' How far do you agree?

4 To what extent did the arms race play a key role in the intensification of the Cold War conflict up to 1962?

5 How important were spheres of influence in Cold War politics after 1945?

Cartoon analysis

The superpowers 'divide up the world'. ▶

Questions

1 Which 'feature' of the Cold War is the cartoonist portraying here?

2 Why are the leaders of the USA and the USSR shown dressed in 19th-century military costume?

Research and presentation activity

The Cold War also had a social and cultural impact on countries inside both the Western and Eastern spheres of influence.

This activity is for you to use to investigate these aspects of the Cold War further.

Part One

Divide the class into two groups.

Group A will research the social, cultural and economic impact of the Cold War on **two** countries in the U.S. sphere of influence. Each of the countries should be from a different region.

Group B will research the social, cultural and economic impact of the Cold War on **two** countries in the Soviet sphere of influence. Each of the countries country should be from a different region.

The two groups should then give brief presentations on the social, cultural and economic impacts of their respective superpowers on their chosen countries.

Part Two

Compare and contrast the impact of the Cold War on countries within the U.S. and Soviet spheres of influence using information from the case studies you have researched.

Overview essay questions

Here are some other essay questions which require you to look at the Cold War as a whole. Plan essay frames in pairs and then feedback to the rest of the class:

1   What do you understand by the term 'containment'? Analyse its importance in Cold War development.

2   When, and for what reasons was there danger of the Cold War escalating into a nuclear conflict?

3   Excluding the superpowers, analyse the role of two countries in the development of the Cold War after 1950. (Germany and China would be good examples to use here.)

● **Examiner's hint:**
Timelines
When planning 'overview' questions on the Cold War, you should have a timeline in front of you. If you refer back to Chapter One, you will find the thematic timeline which outlines the different 'eras' in the Cold War. In the Appendices, you will find a timeline with the key events from 1945 to 1999. However, to assist you with revision you should also create your own timelines. These timelines can be done in different ways:
- different colours for USA actions and USSR actions
- actions of the USA on one side of the line and the actions of the USSR on the other side
- colour codes to show times of tension versus times of 'relaxation'
- different timelines for different parts of the world.

Chapter Nineteen
Theory of Knowledge

Why study History?

Many elements of the IB History course link in well to exploring Theory of Knowledge, including the question of why it is important to study history at all.

American historian John Lewis Gaddis argues:

…the study of history is…to achieve the optimal balance, first within ourselves, but then within society, between the polarities of oppression and liberation.
John Lewis Gaddis, The Landscape of History *(OUP, 2002)*

Over 60 years ago the British philosopher and historian R.G. Collingwood also defended the study of history, saying:

What is history for? … Knowing yourself means knowing, first, what it is to be a man; secondly, knowing what it is to be the kind of man you are; and thirdly, knowing what it is to be the man YOU are and nobody else is. Knowing yourself means knowing what you can do; and since nobody knows what he can do until he tries, the only clue to what man can do is what man has done. The value of history, then, is that it teaches us what man has done and thus what man is.
R. G. Collingwood, The Idea of History *(OUP, 1946)*

So, history helps us understand ourselves and our own individual 'histories', and is, therefore, important in helping us clarify our understanding of the world we live in. History is used to argue and justify political positions, economic policies, international relations between countries and religious perspectives. In fact, most other areas of knowledge rely to a certain extent on the use and application of history. For example, it would be difficult for a scientist to add to the body of knowledge in his or her subject in a meaningful way without knowing what had come before.

Historians are dangerous people. They are capable of upsetting everything.
Nikita Khrushchev

What is the historian's methodology? How do historians work?

An important question for ToK students to examine is to what extent history is discovered or invented. Below is a list of some of the steps a historian might go through in attempting to find 'historical truth':

- Plan research.
- Create organizing questions.
- Research/investigate evidence.
- Build a body of evidence.
- Evaluate sources for value and limitation.
- Consider different perspectives.
- Apply methodology from different areas of knowledge.
- Consider which lines of argument seem most important.
- Select evidence and lines of argument.

Questions

1 How far does opinion impact on each part of the method?
2 New evidence leads to new historical interpretations. However, should you also consider the extent to which the 'context' of the historian leads to new historical interpretations?

Question

'…if there is to be an acceptable bias in the writing and teaching of history, let it tilt towards liberation.'

- What do you think John Lewis Gaddis means in this quote?

Can we find historical truth?

- What is the difference between known facts, like the exact date of a battle, and the background 'facts' of what caused the battle?
- Sometimes the evidence is scarce, and the historian may have to 'fill in the gaps'. Where there seems to be too much detail the historian may have to be more 'selective' to build a line of argument with the information chosen.
- The problem of reliability of source information is key to the work and method of the historian. Historians acknowledge these problems and attempt to limit them as much as possible, through cross-referencing and interpreting the extent of the limitations of each source.
- The role of the historian in attempting to identify 'themes' and categories' is likely to be affected by the historian's own cultural paradigms and/or religious context. Indeed, any 'selection' of evidence might always be open to some degree of bias.

British philosopher and historian, ▶
R. G. Collingwood (1889–1943).

British historian E.H. Carr described how historians 'catch' the facts in this way:

> The facts are like fish swimming in a vast murky ocean, and what the historian catches will depend partly on chance, but mainly on what part of the ocean he chooses to fish in and what bait he chooses – these two facts of course being determined by the type of fish he wants to catch. By and large the historian will get the facts he wants.
>
> *E.H. Carr, 'What is History?' (from a lecture given in 1961)*

American's enjoy a jazz festival in 1931

August 1939

The 1936 Olympics are held in Germany

August 1938

Stalin initiates collectivization in the USSR in 1928

January 1933

Anglo-German Naval agreement

Abyssinia appeals to the League of Nations

Munich Agreement in September 1938

Japanese invasion of Manchuria

League of Nations and economic sanctions

The USA pursues a policy of isolation

Washington Agreements

Questions

1 Which of these key dates and events would you choose in attempting to explain why World War Two broke out in Europe in 1939?

2 Why might other people select differently from you?

It is surprising that history is so dull considering that so much of it is invented.
British novelist Jane Austen (1775-1817)

Question

- To what extent is history invented or discovered?

Problems of knowledge

History has, of course, already happened, and so you might therefore reason that the 'truth' in history should be clear. However, there are similar problems of knowledge in history as there are with the other areas of knowledge. As already discussed, there are problems with the process of researching evidence, the evidence itself and the selection and interpretation of the evidence. It must also be considered that most sources of evidence are themselves interpretations. This is because the sources have been created by individuals, and these individuals are liable to bias due to their own backgrounds, views and opinions.

The ways of knowing: reason, emotion, language and sense perception

Questions

1 Which of the four 'ways of knowing', listed in the heading above, are used by historians when attempting to find historical truth?

2 What problems are associated with these ways of knowing?

3 Which of these four is the most important to the historian?

4 Historians label history into periods or thematic areas. It has also been done in this book. For example, 'Origins of the Cold War' or 'Détente'. Why do historians do this? Would people who lived through these events recognize these labels?

5 'Historians seek to be detached, impassionate, impartial. In fact, however, no historian starts with his mind a blank, to be gradually filled by the evidence.' (Historian AJP Taylor, in *The Times Literary Supplement*, 6 January1956) What does Taylor mean by, 'no historian starts with his mind a blank'?

History is as much an art as a science.
French philosopher Ernest Renan (1823-92)

Links with other Areas of Knowledge

Historians have their theories, their arguments and accounts 'tested' by other historians in their field. Perhaps in this way history can be considered similar to science in that it is open to criticism, correction and revision. In addition, scientific methods can be used to support historical theories, for example, to test the authenticity or age of documents.

Also, history, like the Natural Sciences, uses **deconstructions**, and **macro and micro scales**. In science, there are 'general laws', but also specific experimentation, while in history you might consider broader factors, for example, causations (macro). These could then be used to consider causal developments in one country, or even one city (micro) as a case study.

However, historical evidence can also be viewed as different from scientific evidence in the way it is 'found'. Scientific experimentation, 'double blind testing' and so on are not methodologies available to the historian.

Case study

Briefly research the impact of Marshall Aid money on one European country. While you are researching consider the following:

- the language used by the historians
- information included or omitted by the historians
- details emphasized by each historian
- analytical concepts used by each historian, and whether such concepts are liable to 'change over time'.

Then find an example from this book, or from your IB History course, and consider the extent to which history can be seen as 'changing' within new theoretical frameworks.

Challenges for historians

Historians, like scientists, search for cause and effect. Most history examination essay questions will ask you to find a number of key causes and analyse their relative importance. The main cause may be found by assessing the most important evidence, and the factor with the greatest amount of relevant evidence.

There are also problems in terms both of scope and depth of causation. For example, how far back do we go to look for causes? How much detail is relevant? This is also a problem in analysing the effects of a past historical episode – how far forward should we look for consequences from the time of the original event? How much detail should we attempt to include as evidence to support our views?

It is also important to consider the role of 'accident' and 'chance' in history. Can you identify any events in the Cold War where there was an element of 'chance' in the factors that caused them? How useful is the consideration of 'accidental' causation to a historian?

Perhaps history has more in common with the Arts than with the Natural Sciences. Is history really more about highlighting and emphasizing the nature of humankind and the human condition in the way that the Arts sometimes does?

The ruined buildings shown below are in the town of Guernica in Spain. The destruction of Guernica and the bombing of civilians there during the Spanish Civil War is the subject of Pablo Picasso's famous anti-war painting.

Recently, when U.S. officials were making a statement justifying the war in Iraq, they realized that they were standing in front of a copy of this painting. The press conference was halted for the painting to be covered over. Why would they be so worried about the impact of this painting?

Do historians paint pictures with their words, highlighting issues and events in ways that might mirror the power that artists can command with their images? If so, does the artistic method have any similarities to the research methods employed by historians?

The difference between history and historiography

In history, there is the narrative, a description of the events that took place. There is also the historiography, the analysis and interpretation of these events.

There are problems with facts in both cases. When writing a descriptive account of events, or even a chronological timeline, the historian might have to be selective, omitting some events that others might think relevant or significant. These additions and omissions create a personal interpretation of the event. A further step away from objectivity is taken when a historian then has to select or identify different themes, causes and effects. The choice of language in which these selections are presented will also impact on objectivity when presenting historical 'truths'.

History is written by the winners.
English novelist and social commentator George Orwell in his essay 'On Revising History' (4 February 1944)

History, power and elites

History often focuses on the roles of great leaders in important world events. It has been suggested that this adds to the limitations of historians' craft. They need to have an understanding of not only the background and context of any individual leader or person of influence, but also to interpret from this information the individual's motivations.

A further problem is that, particularly before mass literacy, much of what we know about the past was recorded by the literate elites in society. In the new brave world of the IT revolution we will have video footage of average families on holiday, at weddings and at school. There will be emails, voicemails and online images of a cross-section of the developed world. But again, just

The belief in a hard core of historical facts existing objectively and independently of the historian is a preposterous fallacy, but one which it is very hard to eradicate.
E.H.Carr, 'What is History?' (1961)

Questions

1 How far do you agree with Carr's assertion that 'The belief in a hard core of historical facts existing objectively and independently of the historian is a preposterous fallacy'?

2 Why does Carr say this view is 'very hard to eradicate'?

as the voices of the poor and of the majority of women were unrecorded in the past, so in our technological age the lives of the dispossessed in the developing world will, to a greater extent, be left unrecorded. As American historian Barbara Tuchman (1912-1989) explained:

> **Each man is a package of variables impossible to duplicate. His birth, his parents his siblings, his food, his home, his school, his economic and social status, his first job, his first girl, and the variables inherent in all these make up that mysterious compendium, personality – which then combines with another set of variables: country, climate, time and historical circumstance. The range of factors available make interpretation very difficult.**
>
> *Barbara Tuchman*

If a certain degree of bias is impossible to avoid, how then can a historian write objective history?   Indeed, historians need to have a viewpoint or a paradigm to provide a structure for their selections of data. Some historians attempt a number of approaches, consciously or not, in addressing different perspectives.

Social determinism

It has been said that any event, once it has occurred, can be made to appear inevitable by a competent historian. Those historians who use the model, of 'social determinism' believe that the 'laws of history' are independent of the actions of individuals or regimes.

Karl Marx believed this. He asserted that the important factors in historical causation are the socio-economic conditions. He was convinced that the development of these factors follows a certain course, which inevitably leads to a new society.

Historians recognize the problems of their methodologies and attempt to limit and overcome them. As we have seen, evidence is often central to reasoning, so the problem of evidence is central to all areas of knowledge. It is not only new evidence that changes our perspective of the past, but our own current world that changes what we consider to be 'historical truth'.

▲ What chance does a woman in rural sub-Saharan Africa have for her opinions or actions to become part of recorded history?

Question
- Have you learned in your IB History course that history is driven more by socio-economic factors, or by individuals and regimes?

Intrinsically it is not a question of the higher or lower degree of development of the social antagonisms that result from the natural laws of capitalist production. It is a question of these laws themselves, of these tendencies working with iron necessity towards inevitable results. The country that is more developed industrially only shows, to the less developed, the image of its own future.

Karl Marx in Capital I *(Preface to the First German Edition, 1867)*

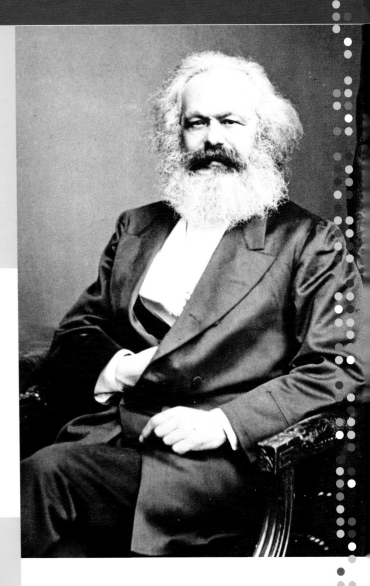

Reading the perspectives and arguments of 21st century historians on the Cold War will tell us not only about the second half of the 20th century, but about the world we live in today. Current attitudes often shape how historians think, and this then shapes our understanding of the 'historical truth'.

Leo Tolstoy also believed in history being inevitably determined. This passage refers to the Napoleonic Wars: The causes of this war seem innumerable in their multiplicity. The more deeply we search out the causes the more of them we discover…And consequently nothing was exclusively the cause of the war, and the war was bound to happen, simply because it was bound to happen.

from War and Peace *by Russian writer and philospher Leo Tolstoy (1828–1910)*

Questions

1 Consider the above quote from Tolstoy – is the idea that history is 'determined' useful to historians or the student of history? Perhaps it is more useful to suggest that history is about the interplay of social and economic forces *and* the actions of individual men, women and regimes.

2 Consider the events during the Cuban Missile Crisis. Which were more important - causes, socio-economic factors or the actions of individuals?

APPENDIX I

Basic timeline

This is for 'quick' reference only. At the beginning of each chapter there is a more specific and detailed timeline. This timeline should be used to put key events into context, and to give you an idea of some of the 'turning point' years in the Cold War.

1944	November	Tehran Conference / Big Three meet
1945	February	Yalta Conference
	April	Roosevelt dies – Truman now president
	May	Germany surrenders, Victory in Europe
	June	UNO formed
	July	Potsdam Conference
	August	Hiroshima and Nagasaki / Japan surrenders, victory in Pacific
1946	February	Stalin's Two Camps speech
	March	Churchill's Fulton Iron Curtain Speech
	June	Baruch Plan proposed
1947	March	Truman Doctrine
	June	Marshall Plan proposed
	July	Kennan's 'Mr X' article
	October	Cominform created
1948	February	Czech Coup: Marshall Plan implemented
	May	State of Israel created
	June	Berlin Blockade (and Yugoslavia expelled from Cominform)
	November	Truman re-elected
1949	January	COMECON founded
	April	NATO established
	May	Berlin Blockade ends
	September	USSR explodes atomic bomb. FDR established
	October	GDR established. Mao proclaims foundation of People's Republic of China
1950	April	NSC-68
	June	North Korea invades South Korea
1951	September	USA and Japan sign mutual security pact
1952	November	Eisenhower elected
1953	March	Stalin dies
	June	East German uprising
	July	Armistice in Korea
1954	January	Dulles announces 'massive retaliation' policy
	May	Fall of Dien Bien Phu
	July	Geneva Conference on Vietnam
	September	SEATO established
	October	West Germany joins NATO
1955	May	Warsaw Pact signed
	July	Geneva Summit
	September	Nasser announces arms deal with USSR
	November	Baghdad Pact

1956	February	Khrushchev's 'de-Stalinization' speech/'peaceful co-existence' promoted
	July	Suez Crisis
	October	Hungarian Uprising suppressed
1957	October	Sputnik launched by USSR
1958	July	Revolution in Iraq
	August	Quemoy and Matsu blockaded
1959	January	Castro takes power in Cuba
	May	Dulles dies
	September	Khrushchev visits USA
1960	May	U-2 spy plane shot down over USSR
	November	Kennedy elected. Sino-Soviet split confirmed
1961	January	USA breaks off relations with Cuba
	August	Berlin Wall built
1962	October	Cuban Missile Crisis
1963	August	Partial Test-ban Treaty signed in Moscow (USA, USSR and UK)
	November	President Kennedy assassinated – Johnson now president
1964	August	Gulf of Tonkin Resolution / USA goes to war in Vietnam
	October	Khrushchev deposed - replaced by Brezhnev
		China detonates A-bomb
	November	Johnson re-elected
1965	August	Fighting between India and Pakistan over Kashmir
1966	September	NATO headquarters moved to Brussels after French withdrawal from military command structure.
1967	June	Six Day War between Israel and Arab states
	August	ASEAN established
1968	July	Brezhnev Doctrine
	August	Warsaw pact invades Czechoslovakia
	November	Nixon elected
1969	November	Nuclear non-proliferation Treaty
1970	April	SALT talks begin
1971	October	UN admits China, expelling Taiwan
1972	February	Nixon visits China
	May	Nixon visits USSR. SALT 1 signed
	November	Nixon re-elected
1973	October	4th Arab-Israeli War (Yom Kippur War)
1974	August	Nixon resigns over Watergate
1975	April	Communists victory in Vietnam & Cambodia
	August	Helsinki Final Act signed
1976	February	SEATO disbands
	September	Mao dies
	November	Carter elected
1977	June	USA plans to deploy cruise missiles
	December	USSR deploys SS-20s in Europe
1978	May	UN special session on disarmament
1979	January	USA and China open diplomatic relations
	June	Carter and Brezhnev sign SALT 2
	November	U.S. hostage crisis in Tehran
	December	Soviet forces invade Afghanistan

1980	May August September November	Tito dies Mass strikes in Poland Iraq attacks Iran Reagan elected
1981	January April November	U.S. hostages released in Iran Argentina seizes Falkland islands Death of Brezhenev, replaced by Andropov
1983	March October December	Reagan promotes SDI U.S. troops invade Grenada Soviets walk out of START talks
1984	February November	Andropov dies, replaced by Cherenko Reagan re-elected
1985	March September November	Death of Cherenko, replaced by Gorbachev USSR criticize SDI at UN Reagan and Gorbachev summit
1986	April	Chernobyl disaster
1987	December	Summit in Washington, Reagan and Gorbachev
1988	February May November	Gorbachev announces withdrawal from Afghanistan Summit in Moscow, Reagan and Gorbachev sign INF treaty Bush elected
1989	April June September October November December	Soviet troops withdraw from Hungary Tiananmen Square massacre Hungary opens border with Austria Honecker forced to resign in East Germany Berlin Wall comes down Czech Communist Party resigns East German, Lithuanian, Latvian parliaments abolish special position of Communist Party. Ceausescu executed in Romania. Havel new Czech president.
1990	January March May June July August October November	Bulgarian parliament abolishes special position of Communist Party Lithuanian parliament declares independence. Estonian parliament votes for secession from USSR Latvian parliament declares independence Bush/Gorbachev summit in Washington NATO declares formal end of Cold War Iraq invades Kuwait German Unification. Gorbachev wins Nobel Peace Prize Signing of CFE Treaty and Paris Charter - ends economic and military division of Europe
1991	February April June August September December	Warsaw Pact disbands. UN forces expel Iraq from Kuwait Georgia declares independence from USSR Yeltsin becomes president of Russia Failed coup against Gorbachev, Yeltsin condemns hardliners. Estonia, Latvia, Lithuania, Ukraine and Belarus declare independence 11,000 Soviet personnel are withdrawn from Cuba Ukraine votes for independence. Russia, Ukraine and Belarus declare USSR no longer exists. Gorbachev resigns as president of USSR.

APPENDIX II

China's Relations with the USA and the USSR

Actions of China	DATE	Actions of USA	Actions of USSR
Mao's Chinese Communist Party takes power People's Republic of China established	1949	USA refuses to recognize legitimacy of PRC	Soviets recognize the PRC as legitimate
The People's Liberation Army invades Tibet PRC warns USA/UN against threatening Chinese border in Korea	1950	USA condemns invasion of Tibet USA commits to protect Taiwan USA under UN flag sends forces to defend South Korea	Sino-Soviet Treaty signed USSR boycott's Security Council in UN due to non-recognition of China USSR condemns USA/UN action in Korea
Accepts truce in Korea PRC constructs 'Third Line' defences	1953	Accepts truce in Korea	Stalin dies
PRC shells Quemoy and Matsu islands off Taiwan	1954	USA threatens massive retaliation if Taiwan is directly threatened	
China attends the Bandung Conference Asserts the USA is the key danger to world peace	1955		
	1956		Khrushchev makes 'de-Stalinization' speech Khrushchev champions idea of 'peaceful co-existence' Soviets crush Hungarian Uprising At conference of world's Communist Parties Soviets angered by Deng Xiaoping's attacks on policies
Mao sees Khrushchev's 'de-Stalinization' speech as attack on own personality cult Mao's sees 'peaceful co-existence' as a betrayal of Marxist ideology Mao views Hungarian Uprising as failure for USSR			
	1957		
At conference of world's Communist Parties Mao condemns the Soviets as 'revisionists'			
Mao launches the 'Great Leap Forward' Khrushchev visits China Mao gives up presidency of PRC PRC shells Matsu and Quemoy: Taiwan Crisis	1958	USA prepares for war with PRC over Taiwan	Khrushchev visits China
	1959		
	1960		Soviets condemn Mao's 'Great Leap Forward' Soviets withdraw scientists working on nuclear programmes in China

Actions of China	DATE	Actions of USA	Actions of USSR
Chinese delegation leave CPSU Congress in Moscow The PRC offer support to Albania	1961	Kennedy becomes president	USSR withdraws aid from Albania
Sino-Indian Border War PRC condemns USSR policy in Cuba Sino-Soviet Border clashes	1962	USA allowed by India to fly U-2 spy planes over China U.S. responds to discovery of Soviet missiles with blockade of Cuba	Soviets give MIG fighters to India in war with China Soviets establish nuclear missiles in Cuba Sino-Soviet border clashes
PRC condemns Soviets for abandoning role as revolutionary leaders by working with west in Test Ban Treaty	1963	USA signs Test-ban Treaty with USSR	USSR signs Test-ban Treaty with USA
A-bomb tested by PRC	1964		
		USA do not want to involve the PRC in escalating war in Vietnam	
Mao launches Cultural Revolution PRC condemn American involvement in Vietnam as 'imperialism'	1966		
H-bomb tested by PRC	1967		
	1968		Brezhnev leader of USSR Soviets crush Czech regime
Mao condemns Soviet actions in Czechoslovakia			
	1969		USSR attempts to exlude PRC from international Communist movement Sino-Soviet Border War USSR threatens rocket attacks on PRC
Sino-Soviet Border War PRC threatens rocket attacks on USSR			
China launches first space satellite	1970		
Sino-USA talks begin PRC takes China seat in UN	1971	Sino-USA talks begin USA accept PRC as 'China' in UN	
U.S. President Nixon visits PRC	1972	U.S. President Nixon visits PRC	
	1973	USA troops begin withdrawal from Vietnam USA final withdrawal of all personnel from Vietnam	
Chiang Kai-shek dies PLA into Cambodia	1975		
	1976		
Zhou En-Lai dies Mao dies Hua Guofeng becomes CCP Chairman Anti-Soviet Gang of Four removed			

Actions of China	DATE	Actions of USA	Actions of USSR
Deng becomes CCP Secretary	1977		
Four Modernizations adopted	1978		Soviets sign military alliance with Vietnam Soviets support Vietnam in invasion of Cambodia
Pro-democracy movement begins Full diplomatic relations between PRC and USA established PRC invades Vietnam PRC condemns Soviet invasion of Afghanistan	1979	Full diplomatic relations between USA and PRC established USA condemns Soviet invasion of Afghanistan	Soviets invade Afghanistan
Gang of Four on trial	1980		
PRC issue Nine Principles on Taiwan	1981		
Margaret Thatcher visits PRC to discuss Hong Kong	1982		
Sino-British declaration in Hong Kong	1984		
Gorbachev visits PRC Tiananmen Square – Pro-democracy demonstration crushed	1989	Moderate condemnation of actions in Tiananmen Square	Gorbachev Visits PRC
	1990		Abandonment of the USSR Communist Party
		USA gives PRC 'most favoured nation status'	
	1992		
Deng Xiaoping dies Hong Kong returned to China	1997		

APPENDIX III

U.S. Presidential Policies During the Cold War

	Truman	Eisenhower	Kennedy	Johnson	Nixon	Carter	Reagan
Key policy ideas/beliefs	Containment – the Truman Doctrine	Containment – the 'New Look', also 'massive retaliation' Domino effect Eisenhower Doctrine Despite Dulles talking about 'rollback', no attempt was ever made to liberate Communist territory	Containment – flexible response Domino effect	Containment Domino effect	'Peace with honour' in Vietnam Need for new relationships with both USSR and China to take account of the changed world situation and remove focus from Vietnam Idea of 'linkage' Nixon Doctrine	Wanted to continue détente and arms control Believed in an 'ethical' foreign policy Carter Doctrine	Re-assertion of U.S. power Reagan Doctrine Reduction of nuclear weapons
How put into practice	Marshall Plan Western Military integration (NATO) NSC-68 – increase in military spending Setting up of military bases around the world Support to groups 'resisting Communism' e.g., in South Korea, Taiwan, Indochina	Continuation of all of Truman's actions But in addition: Increased reliance on nuclear weapons Use of covert operations by the CIA Economic aid and intervention in Middle East More prepared to negotiate with the USSR e.g., Geneva Summit	Continuation of all of Truman's actions. Continued with Eisenhower's policy of increasing reliance on nuclear weapons but also built up conventional forces Continued use of CIA Also prepared to negotiate with the USSR Introduced Green Berets as counter-insurgency force Wanted to give aid to developing countries (Alliance for Progress) Peace Corps; sending young Americans to Third World countries to give aid	Continuation of all of Truman's actions plus USA's commitments in Middle East and Asia Stepped up involvement in Vietnam by sending troops Helped anti-Communist governments in Latin America e.g. in Dominican Republic	Withdrawal from Vietnam by 1973 Détente with USSR through arms and trade agreements and summits Détente with China through summit and trade agreements	Linked arms control reduction to human rights issues (annoyed Soviets) After Soviet invasion of Afghanistan stopped exports to USSR and increased defence budget	Defence spending was increased New missiles developed Star Wars (SDI) Use of CIA covert operations Support to anti-Communist insurgents in Central America After 1985, involved in arms reduction talks with USSR in a series of summits

	Truman	Eisenhower	Kennedy	Johnson	Nixon	Carter	Reagan
Successes	Containment – successful in Europe. Marshall Plan rebuilds European economies Berlin blockade resisted West Germany created as democratic and economically stable country In Asia, Japan emerging as powerful anti-Communist country Communism in Korea contained	Containment – successful in Europe; West still in Berlin Strengthened NATO Korean war ended Massive retaliation policy deterred Chinese actions against Taiwan Lebanon and Jordan secured as allies in Middle East Secured friendly government in Iran after CIA coup of 1953 Competent handling of Suez crisis Attempted to control military spending Achieved warmer relations with the USSR	Containment – successful in Europe; Safeguarded West's position in Berlin Successful handling of Khrushchev at Vienna Summit Skilful handling of Cuban Crisis USA maintains its nuclear supremacy Starts space programme Arms agreements with USSR Hot-line established	Containment – continues to be successful in Europe (though no major crises occur under Johnson)	Withdrawal of U.S. troops from Vietnam Improved relations with USSR and China – significant arms agreement with SALT I	Raised awareness of human rights issues around world Camp David Agreement; peace treaty between Israel and Egypt Panama Canal Treaty which ended dispute about control over the Panama canal by agreeing to hand it over to Panama by 1999 as long as it remained neutral territory Helsinki Agreement USA formally recognizes Communist government in China	Star Wars helps bring USSR to negotiating table (according to some historians) INF Treaty signed with USSR reduces nuclear stocks Cold War hostility greatly reduced through meetings with Gorbachev
Failures	Involved USA in Indochina – failed to appreciate complexity of Asian nationalism Massive increase in military spending with implementation of NSC-68 China is now an enemy	Indochina: failure to take part in 1956 elections discredited U.S. aims in Vietnam Supported Diem – repressive ruler CIA intervention in Iran and Guatemala condemned as examples of U.S. imperialism Reliance on covert operations made powerful CIA too powerful Embarrassment over U-2 flight	Economic aid to Latin America never achieved aims Bay of Pigs – humiliation for USA Significantly increased aid to South Vietnam – tied into supporting South Vietnam government after assassination of Diem	Intervention in Dominican Republic to support a conservative junta against a counter-coup to restore the democratic government of Bosch led to complaints from Bosch that 'this was a democratic revolution smashed by the leading democracy in the world'. Vietnam – failed to stop escalation of the conflict. Tet Offensive seen as a major U.S. failure.	Unable to secure financial support for South Vietnam which fell to Communist rule in 1975 Invasion of Cambodia was a failure and helped lead to Pol Pot's victory SALT agreement – not comprehensive (Some critics would regard détente as a failure – see Chapter Thirteen.)	Lacked ability to have a clear approach to Soviets due to divisions in own administration SALT II never ratified On-going hostage crisis in Iran (though this was resolved on Carter's last day in office)	In early 1980s his approach to USSR – 'evil empire' – raises tensions Policy in Central America received a lot of criticism – USA seen as supporting narrowly based right-wing governments

	Truman	Eisenhower	Kennedy	Johnson	Nixon	Carter	Reagan
legacy	Huge commitment to defence of democracy and anti-Communist governments worldwide Commitment in Indochina Huge expenditure on military	Left Kennedy a difficult legacy: unsolved problems in Cuba, Vietnam, Laos Also a crisis in U.S.-Soviet relations following U-2 incident Also CIA planning invasion project for Cuba	Improved relations with USSR; new acceptance of danger of nuclear weapons and beginning of arms control agreements Germany removed as an issue Cuban crisis resolved Space programme established But USA in increasingly difficult position in Vietnam	Divided opinion over USA's role in the world; a questioning of USA's involvement in Vietnam	Significant arms agreements, but a continuing arms race PRC now in UN Increasing concern from many in USA that détente was benefiting the USSR	Belief that USA needs to assert itself in the world – hence election of Reagan	End of Cold War

SELECTED BIOGRAPHIES

Willy Brandt (1913-1992) West German Chancellor 1968–74. Brandt's public opposition to the Nazis forced him to live in exile from 1932 to 1945 during which time he linked up with the wartime German resistance movement from Sweden. He lived in West Berlin after 1945 and became its mayor 1957-1966 during the crisis of the building of the Berlin Wall. As Chancellor of Germany from 1968, he promoted the policy of *Ostpolitik,* which brought closer relations between East Germany and West Germany. In 1980 he produced the Brandt Report on the world economy for the UN; this advocated a major redistribution of economic wealth from rich to poor countries.

Leonid Brezhnev (1906-1982) Soviet leader 1964-82 who succeeded Khrushchev. Military expenditure remained a huge burden under Brezhnev and the Soviet economy stagnated. He was largely responsible for the Warsaw Pact decision to invade Czechoslovakia and issued the Brezhnev Doctrine to justify this. Brezhnev contributed to the policy of détente in the 1970s,which led to the SALT Treaties of 1972 and 1979. He was also responsible for the Soviet invasion of Afghanistan. Brezhnev died in 1982 after a long illness. This contributed to the lack of direction by the Soviet government at the time.

Chiang Kai-shek (1887-1975) Chinese nationalist general of the Guomindang Party (GMD). He fought against the Chinese Communists until his defeat in the Chinese Civil War in 1949, after which he founded a nationalist Chinese enclave on the island of Taiwan.

Winston S. Churchill (1874-1965) Prime Minister of the United Kingdom during World War Two. He was strongly anti-Communist, but nevertheless was prepared to work with Stalin against the Nazis. Churchill lost power in the 1945 British General Election. After the war he viewed the actions of Stalin with great suspicion. In his famous Iron Curtain speech in 1946, Churchill was the first to speak openly of Soviet expansion and call for an alliance to stop Stalin. He was elected British Prime Minister again in 1951 during which time he stressed the need for Western unity and a special relationship between the USA and the UK.

Deng Xiaoping (1904-1997) Leader of Communist China 1977-98, who rose to political power following the death of Mao Zedong. He started to improve international relations with the West and the USSR, and also began the relaxation of government control over the economy. However, Deng strongly resisted calls for political reform and was responsible for ending student protests by force in 1989.

John Foster Dulles (1888-1959) Served as Secretary of State under President Eisenhower from 1953 until 1959. He was very anti-Communist and championed a more assertive attitude to Communism in foreign affairs, developing the policy of Brinkmanship.

Mikhail Gorbachev (1931-) Soviet leader from 1985 until 1991. He replaced Chernenko and ended a long period of rule by elderly Communist politicians. He introduced the new policies of *perestroika* (restructuring) and *glasnost* (openness). *Perestroika* aimed to invigorate the Soviet economy and to rid the system of corruption and inefficiency. Through *glasnost* he sought better relations with the West, partially in an attempt to reduce Soviet arms expenditure. His policies ultimately led to important arms agreements with the West (START), but also contributed to the break-up of the Soviet Union when he refused to use the Red Army against democratic movements in Eastern Europe in 1989. Gorbachev survived a coup against him by conservatives in the Communist party, but resigned in 1991.

Lyndon B. Johnson (1908-1973) President of the USA 1963–69. He took office after Kennedy's assassination. Johnson was committed to carrying out his domestic policy of 'The Great Society', which was an attempt to tackle American social problems. However, the resources needed to put the Great Society into practice were instead diverted to the Vietnam War, which escalated under his presidency. Due to failures in the Vietnam War – in particular the Tet Offensive – Johnson did not stand for re-election in 1968.

George Kennan (1904-2005) Deputy Chief of Mission in the U.S. Embassy in Moscow in 1946. Kennan gave his analysis of Soviet foreign policy in his Long Telegram. He believed that the USSR was naturally expansionist and needed to be resisted by strong action. The Long Telegram had a significant influence on Truman's foreign policy and led to containment. Kennan returned to the Soviet Union, serving as U.S. Ambassador in 1952-53.

John F. Kennedy (1917-1963) President of the USA 1961-1963. He was the first Catholic and the youngest President ever of the United States. His youth, vigour and charm created a new hope for Americans that both domestic and foreign problems could be effectively tackled. He followed a policy against the Soviets of 'flexible response', which meant relying on a range of responses to deal with Soviet actions. Kennedy resisted threats from Khrushchev for the U.S. to leave Berlin and later played a key role in the resolution of the Cuban Missile Crisis. However, he increased U.S. involvement in Vietnam. Kennedy was assassinated in 1963.

Nikita Khrushchev (1894-1971) Emerged as the leader of the Soviet Union after the death of Stalin in 1953. His denunciation of Stalin at the Twentieth Party Congress in 1956 led to the policy of destalinization . However, when Hungary went too far in the process of liberalization, he sent in Soviet tanks. In international affairs, Khrushchev followed a policy of 'peaceful co-existence' believing that the superpowers could exist side by side without destroying each other. Despite this, he still threatened the West over Berlin and took a huge risk by planning to put nuclear missiles in Cuba. The Soviet climb-down during the Cuban Missile Crisis of 1962 contributed to his downfall. Khrushchev was sacked by the Soviet Politburo in 1964 and died in 1971.

Mao Zedong (1893-1976) Leader of the Chinese Communist Party in its 1949 victory against the nationalist Guomindang in the Chinese Civil War. He has been regarded as a great revolutionary leader, military strategist and political thinker. Although many of his social, political and economic reforms were severely criticized for causing great suffering and famine in China, it was under Mao's leadership that China became a great power during the last half of the 20th century. Mao remained leader of the People's Republic of China until his death in 1976.

George Marshall (1880-1959) Successful American military leader in World War Two before he became Secretary of State and then Secretary of Defence. As Secretary of State during the early onset of the Cold War, he is closely associated with the economic aid plan for post-war Europe that was named after him – the Marshall Plan.

Karl Marx (1818-1883) 19th century political philosopher and economist. His most famous writings include the 'Communist Manifesto', which set down his theory that Capitalism would ultimately be replaced by Communism, where the working classes rule by themselves for themselves. Marx believed that Capitalism would eventually fail due to its own inherent weakesses. However, he also foresaw revolutions as the precursor to the 'dictatorship of the proletariat'. Marx was the inspiration for many of the 20th century's socialist and Communist parties.

Joseph McCarthy (1908-1957) Lawyer who was elected to the U.S. Congress as Senator for Wisconsin in 1948. He was fiercely anti-Communist and contributed to the 'red scare' in America by claiming that there were Communists working in the U.S. State Department and elsewhere. No evidence was produced to back up his claims, but they helped create hysteria about a Communist conspiracy within the USA. McCarthy's credibility was finally challenged when he accused the U.S. Army of Communist infiltration. It became clear that his extravagant and unsubstantiated claims were ridiculous and his influence rapidly diminished. He died of alcoholism in 1957.

Richard Nixon (1913-1994) President of the USA 1969-1974, vice-president 1953-1960. As president he developed a close working relationship with his chief adviser – Henry Kissinger. Together they pursued a policy of détente with the USSR, and also initiated diplomatic relations with the People's Republic of China. However, following the Watergate scandal, Nixon became the first U.S. president to resign from office.

Ronald Reagan (1911-2004) President of the USA 1981-90. He was known for his anti-Communist views. Reagan was President during the second Cold War of the early 1980s when the United States stepped up arms production and initiated the SDI (Strategic Defense Initiative). However, he was also responsible for negotiations with Gorbachev, which led to START (Strategic Arms Reduction Talks).

Franklin D. Roosevelt (1882-1945) President of the USA 1933-1945 (elected for an unprecedented four times). He was responsible for leading the USA out of the Great Depression though his New Deal policies, and for taking the USA into World War Two. Roosevelt then played a key role in making decisions about the post-war world at the conferences of Tehran and Yalta. He died in office in 1945.

Marshal [Josip Broz] Tito (1892-1980) Liberated Yugoslavia at the end of World War Two and established the Federal Communist Republic of Yugoslavia, becoming Prime Minster and President. Although Communist, he wanted to retain independence from Stalin, who then expelled Yugoslavia from Cominform. Tito played a key role in the formation of the Non-Aligned Movement. After Tito's death in 1980, Yugoslavia eventually broke up into a number of independent states.

Harry S Truman (1884-1972) Became U.S. President from the death of Roosevelt in 1945 until 1952. He had been vice-president to Roosevelt from the election in 1944. Truman authorized the use of nuclear bombs against Japan in August 1945 and was responsible for introducing the Truman Doctrine and the Marshall Plan. Truman also led the Western Allies in the Berlin Airlift and the Korean War.

Zhou En-lai (1898-1976) Played a prominent role in the Chinese Communist Party during the Civil War, and became Premier of the People's Republic of China from 1949 until his death in 1976, the same year as Mao. He was also China's foreign minister from 1949 to 1958, and continued to play a pivotal role in foreign relations into the 1970s. Zhou was a highly skilled diplomat and negotiator. He represented Communist China in crucial talks, such as the Geneva Conference in 1954, and the secret talks with Henry Kissinger, which engineered Sino-American rapprochement.

FURTHER READING

Books

These books offer good overviews of the Cold War:

America, Russia and the Cold War 1945-2006, Walter LaFeber, (McGraw-Hill, 1996)

The Cold War, John Lewis Gaddis (Penguin, 2005)

The Cold War, John Mason (Routledge, 1996)

The Cold War, Martin Walker (Vintage, 1994)

The Fifty Years War, Richard Crockatt (Routledge, 1995)

The Global Cold War, Odd Arne Westad (CUP, 2007)

International Relations since 1945: A Global History, John W. Young and John Kent (OUP, 2004)

Rise to Globalism, Stephen Ambrose and Douglas Brinkley (Longman, 1998)

These books contain more in-depth analysis and are useful for Individual Assignments, Internal Assessments or extended essays with Cold War themes:

Argument Without End: In Search of Answers to the Vietnam Tragedy, Robert McNamara (Westview Press, 2000). McNamara's documentary, Fog of War, is also worth watching for his perspective on different events in the Cold War.

The Cold War, Klaus Larres and Ann Lane, eds. (Blackwell, 2001)

Colossus: The Rise and Fall of the American Empire, Niall Ferguson (Penguin, 2004)

Eastern and Central European States 1945-92, John Laver (Hodder and Stoughton, 1999)

Europe and the Cold War, David Williamson (Hodder and Stoughton, 2001)

Inside the Kremlin's Cold War, Vladislav Zubok and Constantine Pleshakov (Harvard, 1996)

The Last Decade of the Cold War, Olav Njolstad, ed. (Frank Cass, 2004)

Seize the hour: When Nixon Met Mao, Margaret MacMillan (John Murray, 2006)

Stalin's Wars, Geoffrey Roberts (Yale University Press, 2006)

Vietnam: The Ten Thousand Day War, Michael MacClear (Methuen, 1981)

We Now Know, John Lewis Gaddis, (OUP, 1997)

This is a book of documents with commentary:

The Cold War: A History in Documents and Eyewitness Accounts, Jussi Hanhimaki and Odd Arne Westad, eds. (OUP, 2003)

It is also a good idea to look at biographies, autobiographies and memoirs by the central figures in the Cold War, such as Mao Zedong, Nikita Khrushchev, Henry Kissinger, Richard Nixon, Ronald Reagan and Mikhail Gorbachev.

This book is good for thinking about Theory of Knowledge in the context of history:

The Landscape of History, John Lewis Gaddis (OUP, 2002)

Websites

To visit the following websites, visit www.heinemann.co.uk/hotlinks, enter the express code **4280P** and click on the relevant weblink.

The Cold War International History Project website – click on weblink 1.

The website accompanying the CNN Cold War television series – click on weblink 2.

The Spartacus Educational website. This has good summaries on key individuals and events – click on weblink 3.

The BBC History website. This useful website also has audio links to speeches, etc. – click on weblink 4.

The website of the Avalon Project at Yale Law School. This is good for documents – click on weblink 5.

The History Department at the University of San Diego. A good overview of events with photos can be found at this site – click on weblink 6.

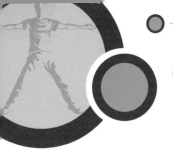

GLOSSARY

38th parallel This is the latitude line chosen to divide Korea after World War Two. North of the line was put under Soviet administration and south of the line was put under American administration. It was intended to be a temporary division, but after the Korean War it became the permanent dividing line between North Korea and South Korea.

Allied Control Council (ACC) This is the council set up to control the whole of Germany after World War Two. Although Germany was divided between the USA, UK, France and the USSR, the overall administration was carried out by the ACC. There was a similar council for Berlin called the *Kommandantura.*

Allies (or Allied Powers) name given to the grouping of the United Kingdom, the USA and USSR that fought on the same side in World War Two

anarchy when there is no government or control in society leading to disorder and confusion

anti-colonialism against the idea of countries having colonies

apartheid racist system of 'apartness' which was introduced by the Nationalist government of South Africa in 1948 to ensure white-dominated political rule

appeasement achieving peace by giving concessions or by satisfying demands. It was the policy used by UK towards Germany before World War Two (see Munich Agreement)

armistice agreement to end fighting

arms race competition to gain weapons superiority that took place between East and West during the Cold War

Austrian State Treaty of 1955 This was signed by the UK, France, the USA and the USSR. At a conference, agreement was made to end the post-war occupation of Austria and to recognize the Austrian Republic.

Bandung Conference This conference in August 1955 in the Indonesian city of Bandung was the first international gathering of independent Asian and African countries. It inaugurated the Non-aligned Movement.

bias opinion taking into consideration only one side of argument

Big Three used to refer to Roosevelt, Stalin and Churchill at the Yalta Conference

bill of rights document that sets out rights for individuals in a country.

Blitzkrieg literally means 'lightning war' and was used to describe the military tactics of the Nazis during the opening stages of World War Two

Bolshevik Revolution This took place in Russia in October 1917 when the Bolshevik Party under the leadership of Lenin overthrew the Kerensky provisional government, which had been in power since the abdication of the Tsar in February 1917. In the aftermath of the revolution, the Union of Soviet Socialist Republics (USSR) was established.

bourgeois relating to the 'middle classes' (bourgeoisie) or association with the middle classes of a country. It is usually used in a negative way in the context of Marxist writings where the bourgeoisie are contrasted with the superior proletariat, or working classes.

boycott when a group of people or country refuse to take part in something or do business or have contact with another group or government

Brussels Pact This was signed in 1949 between Belgium, France, Luxembourg, the Netherlands and the UK. It was designed to organize a system of European mutual defence and was thus a precursor to NATO, which was set up later in 1949.

catalyst something that speeds up or causes the action of a process or event

censorship control by the government of the content of films, newspapers, books, etc., and by this action suppression of anything considered a threat to the power of the state

clique small, exclusive group of people that is apart from the main group

collectivization process by which all private farmland in the Soviet Union was put into large collective farms controlled by the state

collusion secret understanding, often for a dishonest purpose

communique official form of correspondence, e.g., a news report

constitution set of rules that lay down how an organization or a country should be governed

counter-insurgency type of military campaign which is used during an occupation or a civil war to put down rebellion

coup or coup d'etat violent or illegal seizure of power

covert secret or hidden

cultural genocide destruction of the culture of a nation, race or religious group. It follows from the word genocide which is usually used to denote the physical destruction of a national, racial, religious or ethnic population.

decolonization process by which colonies or lands that had been controlled by European powers regained their independence after 1945

deconstructions taking things apart in order to look at them in more detail

defoliants chemical sprays that destroy plants. Agent Orange was a defoliant used in the Vietnam War which to destroy the jungle

demobilize when an army disbands and goes home

domino effect belief that if one country fell to Communism, then all countries in the area would also fall to Communism, like a row of dominoes falling over after one is knocked

domestic concerned with what is going on inside a country itself, as opposed to its international relations

economic sanctions sanctions imposed against a country in an attempt to force it to change its policies. It usually relates to trade meaning that certain goods will not be sent to or traded with the country.

expansionist policy of expanding or increasing power or territory

fallout shelter place built to protect people from a nuclear attack

fanaticism extreme opinions, usually referring to politics or religion

first strike refers to the ability to launch the first nuclear strike in a nuclear war

Gang of Four This was a group that gained political power and influence during the Chinese Cultural Revolution (1966-1976). It was made up of Jiang Qing (the wife of Mao Zedong), Wang Hongwen, Yao Wenyuan and Zhang Chunqiao. They were all radical supporters of the Cultural Revolution and became its main driving force in the 1970s. Its main power rested in its influence and access to Mao and its control collapsed less than a month after his death. The Gang of Four was arrested and imprisoned.

glasnost policy of 'openness' introduced by Mikhail Gorbachev when he became Soviet president in 1985

GNP (gross national product) annual total value of goods and services produced in a country

Grand Alliance name given to the alliance of the USA, UK and the USSR during World War Two

Guomindang (GMD) This is the name of the Nationalist party led by Chiang Kai-shek that fought against the Communists in the Chinese Civil War. After it lost to Mao Zedong's Communists in the Civil War, it set up a Chinese Nationalist government on the island of Taiwan.

hegemony leadership by one state over a group of states

historiography study of the writings of historians

Ho Chi Minh Trail This is the supply route between North Vietnam and South Vietnam used by the Vietcong. It ran through Laos and Cambodia in an attempt to avoid U.S. bombing raids.

humanitarian concerned with improving the lives of people and reducing suffering

ideological conforming to an ideology, which is a set of beliefs shared by a group of people. It is a means of explaining how society works or ought to work. For example, the Soviet ideology was based on Marxism and the American ideology was based on Capitalism and liberal democracy.

imperialism policy of gaining colonies (control over other countries) and thereby creating an empire. The United States was accused of imperialism during the Cold War, in this case not by ruling directly over other countries, but by influencing them economically and ideologically.

inauguration ceremony during which a U.S. president officially takes office after having been elected

isolationist when a country keeps out of conflicts in foreign affairs and does not get involved in military alliances. After World War One, the United States took an isolationist position.

junta group of military officers who rule a country after taking power by force

League of Nations international organization set up after World War One which was intended to maintain peace and encourage disarmament

London Conference of Ministers This was a meeting of British, French, American and Soviet representatives in 1947. As agreed at the Potsdam Conference, ministers continued to meet to discuss post-war issues. At the London Conference, there was a marked deterioration in relations between the West and the Soviets.

macro and micro scales looking at a situation close up (micro) and in broader context (macro)

martial law military rule established in a country, usually as a temporary measure during a political crisis

modus operandi particular way of working or dealing with a task

monolithic (Communism) single huge organization. The Americans believed that all Communist states were part of one massive organization controlled by the Soviets.

monopolize to have or to take the greatest share of something so that others are prevented from a fair share

most favoured nation status granted to a country as part of a trade agreement with another country. It means that it will get better trading conditions than other countries that do not have this status.

Munich Agreement 1938 This was signed between the United Kingdom, Germany, France and Italy. It forced Czechoslovakia to give an area called the Sudetenland (which contained German speakers) to Germany. This was part of the UK policy of appeasement. The then Prime Minister of Britain, Neville Chamberlain, believed that by giving Hitler and Nazi Germany what it asked for, a European war could be avoided.

napalm gel made from petrol that readily catches on fire. It was used by U.S. forces during the Vietnam War. It sticks to the skin and causes terrible burns.

nationalization when a government takes over private industry or land so that it is owned by the state

Nazi-Soviet Pact see **Non-Aggression Pact**

Non-Aggression Pact 1939 (Nazi-Soviet Pact) This was the agreement signed between the Soviets and the Germans in August 1939 in which they agreed not to attack each other. Secret clauses of the agreement provided for a joint military action against Poland.

nuclear holocaust term used for what would happen if there was a nuclear war, such as total destruction and great loss of human life

Ostpolitik policy followed by West German Chancellor Willy Brandt in the 1970s which aimed to improve West German relations with East Germany

pacifist someone who does not believe in fighting in a war

paradigm philosophical or theoretical framework or model

paradox when something contains opposite ideas that make it seem unlikely or strange, even though it may be true

paranoia abnormal tendency to be suspicious of and lack trust in other people

perestroika Soviet leader Mikhail Gorbachev's policy of 'restructuring' the economy of the Soviet Union

polemic speech or piece of writing which contains very forceful arguments for or against something

purges term used to describe the mass killings carried out in the USSR by Stalin from the mid-1930s.

quarantine state of forced isolation. This term was used for the blockaded zone that the U.S. military formed around Cuba during the Cuban Missile Crisis.

realpolitik approach to politics which is based on practical concerns and the actual circumstances of the time rather than on ideology

reactionary political term for someone who is opposed to progress or reform, or who wants to put things back to the way they were

reconnaissance when one side checks out or surveys the strength of the other side, for example, using aircraft

regime change when there is a change in the government of the country

reparations payments that are imposed on countries that have been defeated in a war by the victors in order to pay for the costs of the war incurred by the victors

repatriation sending someone back to his or her own country

revisionists critical term used by Communist governments to describe those they believed had deviated from the true Marxist path

Russo-Polish War of 1821 This war was started by the Poles to gain land from the new Soviet Bolshevik state. After the Poles' initial progress had been checked by the Red Army (which nearly captured Warsaw), the Curzon Line was proposed as the frontier between the two states. However, this was never ratified and the Poles were actually able to get much more Russian territory by the Treaty of Riga. The Soviet Union only reacquired this land as a consequence of the Nazi-Soviet Pact and its invasion of Poland in 1939.

saboteurs people who secretly and deliberately damage something

search-and-destroy-missions key part of U.S. strategy in Vietnam. U.S. soliders would look for the Vietcong (often by helicopter) and then destroy their bases or the areas in which they believed that the Vietcong had been hiding.

self-immolation act of suicide by setting oneself on fire

show trial public trials used in the Soviet Union in the 1930s for propaganda purposes to show to the world that key political opponents of the ruling elite were indeed guilty

single polar one source of influence, where only one country dominates. This is as opposed to bi-polar or multi-polar.

sphere of influence area over which a country has influence. For example, Eastern Europe was within the Soviet Union's sphere of influence after 1945. Both the Soviet Union and the United States tried to increase their spheres of influence during the Cold War.

superpowers term given to USSR and USA (and eventually the People's Republic of China) after the end of World War Two. It signifies their immense economic, political and military power compared to other countries.

total war war in which the government of a country uses all the economic and human resources it has in order to win

Trotskyist someone supporting the ideas of Leon Trotsky. Trotsky had been a rival to Stalin for the leadership of the Soviet Union after the death of Lenin. Stalin used the term Trotskyist in the 1930s to his attack political opponents.

veto right to reject or forbid a decision.

white paper government report outlining policy

Zionism belief that Jews should create a homeland in Palestine

Index

Italic page numbers indicate illustrations.
Bold page numbers indicate information boxes.

Photo acknowledgments

The authors and publisher would like to thank the following individuals and organizations for permission to reproduce photographs:

© AKG p.84 (border guard); © Alamy / Interfoto Pressebildagentur p.233; © Art Archive p.104; © Bridgeman Art Library p.158; © Corbis pp.3, 17, 38, 41, 63, 72, 75, 83, 160, 190 (Tito), 190 (Nehru), 207, 209, 216, 217 (Velvet Revolution); © Corbis / Bettman pp.79 (Francis Gary Powers), 86, 226, 229, 230; © Corbis / Craigmyle p.231; © Corbis / Sygma p.87; © David King pp.22, 27; © Getty pp.20 (George F. Kennan), 62, 93, 96, 112, 117, 143, 154, 200, 202; © Getty / AFP / Pascal Guyot p.178; © Getty / Hulton Archive p.176; © Getty / Time Life pp.68, 84 (Berlin Wall); © Herbert Block Foundation pp.49 (Cartoon by Herblock), 74, 78, 79 (Cartoon), 125 203; © Illustrated London News p.16; © iStockPhoto. com / Ufuk Zivana p.163; © Kent University Cartoon Archive pp.122, 224; © Library of Congress pp.137, 139; © McCord Museum Montreal / John Collins 'Bicycle Built For Two' p.169; © McCord Museum Montreal / John Collins 'Big Game Hunter' p.179; © McCord Museum Montreal / John Collins 'Emerging From The Ice Age?' p.110; © McCord Museum Montreal / John Collins 'Fifty Years of Progress' p.111; © McCord Museum Montreal / John Collins 'International Downhill Race' p.110; © McCord Museum Montreal / John Collins 'Tank Trap' p.172; © McCord Museum Montreal / John Collins 'The Voice From The Floor' p.191; © Milwaukee Journal Sentinel p.45; © NASA / Johnson Space Center p.156; © National Records and Archives Administration pp.49 (Shell Explosion), 49 (General McArthur); © PA Photos pp.67, 155, 192, 210; © Patrick Chapatte / Globecartoon. com pp.131, 144; © Photoshot / UPPA p.177; © Poster of the Group Paix et Liberte p.20 (Caucasian Dance); © Punch Library pp.28, 66, 201; © Still Pictures / Charlotte Thege / Das Fotoarchiv p.232; © Thoemmes Continuum p.227; © Tony Auth pp.215, 217 (Cartoon); © Topfoto pp.94, 113, 130, 151; © Tribune Media Services / Jeff MacNelly p.152; © With permission from the Doug Marlette Foundation p.70.

Cover photograph of a soldier on Berlin Wall reproduced with kind permission of © Alamy / Popperfoto.

Every effort has been made to contact copyright holders of material reproduced in this book. Any omissions will be rectified in subsequent printings if notice is given to the publishers.